13th Updated Edition

Unbelievably Good Deals and Great Adventures That You Absolutely Can't Get Unless You're Over

50

JOAN RATTNER HEILMAN

CB

CONTEMPORARY BOOKS

Library of Congress Cataloging-in-Publication Data

Heilman, Joan Rattner.
    Unbelievably good deals and great adventures that you
absolutely can't get unless you're over 50 / Joan Rattner
Heilman.
    — 13th updated ed.
        p.   cm.
    Includes index.
    ISBN 0-8092-9498-2
    1. Travel.   2. Discounts for the aged.   I. Title.
G151.H44   2001
910'.2'02—dc21   00-52336
                                                              CIP

Contemporary Books
*A Division of The **McGraw-Hill** Companies*

1 2 3 4 5 6 7 8 9 0   MV/MV   0 9 8 7 6 5 4 3 2 1

ISBN 0-8092-9498-2

This book was set in ITC Berkeley Oldstyle
Printed and bound by Maple-Vail Book Manufacturing Group

Cover design by Kim Bartko

McGraw-Hill books are available at special quantity discounts to use as premiums and
sales promotions, or for use in corporate training programs. For more information, please
write to the Director of Special Sales, Professional Publishing, McGraw-Hill, Two Penn
Plaza, New York, NY 10121-2298. Or contact your local bookstore.

This book is printed on acid-free paper.

Contents

1

Introduction to Good Deals and Great Adventures

This book is for people who love to do interesting things and go to new places—and don't mind saving a little money while they're at it. It is a guide to the perks, privileges, discounts, and special adventures that are now yours simply because you've been around for a while.

On your 50th birthday (or on your 60th, 62nd, or 65th), you qualify for hundreds of special opportunities and money-saving offers that have lots of younger people wishing they were older—all for a couple of good reasons. First, as a person in your prime, you deserve them.

Second, as part of the fastest-growing segment of the American population, you represent an enormous market of potential consumers, a fact that has become quite apparent to the business community. More than a quarter of the U.S. population today is over 50. By 2020 that proportion is expected to increase to a third as the baby boomers turn 50 (one every 7.6 seconds). About 35 million Americans—almost 13 percent of the total population—are now over 65, and it is estimated that by 2030 that number will double. Besides, life expectancy is higher today than ever before (about 65,000 Americans are over 100), and most of us can expect to live a long, healthy, and active life.

Those of us over 50 control most of the nation's wealth, including half of the discretionary income (the money that's left over after essentials have been taken care of) and almost 80 percent of its financial assets. Very often, the children have gone, the mortgage has been paid off, the house is fully furnished, the goal of leaving a large inheritance is not a major concern, and the freedom years have arrived at last.

As a group, we're markedly different from previous older generations who pinched pennies and saved them all. We, too, know the value of a dollar, but we feel freer to spend our money because we're better off than our predecessors, a significant number of us having accumulated enough resources to be reasonably secure. We also are far better educated than those before us, and we have developed many more interests and activities. Besides, we have more time to enjoy ourselves. The average age of retirement has dropped to 61.

Most important, we as a group are remarkably fit, healthy, and energetic. We're living longer and feeling better. In fact, a survey has shown that most of us feel at least 15 years younger than our chronological age and rate our health as good or excellent.

The business community is actively courting the mature population because now many of us have the time to spend our money doing all the things we've always put off before.

With the recognition of our numbers, our flexible schedules, and our vast buying power, we are finally being taken very seriously. To get our attention, we are increasingly presented with some real breaks and good deals, all detailed on these pages. We are also invited on trips and adventures specifically tailored to suit our interests, needs, and abilities.

In this book, you will learn how to get what's coming to you—the discounts and privileges that are among the advantages (besides having the children move out) of getting older. Here are some that you absolutely couldn't get if you were younger:

■ Discounts at hotels and motels, at car-rental agencies, on buses, trains, and boats
■ Price breaks on airfares from virtually all airlines
■ Colleges and universities that offer you an education at bargain rates
■ Insurance companies with discounts for people who are 50 or thereabouts
■ Travel adventures all over the world designed specifically for older travelers
■ Clubs, trips, and services for mature singles
■ Ski resorts where you can ski for half price—or nothing
■ Tennis tournaments, golf vacations, walking trips, bike tours, and senior softball leagues designed for you
■ And much more!

Because every community has its own special perks to offer you, make a practice of *asking* if there are breaks to which you are entitled wherever you go, from movies to museums, concerts to historic sites, hotels to ski resorts, restaurants to riverboats, in this country and abroad. Don't expect clerks or ticket agents, tour operators, restaurant hosts, or even travel agents to volunteer them to you. First of all, they may not think of it. Second, they may not realize you have reached the appropriate birthday. And third, they may not want to call attention to your age, just in case that's not something you would appreciate. You never know if you're being offered the best possible deal unless you ask. Many bargains and privileges are available only to people who speak up.

Remember to request your privileges *before* you pay or when you order or make reservations, and always carry proof of age or an over-50-club membership card, or, better yet, both. Sometimes the advantages come with membership in a senior club, but usually they are available to anyone over a specified age.

To make sure you're getting a legitimate discount when you want to take advantage of your over-50 privileges when you travel, call the hotel, airline, car-rental company, or tour operator and ask what the regular or normal prices are. Find out if there's a special sale or promotion going on. Ask about other discounts—corporate, weekend, government, auto-club membership breaks, for example. Most important, always ask for *the lowest available rate* at the time you plan to travel and compare that with the discounted senior rate. Then decide whether you are getting a good deal. Sometimes you'll find that even better specials are available.

With the help of this guidebook, completely revised and updated at least once a year, you will have a wonderful time and save money too.

2

Travel:
Making Your
Age Pay Off

People over 50 are the most ardent travelers of all. We travel more often, farther, more extravagantly, and for longer periods of time than anybody else. Now that the travel industry has discovered these facts, it's going after our business.

The travel industry has fallen in love with our age group because we have more discretionary income than people of other ages and more time to spend it. Besides, we are remarkably flexible. Many of us no longer have children in school, so we're free to travel at off-peak times or whenever we feel the need for a change of scenery. In fact, we much prefer spring and fall to summer. Some of us have retired, and others have such good jobs that we can make our own schedules. We can take advantage of midweek or weekend slack times when the industry is eager to fill space.

But, best of all, we are energetic, and we're not about to stay home too much. People over 50 account for about one-third of all domestic travel, overseas packaged tours, air travel, and hotel/motel nights, as well as 70 percent of bus trips and cruises.

Contrary to what a younger person might think, people in the mature generation aren't content with watching the action. Instead, we like to get right into the middle of it. There's not a place we won't go or an activity we won't try. Though many of us prefer escorted tours, almost half of us choose to travel independently.

Not only that, we're shrewd—we look for the best deals to the best places. We are experienced comparison shoppers and want the most for our money.

For all of these reasons, we are now offered astonishing numbers of travel-related discounts, reduced rates, special tour packages, and other perks. Many agencies and tour operators have designed all or at least part of their trips to appeal to a mature clientele. Others include older travelers along with everyone else but offer us special privileges.

Most major airlines sell senior coupon books, good for a year, that allow us to travel much more cheaply than other people or, instead, give those of us over 62 a 10 percent reduction on regular fares. Several have established senior clubs which can sometimes provide even better savings. Practically all hotel and motel chains—as well as many individual establishments—now offer similar inducements, such as discounts on rooms and restaurants.

There are so many good deals and great adventures available to you when you are on the move that we'll start right off with travel.

But, first, keep in mind:

■ Rates, trips, and privileges tend to change at a moment's notice, so check out each of them before you make your plans. Airlines and car-rental agencies are particularly capricious, and it's hard to tell what they offer from one week to the next. The good deals in this guidebook are those that are available as we go to press.

■ Always ask for your discount when you make your reservations or at the time of purchase, order, or check-in. If you wait until you're checking out or settling your bill, it may be too late.

■ Remember that discounts may apply only between certain hours, on certain days of the week, or during specific seasons of the year. Research this before making reservations and always remind the clerk of the discount when you check in or pay your fare. Be flexible when you can and travel during the hours, days, or seasons when you can get the best deals.

■ It's particularly important when traveling to carry identification with proof of age or membership in a senior club. In most cases, a driver's license or passport does the job. In some cases, the organization's membership card, a birth certificate, a resident alien card, or any other official document showing your date of birth will suffice. If you're old enough for a Medicare card or Senior ID card, use that.

■ Don't always spring for the senior discount without checking out other rates. Sometimes special promotional rates or discounts that are available to anybody of any age turn out to be better deals. The car-rental companies and airlines, for example, are famous for this. Ask your travel agent or the ticket seller to figure out the *lowest possible available rate* for you at the time you want to travel.

■ Pay for all travel with a major credit card if possible. If there are problems or disputes, you will have less difficulty resolving them.

■ Some of these bargains are yours at age 50, usually but not always tied to membership in a senior organization. Others come along a little later at varying birthdays, so watch for the cutoff points. Also, in most cases, if the person purchasing the ticket or trip is the right age, the rest of the party, a traveling companion, or the people sharing the room are entitled to the same reduced rates.

3

Airfares: Improving with Age

O ne thing that improves with your age is airfare. Almost every airline, domestic or foreign, gives people at age 60 or 62 and a traveling companion a 10 percent discount off published fares. And if two of you traveling together qualify for the discount, each can take along a younger companion at the same lower fare.

Virtually every major U.S. airline also offers travelers over the age of 62 booklets of coupons, each good for a one-way trip within the lower 48 states and sometimes beyond. On long flights they can usually save you considerable money. They have other advantages, too. For example, unlike other low-fare tickets that require round-trip reservations, you use your coupons one at a time so you can book a one-way flight and decide later when you want to return or come back by car or bus. There is no minimum or maximum stay. You don't have to stay over a Saturday night, and you must make your reservations only 14 days before departure. Another important point: you can travel any day of the week, and you can also use them to fly standby. This is infinitely cheaper than the usual last-minute fares and allows you to stay longer or return home sooner than you had planned.

Good as they are, senior coupons aren't always the best way to go. Three major U.S. carriers now have senior clubs, each with different offers and annual membership fees and all of them definitely worth considering if you do a lot of flying. The cost of a flight, long or short, can sometimes be much less than even the coupon price. Moreover, these clubs also offer cut-rate international travel that isn't available with the coupons.

Many airlines also offer special senior fares—some, such as Southwest, on all flights and others periodically. They can turn out to be very good buys if they are available for your itinerary at the time you want to fly.

You get all of these enticements because you, members of the mature population, have proved to be the hottest travel market around, a vast and growing group of careful consumers with money in your pockets and time on your hands. Besides, your schedule tends to be more flexible than those of younger adults so you can often fly midweek and in off-peak travel periods, just when the airlines are eager to fill up seats that would otherwise go empty.

But, first, keep in mind:

■ Make sure you are getting the *lowest possible fare* to your destination at the time you want to fly. Ask about a senior discount, but be prepared to jump ship if you can get a better deal with a short-term sale rate or a supersaver fare—although sometimes your discount can cut these low fares even lower. Most airlines now offer sale fares during off-peak seasons, sometimes specifically for seniors. Watch for them because they are usually the cheapest way to go, although in most cases you can't deduct the regular senior discount from them.

■ Keep in mind that the restrictions you must fly by may not be worth the savings. Always examine the fees and conditions and decide whether you can live with them. There may be blackout periods around major holidays when you can't use your privileges, departures only on certain days or hours, restrictions on the season of the year, or stiff penalties for flight changes. In some plans, you must travel the entire distance on one airline even if connections are poor. It's not always easy to sort out the offers.

■ A 10 percent senior discount is obviously better than nothing, but on high-mileage trips you'll probably do much better with a senior club or a coupon book.

■ Be prepared to present valid proof of age at the check-in counter. It's possible that your discount will not be honored if you don't have that proof with you, and you will have to pay the difference.

■ Virtually all airlines, foreign and domestic, allow younger travel mates to travel with the same senior discount when you fly together for the entire trip. In other words, it pays to fly with a "senior."

■ Be flexible. To get seats and the best fares when you use your senior discount, plan to fly at off-peak times, when the rest of the population isn't rushing off to faraway places. For example, noontime or late-night flights can be much cheaper than early-morning or dinnertime flights. Consider leaving on a different day—fares are often lower midweek or on Saturday. Avoid Monday mornings and Friday afternoons. And obviously, flying off-season, when children aren't on vacation and there are no major holidays, may pay off with better prices.

■ For cheaper airfares, check out the many rapidly proliferating low-cost airlines, such as Southwest, American Trans Air, and JetBlue. They all have limited routes and may not fly out of a city or airport that's convenient for you—nor do they feed you more than a minor snack—but they usually offer other important advantages besides cheap tickets. For example, on some of these niche airlines, you may fly only one way, paying just half the round-trip fare, book your trips at the very last minute without penalty, and have no worries about Saturday-night or minimum stays. Some offer special senior fares that can't be beat, and at least one will give you a senior discount on top of its cheap fare.

■ Senior airline coupon books remain a good buy today, although their prices have gone up over the years. With coupons, a 62-plus traveler can fly long distances for much less than the regular coach fares and often less than short-term sale fares. There are no senior coupons for travel to Europe, Asia, or other distant overseas destinations. Each coupon is good for a one-way trip, including connecting flights as long as you don't stop over at a connection point. Two coupons are generally required each way for Alaska and Hawaii. There is no limit on the number of times you can visit one city.

■ The coupons have additional advantages, as we've mentioned. With two exceptions, coupons for younger companions are not available, but you will get frequent-flyer mileage for the miles you fly. Each traveler requires a separate coupon book, which can't be shared with a spouse or anyone else, except on America West and US Airways, where seniors may use their coupons for children under 12 who accompany them.

■ Coupons usually require a 14-day advance reservation, but they also permit you to travel on an earlier flight on a standby basis. Without a reservation, you may use a coupon to fly standby at any time. The usual routine (but call your chosen airline first, to be sure): Go to the airport and ask to be wait-listed on the next flight to wherever you're going. If the flight is "wide open," you may be ticketed then and there. If not, you go to the gate as a standby. This is especially important when you want to fly at the last minute.

■ After you've used the first coupon in your book, the remaining vouchers become nonrefundable, so don't buy a book unless you are sure you will use them all. Once issued, the coupons must be redeemed for tickets and reservations made within a year, but in most cases you have another year to travel because you can book flights 12 months ahead. Buy the booklets from your travel agent or the airline.

■ Totally unused and unexpired coupon booklets are "fully refundable." However, two airlines now charge sizable service fees (up to $75) for the privilege. Most airlines also charge fees—from $50 to $75—to change your reservations once a ticket has been issued.

- Remember that it costs the same for a few hundred miles as for several thousand, so don't waste your coupons on short trips. In other words, the longer the distance, the greater the savings. For shorter trips, you may be better off with the 10 percent senior discount.

- When you compare prices for coupon booklets, ask whether the quoted rate includes fees, taxes, and special surcharges. Some airlines quote rates that include them; others do not.

- Book your flights as early as possible for the best fares and the most available seats. Seats for travel on senior coupons or senior discounts are limited and may not be reserved at all on some flights.

- Three U.S. airlines—Continental, Delta, and United—now have clubs for seniors, all described on the following pages. They provide benefits that include significant savings on airfares, sometimes much better than the fares you pay using senior coupons, although sometimes not. Besides, they include flights to international as well as domestic destinations.

- Membership in a private airline VIP club means you can spend your waiting time at the airport in comfort, complete with snacks and free drinks, copy machines, private telephones, luggage storage areas, and sometimes even showers. At this writing, you can buy a lifetime club membership at age 62 or more from any of four major airlines—America West, Continental, Northwest, and TWA—for less than half what other adults pay. The break applies to single memberships as well as those that include your spouse. Not only that, but you may also bring guests to the lounges and sometimes use the clubs even when you are not ticketed for a flight that day.

■ Many European airlines give discounts on fares for domestic flights within their borders or to other cities in Europe to both residents and visitors. Check them out in this chapter.

Now for some of the good deals awaiting you. Be advised that airfares and airline policies can change overnight—and often do—so always call the airline that interests you for an update.

U.S. AIRLINES

ALASKA AIRLINES

Fly on Alaska Airlines if you're 62 or older and you'll get 10 percent off on almost every published fare and so will a traveling companion of any age. However, special discounted senior fares that give you more than 10 percent off are often posted on certain routes for passengers over 65 by this airline, which serves 41 cities on the West Coast from Alaska all the way to Mexico.

For information: Call 800-426-0333; www.alaskaair.com.

AMERICA WEST AIRLINES

America West's Senior Saver Pack, for travelers 62 and over, is a packet of four one-way coupons good for coach travel on any of the airline's flights within the 48 contiguous United States and between those states and Vancouver, B.C. The coupons must be exchanged for tickets within a year. Two coupons are required for flights to Alaska or Mexico.

An advantage of flying with this smaller airline is that you may also use your coupons for one or two grandchildren between the ages of 2 and 12 when they travel with you. Also included in the packet are coupons for bonus miles and discounts on land packages and car rentals. You may fly any day, anytime if seats are available. Reservations must be made at least 14 days in advance, although you may use your tickets to fly standby on valid travel days. You're entitled to frequent-flyer points for your miles.

If you don't purchase a coupon book, remember that you and a younger companion can count on a 10 percent discount on most published fares. But first ask about the special senior fares offered occasionally.

Another perk for seniors is a break on a lifetime membership in the America West Club, the company's private airport lounge facility. If you've reached age 62, you'll pay less than half of what younger adults pay for the same privilege.

For information: Call 800-235-9292; www.americawest .com.

AMERICAN AIRLINES

American Airlines has a couple of senior programs for passengers over 62. The first is 10 percent off most domestic fares for you and a traveling companion of any age.

The second is its Senior TrAAveler Coupon Books, which give you four coupons per book, each to be traded within a year for a one-way coach ticket for travel in the contiguous 48 states, Puerto Rico, or the U.S. Virgin Islands. Flights to and from Hawaii or Alaska require two coupons in each direction.

You may travel any day of the week with coupons, but you must exchange your coupons at least 14 days in advance of your flight or use them to fly standby. There is no refund on the coupons and no change of itinerary on one-way tickets, although if you don't take your reserved flight, you may use the ticket for an earlier standby seat to the same city. Seats are limited for coupon users, but you will get frequent-flyer credits for all the miles you fly. The same privileges apply to flights on American Eagle, AA's commuter airline affiliate.

AA is the first airline to allow you to book a flight using coupons that have expired before you have used them all up, but you must pay a service fee of $75. On the other hand, there is also a $75 fee when you turn in a totally unused coupon booklet for a refund.

The AActive American Traveler Club is no longer in operation.

For information: Call 800-433-7300 for reservations; www.aa.com. For the Senior TrAAveler Coupon Books, call 800-421-5600.

AMERICAN TRANS AIR (ATA)

A low-fare airline based in the Midwest, ATA flies primarily to vacation destinations—Florida, New York, Las Vegas, Los Angeles, Phoenix, San Francisco, Hawaii, and the Caribbean. It offers not only cheap tickets, even at the last minute, but also occasional senior specials and a 10 percent discount to passengers over the age of 62 and their younger companions. You may purchase one-way tickets with no penalty and will rarely have to stay over a Saturday night.

For information: Call 800-435-9282; www.ata.com.

CONTINENTAL AIRLINES

Continental Airlines offers several excellent deals for senior travelers. First, there's the 10 percent discount on all fares, even the lowest, for you and a younger companion if you are at least 62. Simply ask for it and be ready to prove your age. You'll get mileage points.

The next choice is Freedom Trips, booklets of four coupons, each to be traded for a one-way ticket on flights between any of the airline's cities including destinations in the continental U.S., Canada, Mexico, the Caribbean, the Bahamas, Puerto Rico, and Bermuda. Two coupons are required for flights to Hawaii and Alaska. You must make reservations or changes at least 14 days in advance or travel standby. You may fly any day except during blackouts around major holidays—or fly standby—and you are entitled to frequent-flyer points for the miles you fly. You must redeem your coupons within a year after purchase, but you have another year to complete your travel.

Continental's Freedom Flight Club is nice and simple. You may join at age 62 and receive a 15 or 20 percent discount off all fares, domestic and international, anywhere, anytime, including both first class and special promotional sales. There is no 14-day advance purchase, no minimum or maximum stay, no Saturday-night requirement. There are no seat limits or blackout dates. If a seat is available, you get it. You also get frequent-flyer credits for your miles but there is no special deal for travel companions. Enrollment in the Freedom Flight Club is limited and may be closed periodically, but you may ask to be placed on the waiting list.

A membership fee of $75 covers domestic travel, while a fee of $125 covers domestic and international travel for a year. For all of the destinations within the 50 states, Canada, Central and South America, and the Caribbean, as a member of the club you get a 20 percent discount for flights Monday through Thursday and on Saturday. On Friday and Sunday, it's 15 percent. For flights to Europe, the discount is 20 percent Monday through Thursday, and 15 percent on Friday, Saturday, and Sunday.

A lifetime membership in Continental's Presidents Club, its airport lounges, costs those over 62 less than half of the regular fee. Join and you can wait for your departures in comfort.

And, if you are a member of AARP, you are also entitled to $25 to $100 savings on Continental Airlines' vacation packages.

For information: Call 800-523-3273; www.flycontinental .com. For Freedom Trips Coupon Books or Freedom Flight Club, call 800-248-8996.

DELTA AIRLINES

At age 62, you have a few good options available from Delta. The first is a 10 percent discount on virtually all published fares, even including most sale fares, for you and a travel partner for flights within the continental U.S. and to Alaska, Hawaii, Puerto Rico, Canada, and the U.S. Virgin Islands. Seats are limited, so book early. Of course you'll be entitled to mileage points when you use the discount.

Your second choice from Delta is the Young at Heart Coupon program, which lets you purchase booklets of four coupons for a flat fee. The coupons must be traded within a year for tickets to any Delta destination in the continental U.S., Puerto Rico, the U.S. Virgin Islands, or Canada, with two coupons required for flights to or from Alaska and Hawaii. You may fly any day of the week and you'll get frequent-flyer credits for your miles. Reservations and/or changes must be made at least 14 days before departure, although standby is permitted anytime before your scheduled flight. Remember that only a limited number of seats are available for passengers using senior coupons, so plan ahead.

Probably the best deal currently offered by this airline is the Delta SkyWise Program, a club for travelers over 62— that is, if you can manage to get enrolled. Like other senior airline clubs, this one has limited membership, and enrollment is closed periodically. If this is the case when you apply, ask to be placed on the waiting list. Members pay $40 a year to get special first-class and economy-zone fares to over 214 destinations in the continental U.S., Alaska, and Hawaii. They also get a flat 15 percent off published economy fares to international destinations except between June 1 and August 31.

An important benefit of this club is that you may enroll up to three companions of any age for $25 each per year and you can all fly together for the same discounted fares. You may change the names of your companions, by the way, as you wish but must register the changes at least two business days before booking a flight. You may travel any day of the week but seats are limited and may not be available on all flights. There are some blackout dates, and standby travel for earlier or later flights on the same day as ticketed is permitted without charge. Round-trip tickets must be purchased 14 days in advance and require a Saturday-night stay. On domestic travel, a surcharge of $20 per person each way is applied for travel on Friday, Saturday, or Sunday.

Finally, members of AARP are entitled to savings of up to $100 per person on Delta Vacations all over the world.
For information: For reservations and Delta Young at Heart coupons, call 800-221-1212; www.delta-air.com. For the Delta SkyWise Program, call 800-325-3750; www.delta-air.com/skywise. For Delta Vacations, call 800-892-5215.

DELTA SHUTTLE

On shuttle flights between New York and Washington, D.C., or Boston, you pay fares that are 10 percent less than younger adults if you are 62 or more.

An even better deal for frequent shuttlers over 62 is the Delta Shuttle Flightpack Booklet that contains four or eight coupons, each to be used for one-way off-peak travel, standby, or with reservations. With the coupons, you may fly all day Saturday or Sunday, or Monday through Friday between 10:30 A.M. and 2:30 P.M. or 7:30 P.M. and 9:30 P.M. And you'll get frequent-flyer mileage.
For information: Call 800-221-1212; www.delta-air.com.

FRONTIER AIRLINES

If you are 62, you and a companion get a discount of 10 percent on this Denver-based carrier.
For information: Call 800-432-1359; www.frontierairlines.com.

HAWAIIAN AIRLINES

Passengers over the age of 60 and younger companions are offered special flat-rate senior fares on flights from the West Coast to Hawaii. These fares are the best you can get except when a promotional seat sale gives you a fare that's even better. Seniors also get a $10 reduction on the cost of the

Hawaiian Island Pass, which allows unlimited travel between the islands for varying numbers of days.
For information: Call 800-367-5320; www.hawaiianair .com.

HORIZON AIR

An airline that serves the Northwest, Canada, and Los Angeles, Horizon Air gives the standard 10 percent discount on most fares to passengers 62 or older and their flying companions of any age. It also has special senior fares to offer occasionally, so ask about them before making a reservation.
For information: Call 800-547-9308; www.horizonair.com.

METROJET BY US AIRWAYS

Passengers older than 62 may use the US Airways Golden Opportunities coupons for flights on Metrojet, a low-cost airline that flies between 23 cities in the Midwest. An alternative option is the senior discount, which takes 10 percent off any regular fare for you and a travel mate of any age.
For information: Call 888-638-7653; www.flymetrojet .com.

MIDWAY AIRLINES

You and a travel mate may take advantage of Midway's 10 percent senior discount on most fares if you are at least 62. At age 60, however, you may buy Midway's Senior Travel Coupon Booklet. This is a packet of four coupons, each redeemable for a one-way flight to almost anywhere this regional airline flies. Restrictions are few and include a 14-day advance purchase, but there is no minimum stay,

Saturday-night stay requirement, or blackouts. To take along a travel mate of any age, you can purchase a companion booklet of coupons for $30 more than yours.
For information: Call 800-44-MIDWAY (800-446-4392); www.midwayair.com.

MIDWEST EXPRESS AIRLINES

Ten percent is the discount on published fares for people over the age of 62 on Midwest Express, an airline that flies out of Milwaukee to many cities in the U.S.
For information: Call 800-452-2022; www.midwestexpress .com.

NATIONAL AIRLINES

Based in Las Vegas, National Airlines services several U.S. cities and offers a senior discount of 10 percent off its lowest available fares to travelers 65 or older and to two of their traveling companions. It also has special senior rates which may be even better, so check them out.
For information: Call 888-757-5387; www.nationalairlines .com.

NORTHWEST AIRLINES

You and a companion of any age get a senior discount of 10 percent, complete with frequent-flyer credits, on most of Northwest's published fares when you've reached the age of 62.

At the same age, you're also eligible to purchase NorthBest Senior Coupons, a booklet of four coupons, each good for a one-way flight within the lower 48 states and Canada and to Puerto Rico on Northwest or its affiliates.

Two coupons are required each way to Hawaii and Alaska. Stopovers require an additional coupon. Reservations must be made 14 days in advance, but you may fly anytime, any day, and collect mileage credits. Or you may fly standby any time. Coupons must be traded for tickets within a year.

Bonus: a lifetime membership at age 62 in Northwest Airlines World Club will cost you less than half of what it costs those who are younger.

For information: Call 800-225-2525; www.nwa.com.

SHUTTLE BY UNITED

Connecting 21 West Coast cities, the Shuttle by United offers a 10 percent discount at age 62 for you and a younger companion.

For information: Call 800-SHUTTLE (800-748-8853); www.ual.com.

SOUTHWEST AIRLINES

Southwest Airlines, a low-cost carrier known for its bargain fares, now flies coast to coast to and from 55 cities. It offers even better bargains—discounted by at least 40 percent and sometimes as much as 70 percent—on every flight, every day of the week, to people who are 65 or older. Advantages: There are few restrictions on tickets, which are fully refundable. Advance booking isn't required (meaning you won't have to pay exorbitant last-minute rates), and you may buy a one-way or round-trip ticket. All seats are coach. Senior fares vary from city to city and change frequently, however, and the number of senior seats is limited on each flight, so reserve your passage as early as possible. Disadvantages:

Few flights are nonstop, no meals are served, the senior fares are not available to younger travel companions, and the senior fares cannot be booked on-line.

For information: Call 800-435-9792; www.southwest.com.

TWA (TRANS WORLD AIRLINES)

TWA reduces the fare by 10 percent for travelers 62 and over and companions of any age on all standard fares in the U.S. and Puerto Rico to Mexico City, Santo Domingo, and Vancouver, and some fares to Europe and the Middle East as well. Ask for the discount when you make reservations. You are entitled to frequent-flyer mileage. TWA also offers occasional senior promotional fares for two people traveling together, when you can save even more.

The Senior Travel Pak is another alternative for travelers 62 or older. It gives you four one-way coupons at bargain prices (if you use them for long trips). Each coupon may be exchanged for a one-way ticket on flights in the mainland U.S. and Canada, plus Puerto Rico, Mexico, and some Caribbean destinations. Two coupons are required each way for trips to Alaska and Hawaii except from Portland, Oregon. TWA's packets include discount certificates for a 20 percent reduction on a ticket to Europe, and a $50 discount on a TWA Getaway Vacation package. You may travel any day of the week except around Thanksgiving and Christmas. Seats are limited so book yours early. Reservations must be made 14 days in advance, but you may travel standby anytime before your scheduled flight after you have traded your coupon for a ticket. You're entitled to mileage points.

A big plus: TWA also sells four-coupon Travel Paks for companions of any age for only $100 more than yours. All of the coupons must be used by the same person and only when you fly together. The discount certificate for travel to Europe is included.

One more benefit of age is a lifetime membership in TWA's Ambassador Club. At age 60, it costs you less than half what it costs those who are younger.

For information: Call 800-221-2000; www.twa.com.

UNITED AIRLINES

United has three programs that benefit mature travelers. The first is a 10 percent discount at age 62 on excursion fares for you and any traveling companion. The discount also applies to United Express, selected fares from regional carriers, and all fares on the Shuttle by United.

The next good deal is the Silver TravelPac program for passengers over 62, which offers packets of four coupons at a flat fee, each coupon good for a one-way ticket within the mainland U.S. and to San Juan or Canada. Two coupons are required each way to Hawaii or Alaska (except from Seattle). They may be used for flights any day of the week, although there are blackouts during holiday seasons, and you must trade them for tickets within a year of the purchase date. Reservations must be made at least 14 days in advance, but you may use the coupons to fly standby. You'll get mileage credits for the miles you fly. Remember, seats at discounted fares are always limited, so plan ahead.

United Airlines Silver Wings Plus is an established membership program for which you become eligible at age 55. It gives you two options: a two-year membership that costs

$75 and includes three $25 certificates to use against future travel and other discounts; and a lifetime membership that costs $225 and gives you three $50 certificates to use against future travel on United, and an additional discount certificate valid for 15 percent off any round-trip system-wide flight. All members also get discounts on hotels, resorts, tours, car rentals, cruises, and flights on partner airlines.

All new members receive a complimentary set of four USA Collection Privilege Certificates that can be used for low-mileage-based fares for the member and a traveling companion of any age to travel within the 50 states and from the U.S. to Canada, Puerto Rico, or the U.S. Virgin Islands. Members age 62 or over may purchase up to three sets of certificates a year for $25 per set.

For information: Call 800-241-6522; www.ual.com. For United Silver Wings Plus, call 800-720-1765; www.silver wingsplus.com. For the Silver TravelPac: 800-633-6563.

US AIRWAYS

If you are over 62, you and a travel companion of any age can count on a 10 percent discount on all US Airways fares, including seasonal sales. The same discount applies to the US Airways Metrojet.

If you plan to fly frequently on this airline, consider the Golden Opportunities Coupon Booklet, a book of four coupons each good for a one-way ticket to any US Airways destination within the continental U.S., Canada, Mexico, the U.S. Virgin Islands, and Puerto Rico. Reservations must be made at least 14 days in advance, but you may travel standby anytime after a ticket has been issued. The coupons may be used for flights any day of the week but must be used within a year of purchase. You will get frequent-flyer points for your mileage. Totally unused and unexpired coupon booklets may be turned in for a refund for a $50 service fee.

Bonus: As many as two of your grandchildren, ages 2 through 11, may fly on your coupons if they make the trip with you.

For information: Call 800-428-4322; www.usairways.com.

US AIRWAYS SHUTTLE

There are three different ways for passengers over the age of 62 to save on US Airways Shuttle flights between New York, Washington, and Boston. The best way is to use the Senior Fare (available only off-peak) because it costs you less than half the regular adult walk-up fare. Second, you can purchase the Flightpass, booklets of four or eight discounted coupons good for one-way trips on all shuttle routes. If you fly the shuttle regularly, these may be your best bet. Using them, you may fly off-peak weekdays between 10 A.M. and 2 P.M., after 6:59 P.M., and anytime on Saturday and Sunday. And last, you may use the senior discount which gives you 10 percent off any fare.

For information: Call 800-428-4322; www.usairways.com.

VIRGIN ATLANTIC AIRWAYS

As soon as you turn 60, Virgin Atlantic gives you and a younger companion a 10 percent discount on all regular fares on all flights between the U.S. and London.

If you are a member of AARP, you—and your spouse or a companion of any age—can now save anywhere from 12 to 25 percent on all 45-day advance-purchase-or-higher economy fares to London, although not in combination with other promotional offers or discounts. When making a reservation, make sure to mention the AARP offer, and be ready to present your membership card when you check in for your flight. The discounts are not applicable for a few weeks around Easter and Christmas/New Year's holidays. As a member, you can also save $50 to $100 on the airline's vacation packages, except on promotional packages, to Great Britain and other European destinations.

For information: Call 800-862-8621 for reservations; www .virgin-atlantic.com. Call 888-YES-VIRGIN (888-937-8474) for vacation packages.

GOOD DEALS IN CANADA

AIR CANADA

If you are over 60, you and any traveling companion are eligible for a 10 percent reduction on all fares, including sale fares, for flights in Canada and the U.S., including Florida, and on trips between Canada and the U.K. and the Caribbean. You'll get mileage credits as well.

For information: Call 800-776-3000 in the U.S., 800-361-8620 in Canada; www.aircanada.ca.

GOOD DEALS ON FOREIGN AIRLINES

Always inquire about special senior discounts when you book your flight. Most foreign airlines offer a 10 percent discount to passengers at age 60 or 62 on transatlantic flights originating in the U.S., although a younger companion may not always be entitled to the same deal. Many foreign carriers will also give you a break on domestic flights within the nation's borders or to other nearby countries. Remember that seasonal promotional fares available to travelers of all ages may be lower than the senior fare, so do your homework before committing yourself.

AEROLINEAS ARGENTINAS

On this airline, passengers over the age of 60 and a companion of any age are offered a 10 percent discount on posted fares for flights originating in the U.S. to any of its South American destinations.

For information: Call 800-333-0276; aerolineas.com.ar.

AEROMEXICO

It's 10 percent off the regular first-class or tourist fares every day on all Aeromexico routes, domestic and international, out of U.S. gateways if you are over 62.

For information: Call 800-237-6639; www.aeromexico .com.

AIR FRANCE

If you're 62, a 10 percent discount is yours on most Air France flights—whether first-class, business, or economy— between U.S. and Canadian gateway cities and destinations in Europe.

For domestic flights within France and to European destinations, you'll get the same 10 percent off if your travel originates in the U.S. or Canada.

For information: Call 800-237-2747; www.airfrance.com.

AIR JAMAICA

Fly to Jamaica and you can take advantage of Air Jamaica's 10 percent discount offered to passengers over the age of 60. A younger traveling companion over the age of 18 gets the same discount you do.

For information: Call 800-523-5585; www.airjamaica.com.

ALITALIA

When you fly on Alitalia to its European destinations or Egypt, you qualify for a 10 percent discount when you are 62, as does a younger traveling companion.

On certain domestic flights within Italy, seniors over 65 are offered special discounted Terza Eta (Third Age) fares. Be sure to ask for them.

For information: Call 800-223-5730; www.alitalia.com.

AUSTRIAN AIRLINES

The Austrian Airlines Group, comprised of Austrian Airlines, Tyrolean Airways, and Lauda Air, serves more than 200 destinations worldwide. On its daily nonstop service to Vienna from its gateway cities, New York, Chicago, and Washington, it offers a 10 percent discount to passengers 62 and over—and their companions of any age—on all but promotional sale fares on transatlantic flights to Vienna originating in the U.S.

In addition, on domestic flights within Austria, women at age 55 and men at 60 can get fare reductions of up to 25 percent off the regular fares. These flights must be booked before departure from the U.S. together with a round-trip transatlantic flight from the U.S.

Austrian Airlines has one more offer to make: "Visit Europe" travel coupons that are sold only to residents of countries outside of Europe, again in conjunction with the purchase of round-trip transatlantic tickets from the U.S. The coupons typically save travelers 50 percent or more per segment on flights to more than 100 destinations in Europe. *For information:* Call 800-843-0002; www.austrianair.com.

BRITISH AIRWAYS

You qualify at age 60 for a 10 percent discount for yourself and a traveling companion when you book an advance-purchase economy-class flight on British Airways from its North American gateway cities to the U.K., Europe, or other parts of the world. Not only that, but the fees are waived for canceling or changing your reservations before your departures. The usual charge of $150 to change your return flight after you've arrived in Europe is reduced to $50 on senior tickets. That means you can buy your tickets without too much worry about having to cancel or make a change.

However, always be sure to check out the 90-day advance-purchase fares and any ongoing promotional sales because these may save you more money than the senior discount.

For information: Call 800-AIRWAYS (800-247-9297); www .britishairways.com.

BRITISH MIDLAND AIRWAYS

British Midland, which flies to 30 European destinations out of London, offers travelers over 55 a 25 percent discount on the Discover Europe Airpass. The airpass is available only to non-European residents and offers low fixed fares from city to city. It must be purchased in the U.S. in conjunction with a transatlantic ticket on any airline. Changes are free of charge when they are made at least 24 hours prior to departure and the itinerary remains the same. Changes within 24 hours of travel cost $40.

Also from British Midland: special senior fares for passengers who are 60 or over on round-trip flights within Europe. These are nonrefundable and no minimum stay is required.

For information: Call 800-788-0555; www.britishmid land.com.

BWIA INTERNATIONAL AIRWAYS

A 10 percent discount is yours if you are at least 62 years old. A younger companion may fly with you at the same fare.

For information: Call 800-538-2942; www.bwee.com.

CAYMAN AIRWAYS

This small airline that flies from Miami, Tampa, Orlando, or Houston to the Cayman Islands will take 10 percent off of most fares for you and a younger travel mate if you are 62.

For information: Call 800-422-9626; www.caymanairways .com.

EL AL ISRAEL AIRLINES

Travelers over the age of 60 and their spouses over 55 are entitled to EL AL's senior fare, which gives you a discount of about 15 percent off the regular or Super Apex fares between the U.S. and Israel. A 14-day advance purchase is required, there is a $50 fee for changing your return flight, and you are allowed one free stopover in or out of New York and one free stopover in or out of Europe.

Look into EL AL's Israel Milk and Honey Vacation packages, available only with a transatlantic ticket from the U.S. *For information:* Call 800-223-6700; www.elal.com. For EL AL packages, call 800-352-5786.

EUROPE BY AIR.COM

Not for seniors only but a good deal anyway is the Flight-Pass issued by europebyair.com, because it lets you fly to any of 130 destinations in 27 European countries on 17 airlines for $99 (at this writing) per one-way flight. You may start anywhere and end anywhere in Europe. Good for 120 days from the start of travel, the pass is sold in countries outside Europe to non-European residents only. Reservations for flights may be made in advance or on the go. There are no charges for changes, no blackout dates, no Saturday-stay requirements, no fare zones. And, unfortunately, no senior discount.

A new option is the FlightPass Unlimited, which gives you unrestricted travel within the network for 15 or 21 days. This pass, too, is sold only in countries outside of Europe, although reservations may be made in advance or as you go.
For information: Call 888-387-2479; www.europebyair .com.

FINNAIR

On flights between gateway cities in the U.S. and Canada and Helsinki, Finland, you will get a 10 percent reduction

off some transatlantic fares if you are 65 or more. Travel companions get the same savings. You'll get an even better discount—a big 75 percent—off the cost of Finnair's domestic flights in Finland. For this you must be 65 and pay for your tickets within three days of booking your flight.
For information: Call 800-950-5000; www.finnair.com.

IBERIA AIRLINES OF SPAIN

Iberia gives you 10 percent off regular published fares for transatlantic flights originating in North America except on promotional sales. On Iberia flights within Europe the discount is the same if your travel originated here. You must have reached 62 to get the privilege, but you may take a younger companion for the same fare.
For information: Call 800-772-4642; www.iberia.com.

JAPAN AIRLINES

JAL has special Silver Fares for passengers over the age of 65 on domestic flights within Japan. With them, you'll get a discount of about 40 percent, depending on the route, time, and date of travel. Best to book them at the same time and in conjunction with your international ticket.
For information: Call 800-525-3663; www.japanair.com.

KLM ROYAL DUTCH AIRLINES

KLM's discount for people over the age of 62 is 10 percent on all nonpromotional fares between the U.S. and its European destinations. Flying on KLM to Paris from the U.S., your discount is even better—30 percent. A companion of any age is entitled to the same reduction in fare if you travel together for the entire journey. On flights within Europe

from Amsterdam, your senior privilege starting at age 60 is a 10 percent discount on almost all fares.
For information: Call 800-374-7747; www.klm.com.

LUFTHANSA GERMAN AIRLINES

After you have turned 62, you get 10 percent off most Lufthansa fares across the Atlantic Ocean to European destinations for you and a travel mate. The same reduction applies to domestic flights inside the German borders.
For information: Call 800-645-3880; www.lufthansa.com.

MALEV HUNGARIAN AIRLINES

On the Hungarian national airline, passengers 60 and over—and travel companions any age—are offered a 10 percent discount on flights between New York and Budapest.
For information: Call 800-223-6884 or 212-757-6480; www.hungarianairlines.com.

MARTINAIR HOLLAND

Martinair flies from nine North American gateway cities to Amsterdam and other European destinations. Travelers over 60 and younger companions pay 10 percent less for tickets except on already discounted promotional fares.
For information: Call 800-MARTINAIR (800-627-8462); www.martinairusa.com.

MEXICANA AIRLINES

A senior discount of 10 percent applies to most Mexicana international flights between gateway cities in the U.S. or Canada and Mexico. You must be 62, but your traveling companion may be younger and fly at the same fare.
For information: Call 800-531-7921; www.mexicana.com.

OLYMPIC AIRWAYS

The national airline of Greece, Olympic Airways gives passengers over the age of 62 and their younger travel mates a 10 percent discount on most flights from its gateway cities of Boston and New York to Athens and other European destinations. Older Canadians departing from Montreal or Toronto also get a special rate.

On domestic flights within Greece, you'll pay only 80 percent of the regular adult fare if you're over 60 and your travel originated in the U.S.

For information: Call 800-223-1226 or 212-838-3600; www.olympic-airways.gr.

SABENA BELGIAN WORLD AIRLINES

Sabena offers all passengers over the age of 62 (60 in Canada) and a traveling companion a discount of 10 percent on virtually all fares for flights from 10 U.S. and Canadian gateway cities as well as on fares for flights within Europe. The discount applies all year and every day of the week.

For information: Call 800-955-2000; www.sabena.com.

SAS (SCANDINAVIAN AIRLINES SYSTEM)

On flights across the Atlantic from gateway cities in the U.S. to Scandinavia or European destinations, passengers over 62 get a 10 percent discount on most fares.

In addition, SAS gives those over 65 special senior fares on domestic flights within Norway on tickets sold in the U.S. Purchase tickets in Norway and you'll get an even better deal—half-fare—if you're over 67.

On domestic flights within Denmark and Sweden, SAS offers special senior fares too, depending on the route, again at 65.

Check out the special senior fares, which vary according to the route, to passengers over 65 on domestic flights.
For information: Call 800-221-2350; www.flysas.com.

SPANAIR

This airline, flying between Washington, D.C., and Madrid, will give you, at age 62, and your travel mate a discount of 10 percent on transatlantic flights except during major holiday periods. On flights within Spain or other destinations in Europe, you need be only 60 to get the discount, although this time a companion is not included. Spanair's periodic sales, of course, may give you an even better deal.
For information: Call 888-545-5757; www.spanairusa.com.

SWISSAIR

If you fly Swissair, you and a traveling companion will get a discount of 10 percent on almost all fares on flights from 10 U.S. and Canadian gateway cities as well as on fares for flights within Europe. It applies all year and every day of the week. Just ask for it. But first find out if the airline is offering one of its occasional senior promotions at the time you want to fly—it will give you the same discount but takes your companion along at half-fare.
For information: Call 800-221-4750; www.swissair.com.

TAP AIR PORTUGAL

If you are at least 62, your discount from this airline is 10 percent off almost any fare on flights between the U.S. and Portugal, Madeira, and the Azores. The discount applies to a younger flying partner as well.
For information: Call 800-221-7370; www.tapairportugal .pt.

TURKISH AIRLINES

You'll get a really good discount—a hefty 25 percent—on most flights to Turkey or other international destinations on Turkish Airlines, the national air carrier. To be eligible for the privilege, you must be 65 or older and fly from one of the three gateway cities—New York, Chicago, or Miami. The discount, however, does not apply to a travel mate, and on some restricted fares it is reduced to 10 percent.

For information: Call 800-874-8875 or 212-339-9650; www.turkishairlines.com.

VARIG BRAZILIAN AIRLINES

On flights originating in the U.S. and flying to Rio de Janeiro or Sao Paulo, Varig gives passengers over the age of 62 a 10 percent discount on most fares.

For information: Call 800-468-2744; www.varig.com.br.

4

Hotels and Motels: Get Your Over-50 Markdowns

Now that you're past 50, you'll never have to pay full price for a hotel room again. Across the U.S. and Canada, and often in the rest of the world today, virtually all lodging chains and most individual establishments go out of their way to give you a break on room rates.

You don't even have to wait until you're eligible for Social Security to cash in on your maturity because most hotels, inns, and motels offer discounts to you at age 50, usually requiring only proof of age or membership in a senior organization. Often the best discounts, sometimes as high as 50 percent, however, are reserved at some hotel chains for members of their own senior travel clubs. Some cost little or nothing to join; others charge a yearly fee.

What all this means is that you should *never* make a lodging reservation without making sure you are getting a special rate—a senior discount of at least 10 percent or an even better deal, such as a promotional sale or a corporate or weekend rate that is lower. Always ask for the senior discount, whether or not one is posted or mentioned in the hotel's literature, and then ask if a better rate is available.

The only bad news is that senior hotel discounts aren't as generous as they were a few years ago and restrictions have increased, for the simple reason that travel is booming and more people are turning 50 than ever before. Even so, dozens of hotel chains and thousands of individual hotels continue to use price incentives to attract over-50 travelers. It makes sense to take advantage of them whenever you can.

But, first, keep in mind:

If you want to take advantage of the privileges coming to you because of your age, you must do some advance research and planning with your travel agent or on your own.

- In this rapidly changing world, rates and policies can be altered in a flash, so an update is always advisable.
- Information about discounts is seldom volunteered. In most cases, you must arrange for discounts when you make your reservations and confirm them again when you check in. Do not wait until you're settling your bill because then it may be too late. Some hotels and motels require that you make advance reservations to get their discounts. "Advance" may mean a considerable period of time such as three weeks, but it may also mean only a week, a day, or even a few hours. Check it out before making your plans.

- Although many senior discounts are available every day of the year, some are subject to "space availability." This means it may be pretty hard to get them when you want to travel because only a limited number of rooms may be reserved for special rates. If these are already booked (or are expected to be booked), you won't get your discount. And some hotels have "blackout" dates during special events or holiday periods when the discount is not valid. So always book early, ask for your discount privileges, and try to be flexible on your dates in order to take advantage of them. Your best bets for space are usually weekends in large cities, weekdays at resorts, and nonholiday seasons.

- It's quite possible that a special promotional rate, especially off-peak or on weekends, may save you more money than your senior discount. Many hotels, particularly in big cities and warm climates, cut their prices drastically in the summer, for example. Others that cater mostly to businesspeople during the week try to encourage weekend traffic by offering bargain rates if you stay over a Saturday night. Resorts are often eager to fill their rooms on weekdays. So always investigate all the possibilities before you get too enthusiastic about using your hard-earned senior discount, and remember to ask for the *lowest available rate*.

- There are several chains of no-frills budget motels that may not offer discounts or too much in the way of amenities but do charge very low room rates and tend to be located along the most-traveled routes.

- If you are traveling with children or grandchildren, remember that at many hotels, children under a specified age, usually 16 or 18, may stay free in your room. And at some big chains, they may eat free, too.

■ In some cases, not every hotel or inn in a chain will offer the discount. Those that do are called "participating" hotels/motels. Make sure the one you are planning to visit is participating in the senior plan.

■ In addition to the chains, many independent hotels and inns are eager for your business and offer special reduced rates. Always *ask* before making a reservation. Your travel agent should be able to help you with this.

■ Some hotel restaurants will give you a discount, too, sometimes whether or not you are a registered guest.

■ By the way, your discount usually applies only to the regular rates and, in most cases, will not be given on top of other special discounts. One discount is probably all you get.

AMERIHOST INN

At these motels concentrated in the Midwest, there's a senior discount of 10 percent on the rates.
For information: Call 800-434-5800; www.amerihost.com.

AMERISUITES

This nationwide chain of all-suite accommodations designed for extended stays offers members of AARP and CARP a 10 to 20 percent discount. Buffet breakfast is included.
For information: Call 800-833-1516; www.amerisuites .com.

ASTON HOTELS & RESORTS

Aston's Sun Club gives travelers 50 and older—and their roommates—25 percent off per night on room rates at its hotels and condominium resorts, budget to luxury, on Hawaii's four major islands, plus a seventh consecutive night free. Ask for these privileges when you make your reservations and pick up a coupon book of discounts when you check in. Sun Club rooms are limited, so reserve early.

For information: Call 800-922-7866; www.astonhotels .com.

BAYMONT INNS & SUITES

At these inexpensive motels located mainly in the South and Midwest, you will get 10 percent off just for being over 55. You'll also get a free continental breakfast. Even better, you'll receive the same discount at only 50 if you belong to AARP.

For information: Call 800-301-0200; www.baymontinns .com.

BEST INNS & SUITES

At these 155 economy inns all over the country, anyone over 50 may take advantage of the Best Guest Silver Edition, a combination of a frequent-stay program and a senior discount. This gives you a 10th night free after staying at any of the chain's inns for nine nights, plus a 10 percent discount off the regular rates.

For information: Call 800-237-8466; www.bestinn.com.

BEST WESTERN INTERNATIONAL

Anyone who's over 55 or belongs to AARP or CARP gets a minimum of 10 percent off the regular rates any day of the year at all of the 4,800 independently owned Best Westerns in 84 countries. Some hotels give extra perks such as complimentary continental breakfast, free local calls, late checkout, and room upgrades. Also ask about other special rates such as weekend, off-season, or government rates. Check the website for detailed routes and driving directions to each location.

For information: Call 800-528-1234; www.bestwestern .com.

BUDGET HOST INNS

A network of about 180 affiliated, mostly family-owned economy inns in 37 states and Canada, most Budget Host Inns offer senior discounts—usually 10 percent off the regular rates—that vary by location. Call the toll-free reservation number and you will be transferred directly to the front desk of the inn, where you can ask about the accommodations, facilities, rates, discounts, and directions to the property.

For information: Call 800-283-4678; www.budgethost .com.

CAMBERLEY HOTELS

Most of these charming upscale hotels, some of them landmark buildings, give AARP members 10 percent off the standard room rates.

For information: Call 800-555-8000; ww.camberleyhotels .com.

CANADIAN PACIFIC HOTELS & RESORTS

See Fairmont Hotels & Resorts. Call 800-441-1414; www.fairmont.com.

CANDLEWOOD SUITES

Travelers 55 and older get a novel deal with Candlewood Suites Senior Value Program. At these midscale all-suite

AMERICAN EXPRESS SENIOR CARD

The major benefit of the American Express Senior Member Card, designed specifically for people 62 or over, is a considerable reduction in the yearly fee—$35 for a standard card or $55 for a Gold Senior Member Card—along with the usual charge privileges and customer services. Other benefits are a quarterly newsletter; savings on travel, shopping, and dining; an urgent-message relay to family or friends; and a hotline open 24 hours a day for emergency assistance on passports and visas, sources of cash, and legal or medical problems.

For information: Call 800-843-2273; www.americanexpress.com/senior.

hotels that feature full kitchens, desks, two separate telephone lines, VCR and CD players, fitness centers, and 24-hour mini-convenience stores, the offer is a two-night stay at half price. To qualify, you must agree to stay an additional day immediately before or after a national holiday—Easter, Mother's Day, Father's Day, Memorial Day, Independence Day, Labor Day, Thanksgiving, Christmas, or New Year's Day. And a first-time stay with Candlewood—anytime—counts as a holiday.

For information: Call 888-226-3539; www.candlewood suites.com.

CASTLE RESORTS & HOTELS

Castle's 18 hotels and resort condominiums in Hawaii, Guam, Saipan, Chuuk, and New Zealand offer the Castle Advantage Program for older travelers. It gives anybody over

the age of 50 a discount of up to 25 percent off the rack rates plus special rates on rental cars during your stay.
For information: Call 800-367-5004; www.castleresorts .com.

CHOICE HOTELS INTERNATIONAL

Choice Hotels is an international group of more than 5,000 inns in 36 countries with brand names that include Clarion, Comfort, Quality, Sleep Inn, Econo Lodge, MainStay Suites, and Rodeway Inns. All of its properties in the U.S. and Canada take catering to older travelers very seriously and offer their Senior Savers Program to anyone over the age of 60. This means you will get 20 to 30 percent taken off the regular room rate when you book at least 24 hours ahead (subject to availability) using the toll-free number below. It's 10 percent for those over 50 without reservations.
For information: Call 800-4 CHOICE (800-424-6423); www.choicehotels.com.

CITADINES APARTMENT HOTELS

When you select one of these studios or apartments in cities and resorts throughout Europe, all with fully equipped kitchenettes, you'll get a 10 percent discount off the published rates any day of the year if you belong to AARP. Advance reservations are required.
For information: Call 800-755-8266; www.apartment hotels.com.

CLARION HOTELS, SUITES & RESORTS

See Choice Hotels International. Call 800-CLARION (800-252-7466); www.clarionhotel.com.

COMFORT INNS & COMFORT SUITES

See Choice Hotels International. Most Comfort Inns are located along major highways and offer a free continental breakfast plus meal discounts at some properties.

For information: Call 800-228-5150; www.comfortinns .com.

CONRAD INTERNATIONAL HOTELS

A subsidiary of Hilton Hotels, many Conrad Hotels in Europe, Australia, Hong Kong, Egypt, Singapore, Turkey, Uruguay, and the Caribbean participate in Hilton's Senior HHonors Worldwide program for over-60s. Members are entitled to up to 50 percent off the regular room rates and 20 percent off the bill for dinner for two. See Hilton Hotels.

For information: Call 800-445-8667; www.hilton.com.

COUNTRY HEARTH INNS

Most of these deluxe economy motels in the South and Midwest take up to 10 percent off the room rates for visitors over 50.

For information: Call 800-848-5767; www.countryhearth .com.

COUNTRY INNS & SUITES BY CARLSON

Each of these independently owned midprice inns all over the world gives you a minimum of 10 percent off the regular rates and a complimentary continental breakfast if you are at least 50 years old.

For information: Call 800-456-4000; www.countryinns .com.

COURTYARD BY MARRIOTT

AARP or CARP members get 10 percent off the regular room rates every day of the year at all of these 500-or-so moderately priced hotels, most of which feature swimming pools and exercise facilities. Advance reservations are recommended.

For information: Call 800-321-2211; www.courtyard.com.

CROSS COUNTRY INNS

If you check in at one of these inns located in Ohio, Kentucky, and Michigan, you will get a discount of 25 percent on the regular room rates every day of the year, but you must be at least 60.

For information: Call 800-621-1429; www.crosscountry inns.com.

CROWNE PLAZA HOTELS & RESORTS

Affiliated with Holiday Inn, Crowne Plaza offers members of AARP a 10 percent discount off the regular room rates any day of the year, subject to space availability. A collection of about 140 upscale accommodations located in 40 countries around the world, these hotels are designed to cater especially to business travelers.

For information: Call 800-227-6963; www.crowneplaza .com.

DAYS INNS WORLDWIDE

Join the September Days Club, open to travelers age 50 and over, and you'll get discounts on the regular room rates of 15 to 50 percent at all 1,900 of the moderately priced Days Inns locations worldwide. Other benefits include a 10 percent discount at participating hotel restaurants and gift shops whether you are a hotel guest or just stopping by. Members are also offered a variety of promotional rates on car rentals, tours and cruises, and airline tickets. A quarterly magazine keeps you up to date. Annual membership costs $15 for one year, $25 for two, $50 for five, and covers you and your spouse, who may be younger than 50.

If you aren't a member of the club but you belong to AARP or CARP or are over the age of 60, you'll get a 10 percent reduction on room rates.

For information: Call 800-DAYS-INN (800-329-7466); www.daysinn.com. In Canada, call 800-964-3434. For details or to enroll in the September Days Club, call 800-241-5050.

DELTA HOTELS

Delta Hotels, Canada's largest first-class hotel company, with over 30 properties across the country, is a subsidiary of Canadian Pacific Hotels & Resorts and Fairmont Hotels. It offers packages at special rates and senior discounts at many of its locations. The discounts vary, however, with some locations giving a big 50 percent off while others offer 10 percent or less, so ask questions when you make your reservations.

For information: Call 800-268-1133; www.deltahotels.com.

DOUBLETREE HOTELS & GUEST SUITES

At all Doubletrees, now part of Hilton Hotels, members of AARP are given a 10 percent discount on corporate and best available rates—anytime, any day, and no advance reservations are required. Members also get 10 percent off food and nonalcoholic beverages at participating Doubletree restaurants if they are hotel guests.

For information: Call 800-222-8733; www.doubletree hotels.com.

DOWNTOWNER INNS

See Red Carpet Inn. Call 800-251-1962; www.reservahost .com.

DRURY INNS

These economy motels concentrated in the Midwest and the South offer a 5 to 10 percent discount on the regular room rates at all of their more than 100 locations to anyone 50 or over. Just ask and have your proof of age handy.

For information: Call 800-325-8300; www.druryinn.com.

ECONO LODGE

See Choice Hotels International. Here you'll get a 15 percent discount—and sometimes as much as 30 percent—if rooms are available when you make an advance reservation using the toll-free number. Without a reservation, the discount is 10 percent every day of the year. Many rooms have been specially designed for mature travelers, with touches such as special lighting and large-face alarm clocks.

For information: 800-553-2666; Call www.econolodge .com.

ECONOMY INNS OF AMERICA

This economy lodging chain, with 20 motels located near major highways in California and Florida, gives 10 percent off the room rates to members of AARP. Just ask for it.

For information: Call 800-826-0778.

EMBASSY SUITES HOTELS

In most of its 150 upscale all-suite hotels in the U.S., Canada, and Latin America, Embassy Suites gives a 10 percent discount to AARP members and others over the age of 50. Amenities for guests include room service, mini-kitchens, complimentary cooked-to-order breakfast every morning, and free beverages every evening.

For information: Call 800-EMBASSY (800-362-2779); www.embassy-suites.com.

FAIRFIELD INN BY MARRIOT

At Marriott's midscale lodging chain, you will get 10 percent deducted from your bill every day of the year if you belong to AARP or CARP.

For information: Call 800-228-2800; www.fairfieldinn.com.

FAIRMONT HOTELS & RESORTS

These 36 luxury hotels and resorts, formerly known as Canadian Pacific Hotels, are located in Canada, the U.S., Bermuda, and Mexico, and give seniors a nice big break. It's 30 percent off the published room rates for members of AARP and CARP seven days a week all year, except for a few blackout periods here and there. And, of course, when space is available.

A second perk: the off-peak packages designed for older travelers at many of these luxurious hotels. Recent packages: the Seniors Spring Fling, the Seniors Fall Getaway, the Sixty-Something room rate, and the Second Honeymoon.

At Fairmont's U.S. City Centre Hotels, situated in many of the larger cities, the 30 percent discount applies only on weekends. Because they are jam-packed with business travelers during the week, the discount on Sunday through Thursday nights is reduced to 10 percent.

For information: Call 800-441-1414; www.fairmont.com.

FOUR POINTS BY SHERATON

Ask for your senior discount at the more than 130 Four Points scattered around the country and you will get 15 to 25 percent off the regular rates, subject to availability. You must be a member of AARP or over the age of 60 to qualify.

For information: Call 800-325-3535; www.fourpoints.com.

HAMPTON INN & SUITES

The Lifestyle 50 Plus program at more than 1,000 moderately priced hotels in the U.S., Canada, and Mexico allows four people to share the same room at a single room rate. Other benefits include rebates on hotel, air, car, and cruise travel booked through the member travel service; $20 in gas coupons; airline and car-rental coupons; 20 percent discount at over 4,000 restaurants; and more. A three-month trial membership costs $1; then, unless you cancel, you are automatically enrolled in the program for $59.95 a year.

For information: Call 800-HAMPTON (800-426-7866); www.hampton-inn.com. For the Lifestyle 50 Plus program, call 800-204-4033.

HAWAIIAN HOTELS & RESORTS

The good news for travelers over the age of 55 is savings of 40 to 60 percent at three full-service oceanfront resorts—

the Royal Lahaina Resort on Maui, Kauai Coconut Beach Resort, and Royal Kona Resort on the Big Island of Hawaii. At the Royal Kona Resort, a full American buffet breakfast for two is included.

For information: Call 800-222-5642; www.hawaiihotels.com.

HAWTHORN SUITES HOTELS

Although there is no official senior discount at these 160 moderately priced suites hotels designed to give guests a home away from home, many properties do offer a 10 percent savings to older travelers. So ask when you are making a reservation. Each suite includes kitchen facilities and offers a hot buffet breakfast daily.

For information: Call 800-527-1133; www.hawthorn.com.

HILTON HOTELS

Hilton's Senior HHonors travel program is a very good deal for those over the age of 60 who do a lot of traveling. It gives you and your spouse up to 50 percent off the regular rates at more than 500 Hilton and Conrad International Hotels around the world. Annual membership for you and your spouse is $55 in the U.S., $75 elsewhere.

As a member, you may reserve a second room at the same reduced rate for family or friends traveling with you and get late checkout privileges when possible. You get 20 percent off the bill for dinner for two at participating hotel restaurants, whether or not you are guests of the hotel. You may also use the health facilities, where available, without charge.

Members are automatically enrolled in Hilton HHonors Worldwide, a guest reward program at Hiltons, Conrads, and the corporation's other brands (Hampton Inn & Suites, Homewood Suites by Hilton, Embassy Suites Hotels, Red Lion Hotels, and Doubletree Hotels & Resorts) all over the world. It gives members hotel points as well as airline frequent-flyer miles for each qualifying stay.

For those who don't join the Senior HHonors program but do belong to AARP, most Hiltons give a discount of 10 to 15 percent.

For information: Call 800-HILTONS (800-445-8667); www.hilton.com. To enroll in Hilton Senior HHonors Worldwide, call 972-788-0878.

HISTORIC HOTELS OF AMERICA

All of these famous landmark hotels are individually owned and make their own decisions about offers to older guests. Here are some examples. The American Club in Kohler, Wisconsin, takes 15 percent off the regular rates for guests over 62. The Hotel Jerome in Aspen, Colorado, offers a 10 percent discount to AARP members, while the Hotel St. Francis in Santa Fe, New Mexico, does the same for visitors over 65. The Eagle Mountain House in Jackson, New Hampshire, offers those over 60 a 20 percent discount on midweek rates and 50 percent off the brunch buffet on Sundays. Both the Landmark Inn in Marquette, Michigan, and the Hotel San Carlos in Phoenix, Arizona, give a 10 percent discount to AARP members.

For information: Call the hotel directly. Or contact National Trust Historic Hotels of America, 1785 Massachusetts Ave., NW, Washington, DC 20036; 800-678-8946 or 202-588-6000; http://historichotels.nationaltrust.org.

HOLIDAY INN HOTELS & RESORTS

At all participating Holiday Inn properties throughout the world, including Holiday Inn Express, members of AARP get a minimum of 10 percent off the regular room rates any day of the year. The privilege is subject, of course, to space availability.

For information: Call 800-HOLIDAY (800-465-4329); www.holiday-inn.com.

HOWARD JOHNSON INTERNATIONAL

At all of Howard Johnson's more than 500 locations in the U.S., Canada, Mexico, and other countries, members of AARP and CARP are entitled to a discount of 15 percent off the regular rates on available rooms every day of the year. Just flash your membership card. All others over the age of 55 also get a 15 percent discount.

For information: Call 800-I-GO-HOJO (800-446-4656); www.hojo.com.

HYATT HOTELS & RESORTS

A collection of upscale hotels in the U.S., Canada, and the Caribbean, Hyatt always gives a discount of 15 to 25 percent off the regular room rates to guests over the age of 62. You must simply ask for it. Many Hyatts, mostly Hyatt Regencies, offer an even better deal, giving those over 62 a special rate of $99 a night when rooms are available.

For information: Call 800-233-1234; www.hyatt.com.

INTER-CONTINENTAL HOTELS & RESORTS

Recently acquired by the Bass Hotels lodging family, most of the 120-or-so upscale Inter-Continentals offer a 10 percent discount off the regular room rates to members of AARP on any day of the year. Present your membership card and ask for it.

For information: Call 800-327-0200; www.interconti.com.

ITT SHERATON HOTELS, INNS & RESORTS

All Sheratons around the world give you a break if you are over 60 or a member of AARP or CARP, and if you request it when you make a reservation. That's 15 to 25 percent off the published room rates, subject to availability. Sometimes, however, these hotels have special sales and packages that are better deals than the senior rate, so always ask for the best available room rate at the time you plan to visit.

For information: Call 800-325-3535; www.sheraton.com.

KIMPTON GROUP HOTELS

Each of the five Kimpton Group hotels in San Francisco as well as others in Chicago and Salt Lake City feature their own special rates or package with a variety of amenities and privileges for mature travelers who are members of AARP or over the age of 55. Hotel Monaco Salt Lake City, for example, includes accommodations and a city tour for two. There is no central contact for this group of boutique hotels; instead, each must be contacted directly to book reservations.

For information: Call 800-546-2622 for the telephone numbers and websites of each of the hotels; or access www .kimptongroup.com.

KNIGHTS INNS

This budget motel chain with about 235 locations, mostly in the East, gives a discount of 10 percent every day of the year to anyone over 50.

For information: Call 800-843-5644; www.knightsinn.com.

LA QUINTA INNS

With over 300 locations in the U.S., these motor inns are inexpensive and become even more so when you ask for your 10 percent discount. You'll get it, except during special events, if you are a member of AARP or a similar organization or if you are 55 and can prove it.

For information: Call 800-531-5900; www.laquinta.com.

LOEWS HOTELS

The three "Generation G" packages recently introduced by Loews Hotels in the U.S. and Canada are designed to encourage grandparents and grandchildren vacationing together. One package is specifically for teenagers, another for children over 10, and the third for all ages. Because each of the 14 hotels is located in a major city with different attractions, each property offers its own activities and rates that may vary during the year. In Orlando, for example, the current package may include Seaworld, Wet N Wild water park, and the Kennedy Space Center; in Santa Monica, it's Universal Studios, the California Science Center, and the Getty Museum; in Denver, a baseball game, Water World, or a play. At several of the hotels, a second room may be reserved at half price.

For information: Call 800-23-LOEWS; www.loewshotels .com.

MAINSTAY SUITES

See Choice Hotels International. Perks include continental breakfast. Call 800-660-MAIN (800-660-6246); www.main staysuites.com.

MARC RESORTS

If you are at least 50, a 25 percent discount is yours, subject to availability, at Marc Resorts' 20 locations on five Hawaiian islands.

For information: Call 800-535-0085.

MARRIOTT HOTELS, RESORTS & SUITES

Marriott's program for over-50s is among the best deals around if you are a member of AARP or CARP and can plan ahead. With a 21-day nonrefundable advance booking and available space, you will get at least half off the regular rates at more than 220 participating locations worldwide. You must pay in advance for the entire stay by check or credit card when you make your reservation.

For those who can't commit themselves three weeks in advance, there is a flat 10 percent discount on regular room rates every day of the year for AARP or CARP card carriers.

In addition, members are offered a 20 percent discount on food and nonalcoholic beverages at the hotel restaurants for up to eight people. This may be used as often as you like, and you are not required to be an overnight guest to get this discount, but you must belong to AARP or CARP. Always ask first if the hotel or resort is participating in the discount plan.

And more: You'll get a 10 percent discount on most items at participating retail shops whether or not you're a hotel guest.

Two hitches: The room discounts may not be available at all times, especially during peak periods; and some Marriotts do not participate in the seniors program, so make inquiries before you book.

For information: Call 800-228-9290; www.marriotthotels .com.

MASTER HOSTS INNS & RESORTS

See Red Carpet Inn. Call 800-251-1962; www.reservahost .com

McINTOSH INNS

At many of these economy inns in New Jersey, Pennsylvania, and Delaware, guests over 50 are offered 10 percent off the regular rates. Continental breakfast is included.

For information: Call 800-444-2775.

MICROTEL INN

At these budget economy hotels there is no official senior program, although some of its 200-or-so properties offer a small discount to travelers over 50. Special features include interior corridors and a complimentary breakfast every morning.

For information: Call 888-771-7171; www.microtel.com.

MOTEL 6

Take advantage of a 10 percent discount off the room rates at any of these more than 850 economy budget motels in the U.S. and Canada by showing your AARP or CARP card.

For information: Call 800-4-MOTEL6 (800-466-8356); www.motel6.com.

MOVENPICK HOTELS

If you're over 65, you pay only 65 percent of the regular weekend room rate on Friday, Saturday, or Sunday nights at the Movenpick Hotels in The Hague and S'Hertogenbosch, both in the Netherlands. But you must book in advance, requesting the senior rate.
For information: Call 800-344-6835; www.movenpick hotels.com.

NATIONAL 9 INNS

You'll get a 10 percent discount at age 50 at most of these motels/hotels concentrated in the West.
For information: Call 800-524-9999.

NOVOTEL HOTELS

Older travelers get up to 50 percent off published rates at nine hotels in the United States and Canada. Show proof that you're at least 55, except at Novotel Hotels in New York City and Montreal, where you must be 60 and 65, respectively.
For information: Call 800-NOVOTEL (800-668-6835); www.accor.com.

OHANA HOTELS OF HAWAII

These moderately priced hotels and suites, part of the Outrigger group, are all located in Waikiki. They offer a straightforward 30 percent discount off the published room rates for anybody over the age of 50. Members of AARP or CARP get an additional 5 percent off the rates.

For information: Call 800-462-6262; www.ohanahotels .com.

OMNI HOTELS

Almost all of these upscale hotels—over 40 of them—take 10 percent off the published room rates every day of the week for members of AARP. To get the special room rate, reserve ahead and request the discount.

For information: Call 800-THE OMNI (800-843-6664); www.omnihotels.com.

OUTRIGGER HOTELS & RESORTS

Travelers 50 and over receive a 30 percent savings off published retail room rates, subject to space availability, when booking the Fifty-Plus Program at any of Outrigger's 13 hotels and resort condominiums on Oahu, Maui, Kauai, and the Big Island of Hawaii. On the Marshall Islands, Guam, or Fiji, the discount is 20 percent. Members of AARP or CARP get an additional 5 percent off the rates at all properties.

For information: Call 800-OUTRIGGER (800-688-7444); www.outrigger.com.

PARADORES OF SPAIN

See Spain, Chapter 8.

PARK INN & PARK PLAZA HOTELS

This group of hotels worldwide gives a 25 percent discount to members of AARP.

For information: Call 800-670-7275; www.parkhtls.com.

PASSPORT INN

See Red Carpet Inn. Call 800-251-1962; www.reservahost .com.

POUSADAS DE PORTUGAL

See Portugal, Chapter 8.

QUALITY HOTELS & SUITES

See Choice Hotels International. At suite hotels, you'll get a free breakfast. Call 800-228-5151; www.qualityinns.com.

RADISSON HOTELS WORLDWIDE

At Radisson's more than 400 locations in 55 countries, take advantage of Senior Breaks, a program that gives you a discount of 25 to 40 percent off the standard rates at age 50 in the U.S. and Canada and 65 in Europe. You'll get the discount year-round, seven days a week, based on space availability. There's no club to join—just carry proof of your age.

In addition, many Radissons offer you and your party a 15 percent discount on dining in hotel restaurants except during peak dining hours, whether or not you are guests of the hotel. All you need is proof of age.

For information: Call 800-333-3333; www.radisson.com.

RAMADA LIMITEDS, INNS, AND PLAZA HOTELS

Anybody may join the Club Ramada—it's free—and enjoy many benefits, but if you are at least 60, you'll get 25 percent off every time you stay at a Ramada property, plus 10 points for every dollar you spend at hundreds of participating Ramadas.

You'll be given 1,000 bonus points when you sign up for the club and another 1,000 on your first stay. Accumulated points can be redeemed for airline tickets, gift certificates at retail stores, lodging, and travel. Included with the membership, too, are discounts on travel packages and car rentals plus a quarterly newsletter.

Members of AARP or CARP who do not belong to the club have 15 percent taken off the regular rates if rooms are available.

For information: Call 800-272-RAMADA or 800-272-6232 for reservations; www.ramada.com. To enroll in the Club Ramada, call 800-672-6232.

RAMADA INTERNATIONAL HOTELS

If you are 60 years old or belong to a senior organization, you will get 10 to 25 percent off the regular room rates at most of these midscale hotels and resorts located mainly in Europe. Ask for it when you make your reservations.

For information: Call 800-854-7854, www.ramadahotels .com.

RED CARPET INN

More than half of the affordable Hospitality International properties—including Red Carpet Inn, Passport Inn, Downtowner Inns, Master Host Inns & Resorts, and Scottish Inn, in the U.S., Jamaica, and the Bahamas—give a discount to seniors. All of the properties are independently owned and so their policies vary, but most give at least 10 percent off the

GOOD DEALS IN RESTAURANTS

Many restaurants offer special deals to people in their prime, but in most cases you must seek them out yourself by reading the menu, asking at the restaurant, or watching the ads in the local newspapers. At some big chains, such as the International House of Pancakes, Kentucky Fried Chicken, Applebee's, and Wendy's, there's a recommended corporate policy of senior discounts or special senior menus. The same is true for some smaller regional chains such as Country Kitchen, Max & Erma's, Chili's Grill & Bar, Black-eyed Pea, and Lyon's.

Sometimes a senior discount is available anytime you decide to dine, but often it's good only during certain hours or as "early bird" specials before 5:00 or 6:00 P.M. The eligible age varies from 55 to 65, and occasionally a restaurant requires that you sign up for its free senior club that issues you a membership card.

In addition, a few hotel chains will give you a break on your meal checks when you eat in their restaurants. For example:

At participating **Hilton Hotels** restaurants in the U.S. and Canada, you're entitled to a 20 percent discount on dinners for two, hotel guests or not, if one of you is a member of Hilton's Senior HHonors Worldwide.

The restaurants in the participating **Marriott Hotels and Resorts** will take 20 percent off your bill, except on alcoholic beverages, for a party of up to eight people if you belong to AARP or CARP, whether or not you are guests of the hotel.

If you join the September Days Club, you'll get room discounts at **Days Inns** worldwide and also a minimum of 10 percent off meals at participating locations.

Doubletree Hotels take 10 percent off the bill for food and nonalcoholic beverages in participating restaurants for members of AARP who are guests at the hotel.

You'll get a reduction of 15 percent on your food bills for yourself and your party when you eat during off-peak hours at participating **Radisson Hotels Worldwide** restaurants, whether or not you are hotel guests. You qualify for the savings at age 50 in U.S. locations and usually at 65 in Europe.

Stop in at a company-owned **Burger King** before 10:30 A.M. and you'll get free coffee if you're a senior. Check yours out—if it's a participating location, you're in luck.

regular rates. Some include a free complimentary breakfast and others allow pets.

For information: Call 800-251-1962; www.reservahost .com.

RED LION HOTELS & INNS

All of these locations in the West give members of AARP and others over 50 a discount of 10 percent off corporate and best available rates.

For information: Call 800-RED-LION (800-733-5466); www.redlion.com.

RED ROOF INNS

Just show proof that you're over 60 and you'll get a discount of up to 10 percent off the regular rates at all 350 of these budget inns in the U.S.

For information: Call 800-RED-ROOF (800-843-7663); www.redroof.com.

RENAISSANCE HOTELS, RESORTS & SUITES

At more than 95 properties worldwide, you are offered up to half off the regular rates, seven days a week, if you belong to AARP or CARP and you make a 21-day nonrefundable advance reservation. You must pay for the entire stay by check or credit card when you make your reservation.

Without an advance purchase, you're entitled to 10 percent off on room rates.

Other savings for members include 20 percent discount on food and nonalcoholic beverages in the hotel restaurants for your party of up to eight people, guests of the hotel or not. And you'll get another 10 percent off most items in participating gift shops, again whether or not you are staying at the hotel.

For information: Call 800-468-3571; www.renaissance hotels.com.

RESIDENCE INN BY MARRIOTT

These extended-stay all-suite accommodations complete with kitchens offer members of AARP or CARP a 15 percent discount on regular rates every day of the year at participating locations. Complimentary continental breakfast and weekday social hours are usually included.

For information: Call 800-331-3131; www.residenceinn .com.

RODEWAY INNS

See Choice Hotels International. These inns, with more than 200 locations worldwide, give you a 15 percent discount— and sometimes 30 percent—if rooms are available when you make an advance reservation using the toll-free number.

Without a reservation, you'll get a 10 percent discount every day of the year. Many rooms feature such senior-friendly amenities as special lighting, grab bars, large-face clocks, big TV control buttons.

For information: Call 800-228-2000; www.rodewayinn .com.

SANDMAN HOTELS

All situated in western Canada, these inns take up to 25 percent off the regular room rate if you are 55 or over. Show proof of age at check-in or, better yet, call the number below and ask for a 55 Plus Card. It's free.

For information: Call 800-726-3626; www.sandman.ca.

SCOTTISH INN

See Red Carpet Inn. Call 800-251-1962; www.reservahost .com.

SHONEY'S INNS

Economy lodgings, Shoney's approximately 75 locations in 18 states take 15 percent off the room rates for members of AARP and CARP anytime, any day of the week. If you are not a member but are at least 55 years old, you will get a 10 percent discount when rooms are available.

For information: Call 800-552-INNS; www.shoneysinn .com.

SLEEP INN

See Choice Hotels International. Continental breakfast is included.

For information: Call 800-SLEEP INN (800-753-3746); www.sleepinn.com.

SONESTA HOTELS & RESORTS

This collection of upscale hotels in the U.S., Egypt, Italy, Peru, Bermuda, and the Caribbean gives members of AARP a 15 percent discount off the regular rates. You must make reservations in advance, of course.

For information: Call 800-SONESTA (800-766-3782); www.sonesta.com.

SPRINGHILL SUITES BY MARRIOTT

Make a reservation at one of these all-suite, moderately priced hotels and you'll get a 10 percent discount on the regular room rate if you belong to AARP or CARP. Included in the package are a complimentary continental breakfast and free local phone calls.

For information: Call 888-287-9400; www.springhill suites.com.

STAYBRIDGE SUITES BY HOLIDAY INN

Designed for extended stays by travelers who require lodging for at least five consecutive nights, Staybridge Suites offer studios and one- and two-bedroom accommodations complete with kitchen facilities. If you are a member of AARP, be sure to get your 10 percent discount any day of the year, subject to space availability.

For information: Call 800-238-8000; www.staybridge.com.

SUMMERFIELD SUITES BY WYNDHAM

These one- or two-bedroom suites are designed to provide privacy and space. Each has its own living room, kitchen, big closet, and private bathroom per bedroom. What's more, when space is available, members of AARP or CARP get a 20 percent reduction on corporate rates Monday through Thursday nights and 20 percent off the lowest weekend rates on Friday, Saturday, and Sunday nights.

For information: Call 800-WYNDHAM (800-996-3426); www.wyndham.com.

SUMNER SUITES

Sumner Suites, a nationwide all-suite hotel chain with about 25 locations in the U.S., offers discounts of 15 percent on weekday rates (Sunday through Thursday) and 10 percent off discounted weekend rates (Friday and Saturday) to AARP members.

For information: Call 800-747-8483; www.sumnersuites .com.

SUPER 8 MOTELS

Virtually all of these over 1,900 no-frills economy motels in the U.S. and Canada give a discount of 10 percent to anyone over the age of 50.

For information: Call 800-800-8000; www.super8.com.

TRAVELODGE HOTELS

All Travelodges and Thriftlodges, more than 550 in the U.S., Canada, and Mexico, have a nice straightforward plan for older travelers. This is a simple unrestricted 15 percent discount off all room rates anytime, any night, for members of AARP and CARP when advance reservations are made through the toll-free number. A 10 percent discount is offered to everyone over 50 without reservations when rooms are available.

For information: Call 800-578-7878; www.travelodge.com.

U.S. CITY CENTRE HOTELS

See Fairmont Hotels & Resorts. Call 800-441-1414; www
.fairmont.com.

VAGABOND INNS

Vagabond's Smart Senior Program is one of the better deals
around. It gives you 30 percent off the standard rates at age
55 at all except one of these economy inns on the West
Coast. This group of hotels also has its Vagabuck Program,
which gives you $5 in play money when you check out to
use the next time you stay at a Vagabond Inn.
For information: Call 800-522-1555; www.vagabondinns
.com.

VILLAGER LODGES & VILLAGER PREMIER

At most of these extended-stay motels and suites, you can
get a room with a kitchenette at a discount of 10 percent
off the daily rate if you belong to AARP or are over the age
of 60.
For information: Call 800-328-7829; www.villager.com.

WESTCOAST HOTELS

If you are over 55, ask for the senior rate at these midscale
hotels in the western states, Alaska, and Hawaii. The rate
varies by location.
For information: Call 800-426-0670; www.westcoasthotels
.com.

WESTIN HOTELS

Members of the ITT Sheraton family, Westin Hotels offer you
the same 15 to 25 percent off the published room rates, sub-

ject to availability, if you are at least 60 or a member of AARP. But before going for your discount, ask if there are any special promotional sales going on at the time you plan to visit—you may find a better bargain. And be sure to request a room with a "Heavenly Bed," a new feature at many Westins.

For information: Call 800-WESTIN-1 (800-937-8461); www.westin.com.

WINGATE INNS INTERNATIONAL

A midscale national hotel chain that features sophisticated technology for business travelers, including free high-speed access connections to the Internet in every room via a lap-top computer, Wingate Inns gives a 15 percent discount off the regular room rates to anybody who is over the age of 60 or a 50-plus member of AARP or CARP. Other amenities include complimentary continental breakfast, wireless phones for use in the hotel, and 24-hour access to self-service business center with free fax, printing, and copying equipment.

For information: Call 800-228-1000; www.wingateinns .com.

WYNDHAM HOTELS & RESORTS

Wyndham's offer to mature guests is generous and simple. Members of AARP get 20 percent off corporate rates Monday through Thursday nights and 20 percent off the lowest weekend rates on Friday, Saturday, and Sunday nights. Rooms at these rates are limited; try to reserve them early.

For information: Call 800-WYNDHAM (800-996-3426); www.wyndham.com.

WYNDHAM LUXURY RESORTS

At most of these upscale resort inns in the U.S., members of AARP are offered 20 percent off corporate rates on weekdays and 20 percent off the lowest weekend rates on Fridays, Saturdays, and Sundays when rooms are available.

For information: Call 800-WYNDHAM (800-996-3426); www.wyndham.com.

5

Alternative Lodgings for Thrifty Wanderers

If you're willing to be innovative, imaginative, and, occasionally, fairly spartan, you can travel for a song or thereabouts. Here are some novel kinds of lodgings that can save you money and perhaps offer adventures in the bargain. Not all of them are designed specifically for people over 50, but each reports that the major portion of its clientele consists of free spirits of a certain age who like to travel, appreciate good value for their money, and enjoy meeting new people from other places.

For more ways to cut travel costs and get smart at the same time, check out the residential/educational programs in Chapter 12.

AFFORDABLE TRAVEL CLUB
Join this bed-and-breakfast club limited to people over 40 and you'll pay a pittance for accommodations, meet

interesting people, and see new places. You may join as a host member, putting up other travelers in your spare bedroom a couple of times a year and providing breakfast and a little of your time to acquaint your guests with your area. Visitors pay $15 for a single or $20 for a double per night for their stay. In return, you get to stay in other people's homes for the same token fee when you travel.

There are currently about 1,400 members in this club in 46 states and 25 countries offering accommodations ranging from simple bedrooms to suites and condos. For a membership fee of $60 a year, you receive a newsletter twice a year plus an annual directory from which you choose your own hosts and from which others may choose you. The club also sponsors a group tour at least once a year.

If you have a pet, you may want to take advantage of the club's house-sitting and pet-sitting service—members move into your house and care for your house and/or pets while you're on vacation, meanwhile enjoying a visit to your neighborhood in exchange.

For information: Affordable Travel Club, 6556 Snug Harbor Ln., Gig Harbor, WA 98335; 253-858-2172.

AMERICAN-INTERNATIONAL HOMESTAYS

AIH matches you with English-speaking hosts in foreign countries where you live in a private home and become part of the family for anywhere from three days to a couple of weeks. Traveling alone, as a couple, or in a group, you'll immerse yourselves in the local culture, your hosts acting as your personal guides and interpreters, in some of the most remote places in the world. Choices include Russia, China, Ukraine, Uzbekistan, Estonia, Mongolia, and the Kirghiz

Republic, among others. At this writing, the cost of a home-stay—including a private bedroom, breakfast, and dinner—is $100 per night single, $175 for two.

For information: American-International Homestays, PO Box 1754, Nederland, CO 80466; 800-876-2048 or 303-258-3234; www.aihtravel.com/homestays.

DEL WEBB'S SUN CITIES

For people thinking of buying a retirement home, the Del Webb Corporation offers Vacation Getaway programs designed to let you experience firsthand the lifestyle in its adult communities. You'll have your own villa for three, four, or seven nights starting any day of the week and enjoy all the facilities: tennis, golf, swimming, aerobics, and socializing with residents and staff. Depending on the season and the location, the rates range from about $199 for three nights to about $675 for a seven-day package in the high season.

The requirements: One partner in a visiting couple must be at least 55 years old, no one in the party may be under 19, guests may stay no more than twice at the same location, and they must agree to meet with a sales representative during their stay.

The communities currently offering Vacation Getaways include Sun City Grand in Phoenix; Sun City Anthem in Las Vegas; Sun City Palm Desert in Palm Springs; Sun City Lincoln Hills in Lincoln, California; Sun City Hilton Head; Sun City Texas in Georgetown, Texas; and Spruce Creek Golf and Country Club in Ocala, Florida.

For information: Del Webb's Sun Cities, 6001 N. 24th St., Phoenix, AZ 85016; 800-433-5932; www.suncity.com.

ELDERHOSTEL HOMESTAYS

Elderhostel collaborates with World Learning, a 65-year-old institution specializing in international education and homestays, to place hostelers in the homes of local families in many foreign countries. The Homestay Programs—two to three weeks long—begin with a week of lectures, classes, and field trips to introduce you to the local history and culture. Then you move into your host home to spend a few days as a member of the family. Those participating in three-week programs meet for an additional week of classes and excursions before heading home.

For information: Elderhostel, Dept. M2, PO Box 1959, Wakefield, MA 01880; 877-426-8056 or 617-426-7788; www.elderhostel.org.

EVERGREEN BED AND BREAKFAST CLUB

This bed-and-breakfast club exclusively for people over the age of 50 was founded in 1982 and now has about 4,000 member families in the U.S. and Canada as well as a few in Mexico and Europe. Whether a host home is elegant or simple, members pay only $10 single or $15 per couple for each overnight stay and bountiful breakfast. In return, they welcome members of the club into their own homes as often as they wish.

When you join, you receive two directories a year with relevant information about all of the host families and the special attractions of their areas. You then make your own arrangements for visits and pay the gratuities directly to the hosts. A quarterly newsletter provides the latest information. Annual club dues are $60 single and $75 per couple.

An important aspect of this hospitality club is the opportunity for members to make new friends and perhaps travel together, as many members do. Group tours and cruises are offered occasionally, too.

For information: Evergreen Bed and Breakfast Club, 201 W. Broad St., Ste. 181, Falls Church, VA 22046; 800-962-2392 or 815-456-3111; www.evergreenclub.com.

NEW PALTZ SUMMER LIVING

Think about spending a couple of summer months in the mountains, about 75 miles north of New York City. Every year, while the usual student occupants are on vacation, 140 furnished garden apartments are reserved for seniors in the village of New Paltz, near Mohonk Mountain and home of a branch of the State University of New York. The rents at this writing for the entire summer (from early June until late August) range from $1,325 to $3,600, depending on the size of the apartment. Living right in town next to the campus, you may audit college courses free, attend lectures and cultural events, and take part in planned activities in the clubhouse. There is a heated pool and a tennis court in the complex. Buses travel to New York frequently for those who want to go to the theater, and there are frequent day trips to places of interest.

For information: New Paltz Summer Living, 19 E. Colonial Dr., New Paltz, NY 12561; 800-431-4143 or 914-255-7205.

ROBSON COMMUNITIES

The Preferred Guest Program invites the prospective adult home-buyers to stay a few days at one of the four Robson

Communities in Arizona. Here they may sample the "active adult resort lifestyle" complete with clubhouses, swimming pools, tennis courts, spas, and golf courses. As a guest, you'll stay on-site in a furnished two-bedroom home, play a round of golf, have a dinner with residents, use the recreational facilities, and spend a few hours with a salesperson. Depending on the time of year, prices currently range from $99 (in summer) to $349 (in winter) for a three-night stay. One person in your party must be at least 40 and no one under 19 may participate.

For information: Robson Communities, 9532 E. Riggs Rd., Sun Lakes, AZ 85248; 800-732-9949; www.robson.com.

ROYAL COURT APARTMENTS

As an alternative to hotels, one-, two-, and three-bedroom apartments are available all year at the Royal Court in central London, one block from Hyde Park, giving you plenty of space and a home at the end of a busy day. You'll get a discount of 10 percent if you are over 50 and mention this book when you make your reservations.

For information: Royal Court Apartments, British Network, Ltd., 112 W. High St., Carlisle, PA 17013; 800-274-8583 or 717-249-5990; www.britishnetworkltd.com.

SENIOR GETAWAYS

If you'd like a complete, all-inclusive winter holiday—no cooking, no driving, no housekeeping—Senior Getaways may be your answer. From November through April, you may stay at the Colonial Bayfront Hotel or the Crystal Bay Hotel in St. Petersburg, Florida, for two weeks to six months. You get accommodations, breakfast and dinner, transportation in the area, sightseeing excursions, exercise classes and other activities, and evening entertainment.

For information: Senior Getaways, 126 Second Avenue NE, St. Petersburg, FL 33701; 800-223-8123; wwwcolonial bayfronthotel.com.

SENIORS ABROAD

Seniors Abroad is a cultural exchange program for people over the age of 50. It pairs American travelers with host families for three-to-four-week homestays in Japan or Great Britain. There, singly or as couples, visitors spend five or six days in the homes of several different families during the trip. In the U.S., host families do the same for foreign visitors. Hosts are volunteers and guests pay only for transportation, tours, hotels between stays, and other expenses.

For information: Seniors Abroad, 12533 Pacato Circle North, San Diego, CA 92128; 858-485-1696.

SERVAS INTERNATIONAL

Servas, the oldest free hospitality organization in the world, is an international cooperative system of peace activists who offer free lodging as a way to promote friendship and understanding across national and cultural boundaries. With over 15,000 hosts in 135 countries who welcome other members into their homes for a day or two without charge, its yearly fee for travelers is $65 (U.S.) or $50 (Canada). This nonprofit, interracial, interfaith organization is open to travelers of all ages who must provide two letters of reference and an interview. Hosts in the U.S. are asked for a voluntary donation of $35 a year to cover administrative costs.

For information: Send a #10 self-addressed, stamped envelope to US Servas, 11 John St., Room 407, New York, NY
10038; 212-267-0252; www.usservas.org. In Canada: Servas Canada, 229 Hillcrest Ave., Toronto, ON M2N 3P3;
www.servas.org.

SUN CITY CENTER

Located about 25 miles outside of Tampa, Florida, Sun City
Center wants you to see what a 5,000-acre, self-contained
retirement community is all about. Its Preferred Guest Program offers an inexpensive vacation package so you can
sample the lifestyle there. You may stay for a few days, lodging at a motel on the grounds, and take part in all of the
activities. A stay of four days, three nights with daily continental breakfast, tennis, swimming, and access to club facilities currently costs $109 to $189, depending on the season.
An extensive tour of the town with a salesperson is on the
agenda.

For information: Sun City Center, PO Box 5698, Sun City
Center, FL 33571; 800-237-8200; www.suncityctr.com.

WOMEN WELCOME WOMEN
WORLD WIDE

WWWWW is a hospitality club with over 2,500 members
in 68 countries who may stay in one another's homes without cost. Dedicated to furthering friendships among women
from different cultures, 5W asks its members for a donation
of $35 in return for a membership list and three newsletters
a year. Members, the majority of them over 50, correspond
with potential hostesses who have offered to share their
homes. Together they arrange their visits at a time conve-

nient to both. The newsletters include notices of 5W gatherings all over the world and a list of women seeking travel companions.

For information: Women Welcome Women World Wide, 203-454-1609; www.womenwelcomewomen.org.uk.

HOME EXCHANGE FOR 50-PLUS

One way to go on vacation without seriously depleting your funds is to exchange homes with someone who lives in a place you'd like to visit and who wants to spend time in your house. No money changes hands and you can save plenty on the cost of hotel rooms and perhaps even car rentals. Although there are many exchange programs ready to serve as matchmakers, we know of only one that deals exclusively with people over the age of 50. Seniors Vacation and Home Exchange provides listings of about 900 houses or apartments all over the world that may be traded for yours for a period of time to be mutually agreed upon. The catch is that you must have access to the Internet, possess an E-mail address, and pay $50 ($75 Canadian) for a two-year membership.

Any arrangement that suits both parties is encouraged—you may trade abodes simultaneously or exchange hospitality by visiting them at one time while they visit you at another. The trades need not come out even, including length of visits, size of homes, or amenities.

For information: Seniors Vacation and Home Exchange, www.seniorshomeexchange.com.

Beating the Costs of Car Rentals

Never rent a car without getting a discount or a special promotional rate. Almost all car-rental agencies in the U.S. and Canada give them to all manner of customers, including those who belong to over-50 organizations (see Chapter 19) or have reached a certain birthday. The discount that's coming to you as a senior member of society can save you some money, although short-term sales will almost always save you more. Refer to the membership material sent by the group to which you belong for information about your discount privileges.

It's almost impossible to sort out the confusing choices of rates, discounts, and add-on fees from the rental companies. To save money, you must shop around, compare costs, and make many decisions that can raise or lower your bill. And then, when applicable, get the senior discount for renters over 50. It may not amount to much, but it will help a little.

But, first, keep in mind:

- Car-rental agents may not always volunteer information about senior discounts or special sales, so always ask for it when you reserve your car.
- Don't settle for a senior discount or senior rate too hastily without investigating the possibility of an even better deal. Shop around yourself or ask your travel agent to find the *lowest available rate or package* at the time you are going to travel, and don't forget to ask about airport fees, taxes, and other extra charges. Senior discounts are usually given on the full published rental rate. So special promotional rates—in other words, sales—or even weekend rates are almost always better, sometimes much better. On the other hand, if you can get the senior discount *on top of the lowest posted rate*, regular or promotional, that's the deal you want.
- Book your car as far in advance as you can, especially if you are traveling during a holiday season. Generally, the later you book the more expensive it will be and the less likely you are to get the car you want. If closer to departure you find a better rate that suits your needs, you can rebook it.
- Remember that weekly and weekend rates are less expensive than daily rates.
- Read newspapers and magazines—especially those targeting over-50s. Look for ads for seasonal sales and clip out "value-added coupons" for additional discounts, cash

savings, or upgrades. Sometimes you'll also get coupons in the mail from clubs, associations, frequent-flyer programs, and credit-card companies. Your travel agent may have some to offer too.

- If you have access to the Internet, check the rental agencies' websites for special deals and last-minute offers. Several car-rental companies give a discount for booking on line.

- Before driving away in your rented car, inspect it for dents, scratches, or other damage. If you find any, ask the agent to sign a statement on the condition of the car and attach it to your rental agreement. That way, you won't be in danger of being charged for the damage upon your return.

- Ask if there is an additional-driver fee and don't sign up for it if you don't need it. If your spouse will be a second driver, rent from a company that allows a husband or wife to drive at no extra cost.

- When you reserve a car, always ask for a confirmation number. When you pick up your car, verify the discount or special rate *before* signing the agreement and ask if a better rate has become available since you booked.

- When you call to ask about rates or reservations, always be armed with your organization's ID number and your own membership card for reference. Present them again at the rental counter when you pick up your car and be sure to confirm your rate before signing the agreement.

- Special savings may not be available at every location, so remember to check them out every time you make a reservation.

- Don't purchase insurance you don't need. Review your personal auto insurance coverage and credit-card policy to determine if you require the optional loss/damage coverage offered by the rental companies. Your home-owner's policy may cover your personal belongings on the road.

- In the U.S., there is no maximum age for renting a car, but there are restrictions in other countries that vary by country and agency. One agency, for example, denies rentals to people over 65 in Greece and Northern Ireland, or over 75 in Ireland and Israel. Another restricts drivers over 60 in Malaysia or the Philippines. In the United Kingdom and Ireland, most agencies will not rent a car to a driver over 75. So make your age clear when you make your reservation. Shop around, and also consider leasing a car, in which case age may not be an issue.

- If you are traveling outside the U.S., don't wait until you arrive at your destination to arrange a rental. Book it here before you go because renting abroad is much more expensive. Remember to request your senior discount. Consult with your insurance carrier and credit-card companies to be sure you are covered overseas. Most personal automobile insurance covers you only for driving in the U.S., and coverage may not include certain types of vehicles.

- If you can drive a stick shift, you can cut the cost of a rental significantly. In other countries, automatic transmissions are not readily available and when they are, they are much more expensive.

ADVANTAGE RENT-A-CAR

A family-owned business, Advantage has about 130 locations in nine western states and gives members of AARP a discount of 5 percent on all retail rental rates. Join its Frequent Rental Club and when you rent four times, you'll earn a free day.

For information: Call 800-777-5500; www.advantagerent acar.com.

ALAMO RENT A CAR

Alamo's offer to seniors who want to take to the road is very simple—it's a discount of up to 15 percent, depending on the season and location, off the regular weekly or daily rates to anybody over the age of 50. When you book your car in advance, mention the rate code BY, ID #173059.

For information: Call 800-GO-ALAMO (800-462-5266); www.alamo.com.

AUTO EUROPE

Rent a car from Auto Europe, a consolidator that rents cars at a discount from 4,000 foreign locations all over the world, and if you belong to AARP or CARP you'll get a discount of 5 percent. Sometimes you'll even get it on top of other promotional discounts or upgrades.

For information: Call 800-223-5555; www.autoeurope .com.

AVIS RENT-A-CAR

If you are a member of AARP or CARP, you'll get a discount of 5 to 20 percent on the lowest available rate from Avis.

All rates include enhanced insurance coverage and unlimited free mileage at participating locations. Watch the coupon ads in over-50 publications that sometimes offer upgrades or more savings on top of your discount.
For information: Call 800-331-1800; www.avis.com.

BUDGET RENT-A-CAR

At its 3,200 locations all over the world, Budget gives a discount of 10 percent off the standard rental rates to members of AARP or CARP, and up to 25 percent to members of Sears Mature Outlook. And don't forget to check out the special deals offered on Budget's website.
For information: Call 800-527-0700; www.budget.com.

DOLLAR RENT A CAR

Join the free Silver Dollar Club if you are over 50 and you'll get a discount of 5 to 25 percent off the regular retail rates, depending on location and season, with unlimited mileage at participating locations and no charge for additional drivers. You must make an advance reservation, request the special rate, and mention the customer discount number SR2000.
For information: Call 800-800-4000; www.dollar.com. You may join the club on-line or by writing to Silver Dollar Club, 113 S. West St., Ste. 301, Alexandria, VA 22314.

ENTERPRISE RENT-A-CAR

Enterprise specializes in renting vehicles in neighborhoods "where people live and work," and that means its 4,000-or-

so branches are located in big cities and small towns as well as at major airports. It offers a discount of 5 percent off the regular rental rates to members of AARP and CARP.
For information: Call 800-RENT-A-CAR (800-736-8222); www.enterprise.com.

HERTZ CAR RENTAL

Members of AARP and NARFE are eligible for savings at 6,500 Hertz locations in 140 countries all over the world. They can get a discount of 5 to 15 percent off the rates with unlimited mileage included for most vehicle classes.
For information: Call 800-654-2200; www.hertz.com.

KEMWEL HOLIDAY AUTOS

This broker rents cars from major car-rental agencies to consumers at a discount in more than 4,000 locations in over 60 countries. Request a senior discount and you'll get an additional savings of 5 percent off the regular rates anywhere in the world.
For information: Call 800-678-0678; www.kemwel.com.

NATIONAL CAR RENTAL

If you belong to AARP or CARP and say so when making a reservation for a rental from National, you will get a discount off the lowest quoted rates of 5 to 20 percent at all locations in the U.S. and Canada. And if you don't belong but are over 55, you'll still get a discount, this time 5 to 25 percent, if you produce proof of your age. If you are going overseas and make your reservation here, you will get your

discount on a car rental in most countries. Value-plus coupons may be applied on top of your discount.
For information: Call 800-CAR-RENT (800-227-7368); www.nationalcar.com.

PAYLESS CAR RENTAL

The free Nifty Fifty Program from Payless gives travelers 50 and over a straightforward 5 percent discount on the lowest applicable rate, even on promotional sales. Simply state your age when you make your reservations for a car from 140 locations in the U.S., Europe, and the Middle East.
For information: Call 800-PAYLESS (800-729-5377); www .paylesscarrental.com.

RENAULT EURODRIVE

As an alternative to car rentals, this company offers short-term leases in more than 30 European countries for a minimum of 17 days and a maximum of 170 days. Designed for leisure travelers who reside outside of Europe, the program includes a brand-new car with unlimited mileage, insurance coverage with no deductible, no VAT, an extensive service network throughout Europe, and 24-hour English-speaking road assistance. Even more important to many travelers, it has no maximum age requirement. In many countries, rentals are limited to people under 70.

Until October 2001, Renault Eurodrive offers a discount of 10 percent to clients paying with the American Express Senior Member card.
For information: Call 800-221-1052 or 212-532-1221; www.renaultusa.com.

RENT-A-WRECK

This car-rental company, whose cars are not wrecks but merely three to five years old, leaves it up to each of its almost 500 franchisees throughout the country to set its own senior discount, usually 5 to 10 percent off the regular rates. Cars must be returned to the lot where they were rented.

For information: Call 800-535-1391; www.rent-a-wreck .com.

THRIFTY CAR RENTAL

Now here's a really good deal. If you are over 55, Thrifty guarantees you a 10 percent discount on all of its rates, even most special promotional rates, at all of its locations throughout the world. When you make an advance reservation, using the toll-free number, ask for the very best rate for the car you want, then make sure you get the additional 10 percent off. You must show identification at the counter when you pick up your car.

For information: Call 800-THRIFTY (800-847-4389); www.thrifty.com.

U-SAVE AUTO RENTAL OF AMERICA

U-Save Auto Rental, with about 1,400 locations—all independent franchises—in the U.S. and Canada, caters to the off-airport or neighborhood market and provides rental cars directly to consumers or local businesses. Many of its locations offer discounts of 5 to 10 percent to older customers, so ask when you call for a car. Ask, too, about special seasonal sales that may save you even more.

For information: Call 800-438-2300; www.usave.net.

7

Saving a Bundle on Trains, Buses, and Boats in North America

Getting around town, especially in a city where driving is not a practical option, probably means depending on public transportation to get you from hither to yon. Remember that, once you reach a particular birthday—in most cases, your 60th or 65th—you can take advantage of some good senior markdowns on trains, buses, subways, and, in some places, even taxis. All you usually need is a Medicare card, a Senior ID card, or your driver's license to play this game, which usually reduces fares by half. Although you may find it uncomfortable at first to pull out that card and flash it at the bus driver or ticket agent, it soon becomes very easy. Do it and you'll realize some nice savings.

And don't fail to take advantage of the bargains available to seniors on long-distance rail, bus, and boat travel as well.

RIDING THE RAILS

Probably every commuter railroad in the U.S. and Canada gives older passengers a break in fares, although you may have to do your traveling during off-peak periods when the trains are not filled with go-getters rushing to and from their offices. New York's Metro North, for example, charges anyone over 65 only half the regular fare for all trains except those arriving in Manhattan during weekday morning peak hours. And on the New York subways and buses, too, you pay only half whether you pay in cash, tokens, or a Reduced Fare MetroCard.

As for serious long-distance journeys, many mature travelers are addicted to the railroads, finding riding the rails a leisurely, relaxed, romantic, comfortable, economical, and satisfying way to make miles while enjoying the scenery.

So many passes and discounts on railroads are available to travelers heading for other parts of the country that sorting them out becomes confusing. But, once you do, they will help stretch your dollars while you cover a lot of ground.

See Chapter 8 for the best deals on transportation in foreign countries for travelers of a certain age.

AMTRAK

To accommodate senior travelers, Amtrak offers a 15 percent discount on the lowest available coach fares, including Explore America Passes, in the U.S., and on some Canadian routes, every day of the week to anyone over 62. The discount is also available on the Metroliner Service on Saturdays and Sundays but does not apply to the Auto Train or sleeping accommodations. Consider taking your children or grandchildren with you because, up to age 15, they ride at 50 percent of the regular adult fare.

Amtrak and VIA Rail Canada have teamed up to offer the North America Rail Pass, which allows you to travel to over 900 destinations, with unlimited stopovers, for 30 consecutive days in the U.S. and Canada. At age 60, you get 10 percent off the regular adult fare. Buy the pass from either company.

The lowest coach fares often sell out quickly, so try to book early. Not all fares are available on every train and some have restrictions that may not suit your plans, which means you should always ask questions before you buy.

For information: Amtrak, 800-USA-RAIL (800-872-7245); www.amtrak.com.

ALASKA RAILROAD

Passengers over 65 are entitled to a reduction of about 25 percent in weekend fares during the winter months—late September through early May—between Anchorage and Fairbanks and anywhere in between. You're encouraged to take food and drink with you because there's limited food service on the train for this 12-hour journey.

For information: Alaska Railroad, 800-544-0552; www .alaskarailroad.com.

ONTARIO NORTHLAND

This passenger railroad serving northeastern Ontario gives travelers over the age of 60 a 10 percent fare reduction any day of the year on the Northlander train running between Toronto and Cochrane. On the Polar Bear Express, a summer excursion line between Cochrane and Moosonee, the discount is about 20 percent. The Little Bear Train runs three times a week from Cochrane to Moosonee, returning the following day, and offers a 25 percent discount for travelers over 60.

For information: Ontario Northland, 555 Oak St. East, North Bay, ON P1B 8L3; 800-268-9281 or 705-472-4500.

VIA RAIL CANADA

The government-owned Canadian passenger railroad offers you, at age 60, 10 percent off any fare every day of the year on top of other discounts that may be available to all passengers. For example, add this 10 percent to the 40 percent reduction on off-peak travel, available to all ages and applicable any day of the week except Friday and Sunday, and you end up with tickets that are half price. Tickets at the off-peak rate must be purchased at least five or seven days in advance. However, the number of seats sold at this rate is limited, so plan ahead and buy your tickets as early as possible.

At 60 you are also eligible to buy three rail passes at a 10 percent discount. The first is the Canrailpass, available for peak or off-peak travel and valid for 12 days within a 30-day period anywhere on VIA Rail's transcontinental system. You may get on and off the train as many times as you wish, stopping wherever you like along the way after reserving your space for all segments.

Second, the Corridorpass, also sold for peak or nonpeak travel, gives you 10 days by train in the Quebec City–Windsor corridor, which includes service to Montreal, Ottawa, Toronto, Kingston, Niagara Falls, Kitchener, Stratford, London, and Sarnia.

And last, the North American Rail Pass, a cooperative venture with Amtrak, allows 30 consecutive days of unlimited travel to over 900 destinations in the United States and Canada. You get as many stopovers as you like but reservations are required for all portions of your journey.
For information: VIA Rail Canada, 888-842-7245; www .viarail.ca.

GOING BY BUS

Never, never board a bus without asking the driver whether there's a senior discount, because even the smallest bus lines in the tiniest communities (and the largest—New York City, for example) in the U.S., Canada, and abroad give seniors a break, usually 25 to 50 percent off at age 60 or 65. In Europe, your senior rail pass is often valid on major motorcoach lines as well, so always be sure to ask.

COACH CANADA

This bus line, which serves southwest Ontario and the Niagara Peninsula and runs between Toronto and Montreal, offers discounts of 10 to 25 percent to passengers over the age of 60. In cooperation with Greyhound Lines (U.S.), it also offers through service to Boston, New York, Washington, and Chicago.
For information: Coach Canada, PO Box 1017, Peterborough, ON K9J 7A5; 800-461-7661 or 705-748-6411.

GREYHOUND LINES

Greyhound Seniors Club, exclusively for those over the age of 62, gives members a 10 percent reduction on any walk-up fare tickets on Greyhound or Peter Pan Bus Lines,

10 percent off on food at company-owned restaurants located in the terminals, 10 percent off on charter services for groups, and 25 percent off on prepaid personal Greyhound Package Express shipments. Sign up at any company bus terminal and for $5 you'll get a club membership card valid for a year. Nonmembers over 62 get a 5 percent discount on the regular walk-up fares.

By the way, seniors also get a 10 percent discount on Greyhound's Ameripass, which gives you unlimited travel for 7, 15, or 30 days to any U.S. destination. Before you do anything, however, ask about the seven-day advance Friendly Fares—they may turn out to be cheaper.

For information: Call your local Greyhound reservation office or 800-231-2222; www.greyhound.com.

CITYPASS: SEE THE SIGHTS FOR LESS

Visitors to Boston, New York, Chicago, Hollywood, Philadelphia, San Francisco, or Seattle who take in several of the city's main attractions during their stay can save time and money with CityPass. That's especially true for those over 65 because they can buy it at a substanial discount. CityPass is a booklet of admission tickets to six of each city's most popular cultural attractions, cutting your cost by at least half the price of box office prices if you use them all. An added benefit is immediate admission without standing in ticket lines.

Tickets may be purchased at any of the CityPass attractions in each city or at city visitor centers, and are available in advance at www.citypass.net or through a travel agent. The booklets have no expiration date but are good only for nine days after you've used the first ticket.

For information: Call 707-256-0490; www.citypass.net.

GREYHOUND CANADA

Here you'll get 10 percent off all regular fares, any day of the week, all year-round, if you are a traveler over 65 with a valid ID. What's more, if you're accompanied by a companion and buy your tickets seven days in advance, the companion travels for half the senior fare. On the family fare, you get 10 percent off and an accompanying child under 16 goes free.

The 10 percent discount also applies to the Canada Pass, good for unlimited travel, with as many stopovers within the country as you like for specified numbers of days; and to the Discovery Pass, which gives you the same privileges on all routes wherever Greyhound goes within the U.S. and Canada.

But hold on. If you are planning to travel long distances within Canada and the U.S., Greyhound Canada offers an even better deal than you'll get using your senior discount. That's the Go Anywhere Fare that lets you take the bus between any two destinations in Canada and the U.S.—no matter how far—for only $139 (Canadian) in the winter and $169 in the summer (mid-June to September) at this writing. No stopovers with this fare, however, and no additional senior discount.

For information: Greyhound Canada, 800-661-8747 or 403-265-9111; www.greyhound.ca.

GRAY LINE WORLDWIDE

Gray Line is an association of 150 independent sightseeing tour companies serving about 200 destinations on five continents. Most of them give a discount of 10 percent on fares for half- or full-day sight-seeing tours to members of

AARP who purchase tour tickets at a Gray Line terminal and present a valid membership card. Some Gray Line companies also give discounts to nonmembers if they are age 55 or 60, so inquire before signing up for a tour.

For information: Call the Gray Line Worldwide office in your area or the corporate headquarters at 303-433-9800; www.grayline.com.

VOYAGEUR BUS LINES

This Canadian motorcoach line's Club 60 offers you a discount of 25 percent on all regular one-way bus fares without prior reservations, seven days a week. Simply present proof of your age when you buy your tickets.

For information: Voyageur Bus Lines; 514-842-2281 in Montreal; 613-238-5900 in Ottawa; www.voyageur.com/info.htm.

GOING BY BOAT

ALASKA MARINE HIGHWAY

Traveling on the Alaska Marine Highway, also known as the Alaska Ferry, in the off-season is a bargain for foot passengers 65 and older. Between October and April, you sail for half the regular adult fare within Alaskan waters. The discount does not apply to vehicle or cabin space. Sometimes in the summer, too, there are half fares for seniors on several of the smaller vessels. The message is: always ask if a senior rate is available.

For information: Alaska Marine Highway, 800-642-0066; www.state.ak.us/ferry.

TOURING BY BOAT, RAIL, BUS
THE ALASKAPASS

With an AlaskaPass, you may travel on many kinds of surface transportation in Alaska and the Yukon Territory for a specified number of days, using gateways in British Columbia and the state of Washington. One set discounted price allows unlimited travel on participating ferries, buses, and trains. You plan your own itinerary, make your own reservations, and pay for your transportation with the pass.

Although the AlaskaPass rates are the same regardless of your age (except for children), two add-ons to the pass cost $20 less than the regular fare for passengers over 60. One is the two-day Canadian Rail Explorer that takes you by rail from Vancouver to Prince Rupert, B.C. The other is the seven-day Washington/British Columbia Rail to Sail Tour, carrying you from Seattle to Prince Rupert by rail, down the Inside Passage of Alaska by ferry, to Victoria by motorcoach, and across Puget Sound by day boat back to Seattle.

For information: Call AlaskaPass, 800-248-7598; www .alaskapass.com.

8

Cutting Your Costs Abroad

The most enthusiastic voyagers of all age groups, Americans over 50—one out of three adults and a quarter of the total population—spend more time and money on travel than anybody else, especially when it comes to going abroad. It's been estimated that more than four out of every 10 passport holders are at least 55 years old. And there's hardly a country in the world today that doesn't actively encourage mature travelers to come for a visit.

Because you are now being avidly pursued, you can take advantage of many good deals in other lands. Airlines, for example, often offer you fare reductions on domestic flights within the country or the continent. Railroad and bus systems in most European countries give seniors deep discounts that are especially valuable if you plan an extended stay in one place. Even ferries and cruise ships are often ready to make you a deal. This chapter gives you a rundown on these and other ways to cut your European holiday costs, especially if you are planning your trip on your own. For the U.S. and Canada, see Chapter 7.

But, first, keep in mind:

■ Always ask about senior savings when you travel on planes, trains, buses, or boats anywhere in the world. Do the same when you buy tickets for movies, theaters, museums, tours, sight-seeing sites, historic buildings, and attractions. Don't assume, simply because you haven't heard about them or the ticket agent hasn't mentioned them, that they don't exist. Senior discounts are becoming more and more common everywhere, and you'll be amazed how much money you can save.

■ Some countries require that you purchase a senior card to take advantage of senior discounts, but most require only proof of age, usually in the form of a passport.

■ Always have the necessary identification with you and be ready to show it. Occasionally you may need an extra passport photograph.

■ For specifics on a country's senior discounts, call its national tourist office here before you go.

■ Call Rail Europe (800-438-7245), which represents most European railways, for information about train passes.

■ Your passport may be required along with your rail pass while you are in transit, so keep it with you.

■ Rail passes, including many national passes, sold in the U.S. and Canada can be bought from any travel agency or directly from Rail Europe. The national passes are often available only at major rail stations or airports within a country. Be prepared to show your passport.

■ Major U.S. hotel chains, such as Radisson, Marriott, Hilton, Choice, and Best Western, offer senior discounts that almost always apply at their participating properties in other countries.

■ Travel passes for sight-seeing are available in confusing profusion, and, since many overlap and some must be purchased before you leave home, it's wise to check them out before you go. Contact the national tourist offices of the countries you plan to visit.

■ Ask about rail pass insurance when you buy your pass, just in case it is lost or stolen during your trip.

■ Be sure your rail pass is validated at a railway ticket office the first time you use it, before boarding the train.

■ Tourist passes usually cost older travelers the same as everyone else, but in most cases they are definitely worth buying. Among the best buys everywhere are the inexpensive, easy-to-use "city cards" available for many major European cities. Usually good for one to four days, they give you free public transportation plus admission to the most important tourist sites. Many also offer discounts on tours, meals, theater tickets, cultural attractions, and shopping.

EUROPE BY RAIL

Rail passes make the going cheaper in Europe, especially if you travel with a companion or a group, and it's easier to use the passes than to buy tickets as you go. Besides, some of them offer senior discounts. It's not a simple matter to sort them all out, however. Some are multinational, good for travel in more than one country. Others are valid only within the borders of one country. These are usually designed for residents but can be useful to tourists as well.

Most passes are available in two different versions: a flexipass that permits travel for a specified number of days within a certain time period, and a consecutive-day pass that is valid on any day within a certain period. Many are not available overseas and must be purchased on this side of the Atlantic before you go. Others may only be purchased in the country that issues them. Be sure to get your rail pass validated at a railway station ticket office the first time you use it—before you board the train.

EURAILPASS AND EUROPASS

The Eurailpass gives you free unlimited first-class train travel on all the major railways of Hungary and 17 western European countries. There is no senior discount on this pass, but it is worth considering if you plan to cover many miles across many borders. On the other hand, if you are visiting just one country, you'd probably do better with that nation's senior discounts or national pass. Available for various numbers of days up to three months, the Eurailpass also entitles you to free or discounted travel on many buses, ferries, steamers, and suburban trains. If you are traveling with at least one other person, you can get a Eurail Saverpass or Eurail Saver Flexipass, which is an even better deal.

Or choose the new Eurail Selectpass which allows you to travel in three adjacent European countries out of the par-

FINDING A DOCTOR OVERSEAS

Before you leave on a trip to foreign lands, it would be wise to send for IAMAT's list of physicians all over the world who speak English; have had medical training in Great Britain, the U.S., or Canada; and have agreed to reasonable preset fees. When you join the free, nonprofit **International Association for Medical Assistance to Travellers** (IAMAT), you will get a membership card entitling you to its prearranged rates, a directory of English-speaking physicians in 125 countries and territories, a clinical record to take along with you, and advice on immunizations and preventive measures for many diseases including malaria. A packet of information about climate, food, water, clothing suggestions, and sanitary conditions in 1,450 cities is given to members who donate $25 or more. *For information:* IAMAT, 417 Center St., Lewiston, NY 14092; 716-754-4883; www.sentex.net/~iamat.

ticipating 17 European nations for 3 to 10 days within a two-month period. This one is also discounted when two or more people travel together.

The Europass, which is less expensive, is another option. It is good for unlimited first-class train travel anytime within a two-month period in five countries (France, Germany, Italy, Spain, and Switzerland). Up to two other countries may be added with a surcharge.

None of these passes is sold in Europe—each must be purchased before you leave home. And none gives seniors a special break.

For information: Rail Europe, 2100 Central Ave., Boulder, CO 80301; 800-4-EURAIL (800-438-7245); www.rail europe.com.

EUROSTAR

The Channel Tunnel train, connecting Paris or Brussels with London, offers many round-trips a day beneath the English Channel. The senior fares—you're eligible if you're over 60—are about 25 percent less than the regular adult fares on first-class tickets. They are also unrestricted and refundable. *For information:* Rail Europe, 800-EUROSTAR or 800-4-EURAIL (800-438-7245); www.raileurope.com.

SCANRAIL SENIOR PASS

Sold only on this side of the Atlantic, the Scanrail Pass provides unlimited travel in Denmark, Finland, Norway, and Sweden. If you're over 60, buy the Scanrail Senior Pass. It offers you the same privileges, but for about 10 percent less than younger adults pay. For more, see "Scandinavia" later in this chapter.
For information: Rail Europe, 2100 Central Ave., Boulder, CO 80301; 800-4-EURAIL (800-438-7245); www.rail europe.com.

THALYS TRAIN

Thalys, the European high-speed rail network, with trains that connect Paris with more than 25 cities in four countries, gives a discount of over 30 percent on the cost of first-class and second-class tickets to travelers 60 and older. Tickets may be booked three months in advance. Up to four children under age 12 travel free when accompanied by an adult with a first-class ticket.
For information: Rail Europe, 2100 Central Ave., Boulder, CO 80301; 800-4-EURAIL (800-438-7245); www.rail europe.com.

COUNTRY-BY-COUNTRY TRAVEL DEALS

AUSTRIA

Women who are at least 60 and men at least 65 can travel around Austria at half fare on trains and buses run by the federal government if they have first purchased an official Senior Citizen Railway Card for about $30. That makes it a good deal for those planning many trips. You can get it at major rail stations in Austria or Germany, or by mail. Contact the Austrian National Tourist Office for instructions.

On its daily nonstop service across the Atlantic to Vienna, Austrian Airlines gives a discount of 10 percent to passengers over 62 and their younger companions on all fares except for short-term sales. On domestic flights within Austria, women age 55 and men age 60 can get fare reductions of up to 25 percent off the regular cost if these flights are booked in conjunction with a round-trip transatlantic flight. And more: this airline's Visit Europe travel coupons, again sold together with round-trip tickets from the U.S., can save you 50 percent or more per segment on flights to more than 100 European destinations.

Although they offer you no discount, the Vienna Card and similar city cards in other Austrian cities and provinces including Salzburg, Linz, and Innsbruck, are very good deals. Sold for varied numbers of days, they give you unlimited travel on all public transportation—no more fumbling for the proper change—as well as free or reduced admission to museums, shops, attractions, and historic sites.

For information: Austrian National Tourist Office, PO Box 1142, New York, NY 10108; 212-944-6880; www .experienceaustria.com.

BELGIUM

For travelers 60 or older, the Golden Railpass allows six rail journeys between any two stations in Belgium for about $37 for second class and $57 first class, a savings of about 50 percent over the usual cost for adults. The pass may also be used by a traveling companion over 55 or under 12.

If you plan to take the train regularly, however, a better choice may be the Half-Fare Card for travelers of any age. It costs about $1.60 and takes 50 percent off the fares on all trips within one month.

Sabena, the Belgian national airline, gives passengers age 62 or older (60 in Canada) and a travel mate a 10 percent discount on most fares every day of the year on flights from North America to Belgium and via Brussels to other destinations in Europe.

Something else to remember: Most hotels in Brussels offer a 50 percent reduction on room rates on weekends and during the months of July and August, when the staffs of many international organizations leave town for home.

For information: Belgian National Tourist Office, 780 Third Ave., New York, NY 10017; 212-758-8130; www.visit belgium.com.

BERMUDA

February is Golden Rendezvous Month in Bermuda, when visitors over the age of 50 are treated to special events and free activities every day. For example, there are complimentary bus tours around the island and talks on the traditions, culture, history, flowers, and wildlife. Plus, there are bridge tournaments, ballroom dancing, and visits to museums. Many hotels offer special packages and rates, while the Visitors' Service Bureau distributes two free ferry/bus tokens per person as well as discount coupon books to use at retail stores and sight-seeing attractions.

For information: Bermuda Department of Tourism, 205 E. 42nd St., New York, NY 10017; 800-223-6106; www .bermudatourism.com.

DENMARK

When you buy tickets for the Danish State Railway system at any train station in Denmark, be sure to ask for the discount for passengers 65 and older. You get a 45 percent reduction on tickets every day except Friday and Sunday, when the discount drops to 20 percent. For information about the ScanRail Senior Pass to be used on the railroads of Denmark, Finland, Norway, and Sweden, see Scandanavia later in this chapter.

When you buy airline tickets, remember that SAS offers passengers over the age of 62 a 10 percent discount on most fares for flights from North America to Scandinavia and other destinations in Europe. For domestic travel within Denmark, the 65-year-old traveler receives 20 percent off certain fares, depending on the route.

Don't forget to buy the Copenhagen Card. Available for 24, 48, or 72 hours, it provides free unlimited travel by bus and train throughout the metropolitan region; free admission to more than 60 museums and historic sites; and discounts on car rentals, canal rides, and ferry crossings. City cards are also sold for Odense and Aalborg.

For information: Danish and Swedish Tourist Boards, 355 Third Ave., New York, NY 10017; 212-885-9700; www.visit denmark.com.

FINLAND

Travel within Finland is discounted, sometimes steeply, for people over 65. Simply show proof of your age—your passport—at the ticket office and you will pay only half fare on all trains and receive a 30 percent reduction on motor-coach journeys of at least 80 kilometers in length.

In addition, Finnair, the national airline, offers you 10 percent off on some translantic fares and a whopping 75 percent discount on domestic flights. You must show identification and pay for your tickets within three days of booking your flight. Cancellations and changes require only a small charge.

Book a voyage on the Silja Line between Helsinki and Stockholm, Talinn, or Rostock, or Turku to Stockholm and you will get a 15 percent discount off the regular fare if you have passed your 65th birthday.

Although the Helsinki Card is not discounted by age, it offers a free city tour and substantial savings on admittance to museums, exhibitions, attractions, buses, trams, and metro and commuter trains within the city limits. Available at the airport, many hotels, and tourist offices, it is sold for periods of one, two, or three days.

For information: Finnish Tourist Board, PO Box 4649, Grand Central Sta., New York, NY 10163; 212-885-9700; www.finland-tourism.com.

FRANCE

Visitors as well as residents over 60 are entitled to discounts on the French National Railroad (SNCF). The Decouverte Senior rate, designed for infrequent travelers, is yours simply by showing ID when you buy your ticket at a railway station. It gives you a 25 percent discount on the standard fares except on trips entirely within the Paris Transport Region.

If you plan to roam around France extensively, however, you may prefer buying a Carte Senior. It is valid for a year and gives you unlimited travel in first or second class at reduced rates—a 50 percent discount on some journeys during nonrush hours and a 25 percent discount on others, including the high-speed TGV trips and sleeping accommodations. The card currently costs 290 francs (about $38) and requires a passport photo when you buy it at any major train station. It also gives you a 30 percent reduction on standard fares on all train trips in 23 other European countries.

And here's a third possibility if you are planning extensive travel by train: it's the senior version of the new France Railpass which, starting at age 60, costs you a little less (about 5 percent) than the regular adult first-class pass. Finally, the France Saverpass, a rail pass that offers a discount for two or more adults traveling together, adds an additional small reduction for those over 60. Both passes must be purchased in the U.S. before you travel.

Wherever you go in France, from museums to historic sites, the movies to concerts, always ask for a senior discount, which usually is offered at age 60. Several hotel and motel chains, too, give special rates that apply at varying ages. And here's something to remember: seniors are permitted, along with the disabled and families with small children, to ride the elevator to the top of the Arc de Triomphe. Everyone else must climb up and down the steep stairs for a spectacular panoramic view of Paris.

The Paris Visite Card (for two, three, or five consecutive days) provides unlimited travel on the Paris metro, RER (suburban rail), and bus system, as well as regular SNCF (French National Railroad) service in the greater Paris region—plus discounts on some tourist attractions. Buy it here from RailEurope or when you arrive in Paris.

On transatlantic flights to Europe, Air France offers a 10 percent discount at age 62 to you and a younger travel mate. It does the same on domestic flights, but only if your trip originates in the U.S. or Canada.

For information: French Government Tourist Office, 444 Madison Ave., New York, NY 10022; 212-838-7800; www .francetourism.com. For the France Railpass: Rail Europe, 800-4-EURAIL (800-438-7245); www.raileurope.com.

GERMANY

Many restaurants in Germany have a *Seniorenteller*, a special menu that offers lighter fare in smaller portions at a lower cost for older guests. Ask to see it and also ask if there are discounts for seniors wherever you go. You'll find they are available in such places as department stores, hair salons, and museums and tourist sites. Even some hotels and spa resorts have them, especially in off-peak seasons.

There is a 10 percent discount on most fares across the Atlantic Ocean to European destinations on Lufthansa for people 60 and older and companions over the age of 18. The same discount applies to domestic flights in Europe.

Finally, check out the city cards, now available at local tourist offices, railway stations, and hotels in Berlin, Hamburg, Frankfort, Munich, Dresden, and Weimar for savings on transportation, tours, and admissions.

For information: German National Tourist Office, 122 E. 42nd St., New York, NY 10168; 212-661-7200; www. germany-tourism.de.

HEALTH COVERAGE ABROAD

When you travel to foreign countries, be aware that the standard Medicare plan, with a few exceptions, does not cover medical care outside the United States. Some Medicare HMOs do cover emergency procedures abroad but not routine care, and many of the available Medigap policies provide 80 percent, after a deductible, of the cost of emergency care incurred in the first two months of a trip outside the country. If you do not carry your own private health insurance that will pay the expenses incurred overseas, talk to your travel agent about temporary health insurance that will cover you for the length of your trip.

For information: Call 800-MEDICARE (800-633-4227); www .medicare.gov.

GREAT BRITAIN

Bargains abound in the U.K., where senior discounts and special rates apply almost everywhere from railroads and bus lines to museums, theaters, and historic sites. For example, visitors over 60 get 25 percent off admission to Windsor Castle. So be sure to ask wherever you go if there is an OAP (old-age pensioner) rate and carry proof of your age with you.

Sometimes you'll get in for nothing at all; 50 national museums and galleries that usually charge admission fees have recently introduced a free admission policy for visitors 60 or older.

For information: British Tourist Authority, 551 Fifth Ave., New York, NY 10176; 800-GO-2-BRITAIN (800-462-2748); www.travelbritain.org. For a free brochure, "Time to Travel: A Guide to Britain for the Mature Traveler," call 888-364-6101 or visit www.travelbritain.org/mature.

Traveling by train: In Britain, where virtually every town may be reached by train, it pays to consider a rail pass, especially since travelers over 60 get discounts of about 15 percent off the regular adult prices.

The BritRail Senior Flexipass allows 4-, 8-, or 15-day unlimited first-class travel within a month in England, Scotland, and Wales. The BritRail Senior Classic Pass, again for unlimited first-class travel, is good for 8, 15, 22, or 30 consecutive days.

If you are traveling with children, your senior pass (or an adult card) allows one accompanying child 5 to 15 years old to travel free; additional children 5 to 15 years of age go at half price; children under 5 are always free.

These passes are not sold in Britain but must be purchased before leaving home. They are not accepted in Ireland or on special excursion trains. With all passes, you may get on and off the trains as often as you like along the way.

Travel passes: Many cost-saving passes are available for seeing the sights in Britain.

Don't leave home, for example, without a Great British Heritage Pass for unlimited free entry to about 600 historic houses, castles, museums, sites, and gardens in England, Scotland, Wales, and Northern Ireland. Buy it from your travel agent, BritRail, or Rail Europe before you leave, or from Tourist Information Centres in Britain. A seven-day pass currently costs about $54.

The London Visitor Travelcard gives you unlimited travel for three, four, or seven consecutive days, for all zones or for the central zone only, on London's buses and subways as well as many trains in the London area. The all-zones card includes transfer via underground from Heathrow Airport to central London. It can be purchased outside of Britain only.

And then there's the London Pass, which you may buy here or in London. With it, you can save on all sorts of things—local transport, tours, and entrance fees to museums, art galleries, and movies. It also is good for all undergrounds, trains, and buses in the London Transport zones 1 through 6. The pass covers about 40 attractions in and around London, bus tours, and canal boat trips. Buy it for one, three, or six days at the British Visitors Center in London or on the Web by visiting www.londonpass.com. Sorry, no senior discount on this pass.

For information: BritRail, 888-BRITRAIL (888-274-8724); in Canada, 800-555-BRIT (800-555-2748). Rail Europe, 800-4-EURAIL (800-438-7245); www.raileurope.com.

Northern Ireland: Seniors pay half price for a Freedom of Northern Ireland Ticket, issued for one or seven days, which gives free access to all services of Citybus, Northern Ireland Railways, and Ulsterbus. Buy the pass at railway stations.

Scotland: Sixty historic attractions, from castles to abbeys and distilleries, are yours to see when you purchase a Scottish Explorer Ticket for 7 or 14 days. Ask for your senior discount, saving about a third of the regular adult cost, when you purchase it at a Historic Scotland property or a Tourist Information Centre in Scotland.

Traveling by bus: If you plan to travel extensively, check out National Express, a long-distance bus operator serving 800 destinations in England, Scotland, and Wales. For travelers over the age of 50, it sells the Advantage 50 Discount Coachcard (currently about $13.50), which provides discounts of up to 30 percent. Get it in the UK at major bus stations.

In the U.S. and Canada, you may buy the Tourist Trail Flexipass before you set forth. The pass, available from British Travel International, gives you unlimited travel for varying numbers of consecutive days and is available at a 25 percent discount off the regular adult price if you are over 50.

For information: British Travel International, PO Box 299, Elkton, VA 22827; 540-298-1395; www.britbus.com.

GREECE

Here, if you are at least 60, you may buy a rail pass, valid for a year at any major railroad station in the country, and use it for five train trips anywhere within Greek borders. Additional trips cost only half fare. Here's the hitch: the pass is good only from October through June and does not include the period around the Easter or Christmas holidays.

At 62, you and a travel companion are eligible for a 10 percent discount on Olympic Airways, the Greek national airline, on transatlantic flights. But on domestic flights when your travel originates here, you'll get 20 percent off the usual fare if you are 60-plus.

For information: Greek National Tourist Organization, 645 Fifth Ave., New York, NY 10022; 212-421-5777; www .gnto.gr.

HONG KONG

In this exciting city, there are several ways to save money on transportation, assuming you are at least 65. The Star Ferry will take you free of charge on the eight-minute crossing from central Hong Kong to Kowloon, giving you a fabulous view of Victoria Harbor. You pay half fare on the Mass Transit Railway, the HYF Ferry to outlying islands, the Light Rail (LR), and the Kowloon-to-Canton Railway (KCR). And on the famous Peak Tram, you are offered a discount of about 60 percent off the regular adult fare. Always be prepared with ID, such as your passport.

Several museums, too, give seniors a break on admissions, charging only half the regular entrance fee.

For information: Hong Kong Tourist Association, 800-282-4582 or 212-421-3382; www.discoverhongkong.com.

IRELAND

Many hotels in Ireland offer senior discounts, especially off-peak, so always inquire about them when making your reservations. In most cases, you must be 65 to qualify. Theaters (midweek), national monuments, and historic sites give you price reductions, too. Always ask. Also, one tour company, CIE Tours International (see Chapter 9), takes $55 off the regular adult fare on a few of its coach tours to the first 15 people over 55 who sign up.

No doubt you'll be spending time in Dublin, so it would be wise to buy a Dublin Supersaver Card, which reduces the admission fees by up to 30 percent for a group of museums, castles, and attractions. Good for a year, it currently costs £16 for an adult pass, but if you are an OAP (Old Age Pensioner, for which you qualify at 65), you'll get it for £12.5. It is available at Dublin Tourism Information Centres around the city.

For information: Irish Tourist Board, 345 Park Ave., New York, NY 10154; 800-223-6470 or 212-418-0800; www.ire landvacations.com.

ITALY

The Silver Card (Carta d'Argenta)—designed for anyone over the age of 60—entitles its holder, tourist or resident, to discounts on tickets on all national and regional trains, including Eurostar Italy and Eurocity. Available only in Italy at railroad stations, it currently costs 40,000 lire (about $25) and is valid for a year. With it, you may buy tickets with a 30 percent discount on the regular adult fare for first class and 20 percent for second class. If all you want, however, is unlimited travel for 4, 8, or 12 days, the Flexi-Rail Pass or Italian Railcard sold in the U.S. by CIT Tours may be a better value for you.

At 62, you're offered a 10 percent senior discount when you fly across the Atlantic on Alitalia, the national airline. At 65, there are discounted Terza Eta (Third Age) fares for some domestic flights.

For information: Italian Tourist Board, 530 Fifth Ave., New York, NY 10111; 212-245-5618; www.italiantourism.com.

JAPAN

Japan has a couple of special privileges for older travelers. First of all, more than 25 museums and art galleries in and around Tokyo offer free or discounted admission to visitors over the age of 65 who present identification with proof of age.

In addition, the Japan Railway Group (JR) offers two senior travel programs available to men over 65 and women over 60—and one companion each—who may ride for half fare on some routes. The Kyoto Yuyu Ticket includes a round-trip on the bullet train between Tokyo and Kyoto or Yokohama and Kyoto in first-class seats; one-day unlimited free rides on Kyoto City bus and subway; discounts on meals, admission fees, etc. The Nara Yuyu Ticket includes the same round-trip, plus a day of unlimited free rides on Kintetsu train line in the Nara area and on Nara City buses; and discounts on meals and admission fees. The tickets may be purchased, with proof of your age, at the Green ticket windows in the JR Tokyo and JR Shin-Yokohama train stations.

Useful for tourists of any age are two free Welcome Cards that you can pick up at your hotel in Tokyo or at a Tourist Information Center. With the Museum Guide Welcome Card, you'll get discounts at 41 museums, as well as a local guidebook and, often, an area map. The Tokyo Bay Welcome Card entitles you to discounted admissions and services, reduced hotel rates, and other privileges in the city's waterfront district.

For a list of free things to do and see in Tokyo and Kyoto, contact the Japan National Tourist Organization or visit its website. The list includes museums, temples, shrines, observatories, markets, and other popular attractions.

And there's more. Good Will Guides System (SCG) connects foreign travelers with local volunteers in 27 cities in Japan who are ready to help you with any problems you may encounter during your visit to their country. The Home Visit System, another volunteer organization, offers you a chance to spend a few hours as a guest in a Japanese home in 14 cities. For these visits, an application and appointment are required.

For information: Japan National Tourist Organization, 1 Rockefeller Plaza, New York, NY 10020; 212-757-5641; www.jnto.go.jp or www.japantravelinfo.com.

LUXEMBOURG

A good investment here is the LuxembourgCard which, for varying numbers of days, gives you free public transportation, free access to museums, castles, historic sites, and cultural attractions, and discounts on sight-seeing tours. Buy it at tourist information centers.

If you plan a long stay in this tiny European country, you may want to purchase a senior card, which currently costs 350 francs and is valid for a year. With the card, you may then buy one-day tickets for journeys on all trains and some buses at half the normal adult price.

For information: Luxembourg National Tourist Office, 17 Beekman Pl., New York, NY 10022; 212-935-8888; www .visitluxembourg.com.

NETHERLANDS

Whenever you go to museums, attractions, and cultural and historic sites or on tours in Holland, always ask if there is a senior discount because people over 65 are usually given a break on admission fees. Have your passport handy to prove your age.

For extensive travel in the country, it may make sense to buy a Holland Railpass, which must be purchased before you go because it is not available in the Netherlands. Travelers over 60 get a discount of about 20 percent off the regular adult price on passes good for three or five days in a month.

At age 60, you are also eligible to buy a "strippenkaart" at railroad stations or post offices in the Netherlands. It allows you to ride buses, metros, and trams throughout the country for about 40 percent off the usual fare.

And consider the Amsterdam Culture & Leisure Pass, which provides vouchers for free or discounted admission to museums, cruises, tours, and more.

KLM, the national airline, gives passengers 60 and over and their travel mates a 10 percent discount on transatlantic flights to any of its destinations in Europe. The same holds true for fares for flights from Amsterdam to other European cities.

For information: Netherlands Board of Tourism, 355 Lexington Ave., New York, NY 10017; 888-GO-HOLLAND (888-464-6552); www.goholland.com.

NEW ZEALAND

Travelers over 60 are entitled to a Golden Age Discount, a 30 percent savings off the standard adult fares on all Tranz Scenic Trains any time of year. Buy your tickets in New Zealand at a railroad station or a visitor information office.

In addition, three brands of CLD Hotels—Millennium, Copthorne, and Quality—throughout the country offer those over the age of 60 a 30 percent discount when rooms are available.

For information: Tourism New Zealand, 501 Santa Monica Blvd., Santa Monica, CA 90401; 877-978-7369; www .purenz.com.

NORTHERN IRELAND

A Freedom of Northern Ireland Ticket, valid on Citybus, Northern Ireland Railways, and Ulsterbus, is sold at railway stations in that country and it's yours for half price if you are 65. You may buy it for one, three, or seven consecutive days. Ask for your senior discount at museums, theaters, and historic sites—you'll usually be admitted for half the regular adult fee.

For information: Northern Ireland Tourist Board, 551 Fifth Ave., New York, NY 10176; 800-326-0036.

NORWAY

In this beautiful country, you're entitled to half fare on buses, any time, any place. For this break, however, you must be at least 67 and ready to prove your age with a proper ID.

At age 60, you can buy a Norway Senior Rail Pass and save about 20 percent over what younger adult travelers pay for the same unlimited first- or second-class rail travel on trains operated by the Norwegian State Railways (NSB), plus a 30 percent reduction on the Flam Railway, for three, four, or five days within one month. It must be purchased in the U.S. or Canada through your travel agent or Rail Europe, as it is not available in Norway.

At age 67, you become eligible for a discount of up to $220 on Norwegian Coastal Voyages (except between June 1 and July 15) that sail up the coast to the Arctic Circle and back.

SAS, the Scandinavian airline, not only offers travelers over 62 a 10 percent discount on flights to Europe, but it also gives special senior fares to those over 65 on domestic flights within Norway if the tickets are purchased in the U.S.

or Canada. If you're already over there, however, you'll do even better once you are 67. Then you and your spouse, who may be younger, will pay only half fare on domestic trips. Passengers on SAS also get special rates at Radisson SAS Hotels if they are over 65.

For information about the ScanRail Senior Pass to be used on railroads in Denmark, Finland, Norway, and Sweden, see Scandanavia later in this chapter.

As for hotels, there are discounts for all of Scandinavia (discussed later in this chapter). In addition, check out the Norway Fjord Pass, which costs about $10 and offers discounts on rooms from May through September in hotels, guest houses, apartments, and holiday cottages.

As you should everywhere, ask if there is a senior discount wherever you go and consider purchasing city cards for Oslo and Bergen. They will provide free public transportation plus free or discounted admission at most museums, historic sites, and cultural attractions.

For information: Norwegian Tourist Board, 655 Third Ave., New York, NY 10017; 212-885-9700; www.visitnorway.com.

PORTUGAL

If you're over 65, there's hardly anywhere you can go in Portugal without being offered a senior discount of 30 to 50 percent off the regular price. So make a point of asking for it when you take a train or a bus and when you go to a museum, a national monument, a theater, a movie, and anyplace else that charges admission.

If you're a mere 60, you can take advantage of a very good deal called the Golden Age Program that gives you a 40 percent discount on the regular rates for accommodations and breakfast for two at all but two of Portugal's famous pousadas. These are the historic government-run inns scattered around the country, many of them in former castles, monasteries, or palaces. The discount applies on Sunday through Thursday nights, with some exceptions, from April through October and sometimes other times of the year, too.

There's also a Tourist Pass available for all ages, which offers free unlimited travel on Lisbon's transportation system. Sold at the airport and tourist information offices, a four-day pass costs about $10.

The Lisbon Card gives you the same access to the underground, buses, trams, and lifts, plus free entry into 26 museums, monuments, and other sites. It also provides discounts on sight-seeing tours, river cruises, and theatrical events. Porto, Portugal's second-largest city, offers the Passe Porto with similar benefits.

And don't forget that TAP Air Portugal, the national airline, will give you and a companion a 10 percent discount on flights between the U.S. and Portugal, Madeira, and the Azores.

For information: Portuguese National Tourist Office, 590 Fifth Ave., New York, NY 10036; 212-354-4403; www .portugalinsite.pt. For pousadas: Marketing Ahead, 800-223-1356.

SCANDINAVIA

Scandinavia—which includes Denmark, Finland, Norway, and Sweden—has many good deals for mature travelers. Here are some that are valid in all four countries. (Those that are unique to the individual countries are described under their own headings throughout this chapter.)

The ScanRail Senior Pass costs tourists over 60 about 10 percent less than what other adults pay for rail travel in Sweden, Norway, Denmark, and Finland. You may travel first or second class anywhere within the four countries for 5 or 10 days within two months, or for 21 consecutive days. Among the added bonuses are reduced fares on some ferries and cruise ships. Reservations are sometimes required and always recommended.

For information: Rail Europe; 1-800-4-EURAIL (800-438-7245); www.raileurope.com.

You and other travelers can also save money in the Scandinavian countries by using hotel passes. The Nordic Hotelpass, for example, gives you discounts of up to 50 percent off the regular room rates at over 90 first-class hotels that are part of Choice Hotels International. The card, valid all year-round, costs about $12 and must be purchased in advance. The Scan+ Hotel Cheque program provides vouchers for discounted rates at about 180 other hotels throughout Scandinavia and is valid May through September. The Scandic Holiday Cheque is a similar program.

SAS (Scandinavian Airlines System) not only gives passengers over the age of 62 a 10 percent discount on fares between North America and Europe but also discounts domestic fares in Denmark, Norway, and Sweden for travelers over 65. Also, Finnair gives you a terrific deal on flights within Finland—75 percent off the regular fares—if you are over 65. You must pay for your tickets within three days of booking.

And, finally, you should seriously consider buying city cards for free public transportation plus free or discounted entry to museums, historic sites, and cultural attractions.

They can be purchased ahead of time in the U.S. or at tourist information offices, train stations, airports, and hotels in Scandinavia. The cities include Copenhagen, Odense, and Aalborg in Denmark; Helsinki in Finland; Oslo and Bergen in Norway; and Stockholm, Gothenburg, and Malmo in Sweden.

For information: Scandinavian National Tourist Offices, 655 Third Ave., New York, NY 10017; 212-885-9700; www.goscandinavia.com.

SINGAPORE

When you send for the Tourism Board's free brochure, "Mature Travelers Guide," for visitors over 55, you will also receive an extensive list of senior discounts, some as high as 50 percent, on admission fees and prices for many of this small island country's attractions, museums, harbor/river cruises, spas, and sight-seeing tours.

For information: Singapore Tourism Board, 590 Fifth Ave., New York, NY 10036; 212-302-4861; www.singapore-usa.com.

SPAIN

In addition to discounts for mature travelers at just about every museum, cultural event, and historic site in Spain, there is another good deal for visitors over 60. The Golden Days Promotion offers a 35 percent discount on the cost of a room and a buffet breakfast at the country's famous paradores. These are government-owned inns, 87 in all, many of them former palaces, castles, convents, or monasteries located in the Spanish countryside. The special rates apply all year except in July, August, September, and Easter and Christmas weeks. Some paradores are available every day of the week; others only from Sunday to Thursday; and still others only on Friday, Saturday, and Sunday.

Also, Spanair, which flies between Washington, D.C., and Madrid, offers 10 percent off transatlantic fares for passengers 62 and older as well as for a companion. Discounts on domestic flights start at age 60.

For information: Tourist Office of Spain, 666 Fifth Ave., New York, NY 10103; 212-265-8822; www.okspain.org. For paradores: Marketing Ahead, 800-223-1356.

SWEDEN

For train trips in Sweden, consider the inexpensive travel card issued by SJ, the state railroad system, which provides substantial discounts. Although the card is valid every day, the discounted seats are limited and you must book your trip at least seven days in advance. The card costs anyone over 65 only about $6, a third less than the regular adult fare.

Hop on a bus in Sweden and, if you're 65, you need only pay half the regular fare.

For seeing the sights in Stockholm, consider buying the SL Tourist Card sold at tourist offices and kiosks, again at half price for seniors (about $10 for three days). With this card, you get free transportation on buses, local trains, subways, and ferry tours.

Take an overnight cruise to Finland on the Viking Line, or a one-day cruise to Denmark on the Stena Line, and, if you are 60, the cost is cut by about half.

SAS, the Scandinavian airline, takes 10 percent off the regular fares for passengers over 62 flying from this side of the Atlantic to SAS destinations worldwide. On flights within Sweden, the airline offers special senior fares, depending on the route, to passengers 65 and older.

And don't forget the city cards—the Stockholm Card, Gothenburg Card, and Malmo Card. Very good deals, they give you free or discounted transportation and admission to places you'll want to visit.

For information: Danish and Swedish Tourist Boards, 655 Third Ave., New York, NY 10017; 212-885-9700; www.go sweden.org.

SWITZERLAND

The Swiss Hotel Association will provide, for the asking, a list of about 400 hotels in 160 cities and towns that participate in a program called *Season for Seniors*. This program gives reduced room rates—sometimes discounted as much as 50 percent—to women over 62 and to men over 65. If two people are traveling together, only one must be the required age. The only catch is that in most cases the reduced rates do not apply during peak travel periods, including the summer months.

The Swiss Museum Passport is good for a month of unlimited visits to about 180 museums. If you are a woman over 62 or a man over 65, you may buy it at a discount at participating museums and tourist offices in Switzerland.

If you fly Swissair and are over 62, remember to ask for your 10 percent discount on most fares.

For information: Switzerland Tourism, 608 Fifth Ave., New York, NY 10020; 212-757-5944; www.myswitzerland.com.

9

Trips and Tours for the Mature Traveler

Many enterprising organizations, tour operators, and travel agencies now cater exclusively to the mature traveler. They choose destinations sure to appeal to those who have already seen much of the world, arrange trips that are leisurely and unhassled, give you congenial contemporaries to travel with and group hosts to smooth the way, and provide many special services you never got before. They also give you a choice between strenuous action-filled tours and those that are more relaxed. In fact, most of the agencies offer so many choices that the major problem becomes making a decision about where to go.

Options range from cruises in the Caribbean or the Greek Isles to grand tours of the Orient, sight-seeing excursions in the U.S., trips to the Canadian Rockies, theater tours of London, African safaris, and snorkeling vacations on the Great Barrier Reef off Australia. There's just no place in the world where over-50s won't go.

Among the newer and most popular trends are apartment/hotel complexes in American and European resort areas, as well as apartments in major cities. Here you can stay put for as long as you like, using the apartment or hotel as a home base for short-range roaming and exploring with the guidance of on-site hosts.

There are many choices, too, for the growing number of intrepid, energetic, courageous members of the 50-plus population who prefer travel that is adventurous and unusual, perhaps even exotic. Many are described in this chapter along with the more traditional variety. Because they are planned specifically for the mature traveler, they usually offer some measure of comfort and convenience even in the wilderness, plus a leisurely pace that allows time for relaxation and independent exploration. Most important, they offer clean, comfortable accommodations, though sometimes rustic or spartan, and, almost always, a private bathroom.

ADVENTURE SOUTH

If you're looking for some excitement and want to travel with a small companionable group of people who are at least 35 years old, consider the 13-day "midlife adventures" in New Zealand. Scheduled for departures during New Zealand's summer—October through mid-April—you'll have moderately paced outdoor experiences as you travel all over the North or South Islands—or both—seeing the sights and visiting five national and two maritime parks. Owned by "a mature couple" and led by "mature" guides, this agency will take you sailing, whitewater rafting, sea kayaking, cave rafting, sight-seeing, hiking, and on glacier walks, bush walks, scenic flights, and a boat trip on a glacial lake. For this you need no previous experience but must be in good physical shape.

For information: Adventure South, PO Box 33# 153, Christ Church, NZ; www.advsouth.co.nz.

AFC TOURS

Specializing in escorted tours designed for mature travelers, AFC schedules trips to all the most popular destinations in the U.S. and Canada and some in other countries. Not only that, but if you live in southern California, where AFC is based, you will be transported free between your home and the airport. Many of the most popular tours are "unpack once," which means you stay in one hotel and take day trips from there. Domestic tours take you to such places as the national parks, Branson, Nashville, New York City, Savannah, New Orleans, and Washington, D.C. International adventures cover all of Europe. Other choices: cruises, steamboating, train tours, holiday tours, and grandparent trips. In other words, almost anything you want. Special for singles: if you sign up four months in advance and a roommate cannot be found to share your room, you need not pay a single supplement.

For information about AFC's new women-only tours, see Wander Women in Chapter 11.

For information: AFC Tours, 11772 Sorrento Valley Rd., San Diego, CA 92121; 800-369-3693 or 858-481-8188; www.afctours.com.

AMERICAN WILDERNESS EXPERIENCE

If you love adventurous vacations and roughing it in style, study the many offerings from AWE, an agency that's spent many years sending travelers on backcountry wilderness adventures and taking care of all the details. Its offerings are gathered from many tour operators and are open to all ages, but some are specifically designed for over-50s, and a few give discounts to seniors. Among these are a canoe trip in the Boundary Waters between Minnesota and Ontario, senior safaris in Alaska, horseback trips in Colorado or New Mexico, and a mountain sports week that combines rock climbing, horseback riding, mountain biking, and whitewater rafting in Colorado. Other trips feature special departures and itineraries for prime timers.

For information: American Wilderness Experience Inc., PO Box 1486, Boulder, CO 80306; 800-444-0099 or 303-444-2622; www.gorp.com/awe.

BACK-ROADS TOURING CO.

Designed especially for adults over 50, the tours planned by Back-Roads Touring Co. take groups of no more than 11 participants on explorations of England, Scotland, Wales, Ireland, Italy, Spain, Portugal, or France, along the back roads to out-of-the-way places. You'll travel by minicoach with a trained guide for one or two weeks, lodge in country inns, guest houses, and small family-owned properties. These are leisurely tours with plenty of time to explore. You'll stay several nights in the same location and spend time with local residents. You may even help plan the itinerary. Add-on stays in London are available, too, and so are four-day "country breaks" and day trips out of London. What's more, if you mention this book, you will get a discount.

A new specialty of this touring company is its Battles for France tour which starts in London, proceeds to General Eisenhower's headquarters in Portsmouth, crosses the channel, and visits famous battlefields in Normandy.

For information: Back-Roads Touring Co., British Network, Ltd., 112 W. High St., Carlisle, PA 17013; 800-274-8583 or 717-249-5990; www.britishnetwork.ltd.com. In Canada, contact Golden Escapes, 75 The Donway West, Ste. 710, Toronto, ON M3C 2E9; 800-668-9125 or 416-447-7683.

CIE TOURS INTERNATIONAL

An agency specializing in escorted vacations in Ireland, Northern Ireland, Scotland, Wales, and England, CIE offers motor-coach tours and fly/drive vacations, some of which come with a "55 and Smiling Discount." This means that on selected departures you get $55 off the cost of the trip if you are 55 or older and are among the first 15 people to book the tour.

For information: CIE Tours International, 100 Hanover Ave., Cedar Knolls, NJ 07927; 800-243-8687 or 973-292-3438; www.cietours.com.

COLLETTE TOURS

Collette Tours, an escorted-tour operator for the past 80 years, offers worry-free vacations for the mature population that include over 125 itineraries in seven continents. It even offers grand tours of South America or East Asia. Its trips move at a relaxed pace, put you up in good hotels, and provide experienced tour guides to see that everything goes well. In such places as Costa Rica, Denmark, Scotland, Portugal, Spain, Switzerland, Israel, and Austria, the agency's "Hub and Spoke" programs feature multiple nights in one place so you don't have to keep packing and unpacking your bags. Meanwhile, day excursions take you to see the sights.

The soft adventures from Collette are for people who love convenience but don't want to be overly organized as they tour the Galapagos, go on safari in Africa, take a trek through the Brazilian rain forest, or view the penguins in Antarctica.

For information: Collette Tours, 162 Middle St., Pawtucket, RI 02860; 800-832-4656; www.collettetours.com.

ELDERHOSTEL

The educational tours from Elderhostel number in the thousands, all of them bargains for adults over the age of 55 (and younger travel mates). Get on this nonprofit organization's mailing list to receive its catalogs or visit its website. Also see Chapter 12.

For information: Elderhostel, 11 Avenue de Lafayette, Boston, MA 02111; 877-426-8056 or 617-426-7788; www.elderhostel.com.

ELDERTREKS

This Canadian-based tour company specializes in adventure getaways for small groups of travelers 50 and over (and companions of any age) who are in reasonably good physical condition and enjoy walking. Featuring exotic adventures all around the world, from Argentina to Mongolia, it stresses cultural interaction, physical activity, and nature exploration. However, itineraries are chosen with older hikers in mind and groups are limited to 15. Trips are rated for difficulty and housing conditions (huts to hotels).

Accommodations for the city portions of the tours are in clean, comfortable, tourist-class hotels and guest houses chosen for charm and location. Accommodations on the adventure portions may be on the floor of a nomadic tent or under a canopy of trees in the jungle, but you can always count on an air mattress. Guides, cooks, meals, and porters are part of the package. Destinations include Bhutan, Borneo, Vietnam, Laos, Sumatra, Java, Bali, Tibet, Nepal, Ecuador, Bolivia, Peru, Madagasgar, Patagonia, Yemen, Belize, Lapland, Guatemala, and Honduras.

By the way, if you are traveling alone and are willing to share, you can avoid a single-supplement charge.

For information: ElderTreks, 597 Markham St., Toronto, ON M6G 2L7; 800-741-7956 or 416-588-5000; www.elder treks.com.

FANCY-FREE HOLIDAYS

Geared for senior travelers, this agency's domestic escorted motorcoach tours, all originating in Chicago, include the usual favorite destinations such as Branson, New England, Alaska, Williamsburg, Asheville, New Orleans, and Washington, D.C. Its fully escorted overseas tours by air, motorcoach, or cruise ship include Ireland, Kenya, Spain, Greece, Germany, and South America.

For information: Fancy-Free Holidays, 24W 500 Maple Ave., Naperville, IL 60540; 800-421-3330 or 630-778-7010; www.fancyfreeholidays.com.

GLOBUS & COSMOS TOURS

This affiliated pair of escorted tour companies, together the largest in the world, offers everything from the traditional escorted tours everywhere in the world to more leisurely vacations that give you a few days in each city on your itinerary. All of them are designed to appeal to over-50 travelers who comprise the vast majority of their clients. The upscale escorted tours from Globus take you to all seven continents of the world including Antarctica, providing accommodations in three- and four-star hotels.

A new Globus specialty is a choice of Tour & Cruise Vacations that combine land tours and cruises. One trip, for example, takes you to Vienna for four nights and then on a Danube River cruise to Budapest and Bratislava.

The company's LeisureStyle Vacations feature two- or three-night stays per city and activities such as cooking classes, golfing, and wine tasting. The Independent City Stays, here and abroad, offer a chance to independently explore with advice and assistance from a professional on-site host.

Cosmos specializes in vacations for cost-conscious travelers and offers traditional escorted motor-coach tours all over the world. By the way, if you are traveling alone and are willing to share a room, you'll get a roommate and pay no single supplement.

For information: Globus & Cosmos Tours, 5301 S. Federal Circle, Littleton, CO 80123; 800-241-9853 or 303-797-2800; www.globusandcosmos.com.

GO AHEAD VACATIONS

Go Ahead Vacations is a division of EF Education, a company that has specialized for over 35 years in intercultural exchange and educational travel. This tour operator plans a wide array of holidays exclusively for the mature crowd. Its European City Stay tours, designed for independent travelers, provide air, hotel, airport transfers, breakfast every day, and an activity coordinator. For a week or more, you can plan your own daily itinerary, doing things on your own or choosing among a variety of optional excursions and tours.

Go Ahead also has a wide range of traditional motorcoach tours and cruises to just about anywhere you've ever wanted to go, including many exotic destinations such as Ecuador and Peru, Thailand, Kenya, China, and Egypt.

If you request a roommate, you'll get one or have your single supplement reduced by half when you sign up during the peak season. Recruit a group of eight people and you go free.

For information: Go Ahead Vacations, EF Center Boston, 1 Education St., Cambridge MA 02141; 800-242-4686; www .goaheadvacations.com.

GOLDEN AGE FESTIVAL TRAVEL

This is another agency that caters to the 50-plus crowd, offering tours to everywhere from Wildwood (New Jersey), Myrtle Beach, Nashville, Maine, and New York to the national parks, Las Vegas, Europe, Greece, China, and Australia—plus plenty of cruises. All packages are escorted and include accommodations, meals, and just about everything else.

In addition, Golden Age Festival offers an innovation— "drive-to tours" for individual travelers, allowing them to take advantage of group discounts that make the trips remarkably inexpensive. On these, all on the East Coast, you drive yourself to your destination—for example, Wildwood, Ocean City, Myrtle Beach, Newport and Mystic Seaport, Hilton Head, Williamsburg—and join others traveling on their own for meals, entertainment, and tours.

For information: Golden Age Festival Travel, 5501 New Jersey Ave., Wildwood Crest, NJ 08260; 800-257-8920 or 609-522-6316; www.goldenagefestival.com.

GOLDEN AGE TRAVELLERS CLUB

This over-50 club specializes in discounted cruises on major cruise lines everywhere in the world, but it also offers land tours from well-known tour operators. When you join the club ($10 or $15 per couple a year), you receive a quarterly newsletter with listings of upcoming sailings. Other inducements are tour escorts and bonus points. Single travelers may choose to be enrolled in the Roommates Wanted list to help them find companions to share cabins and costs. For members in the San Francisco and Sacramento areas, there are one-day travel shows where you may meet fellow travelers and share a snack.

Especially intriguing to mature travelers are the agency's long-stay trips. On these, you stay put—for example, in Spain, Portugal, Guatemala, Australia, Costa Rica, or Argentina—at the same hotel for two or three weeks and, if you wish, take short side trips. The packages include air, hotel, and sometimes meals.

For information: Golden Age Travellers Club, Pier 27, The Embarcadero, San Francisco, CA 94111; 800-258-8880 or 415-296-0151; www.gatclub.com.

GOLDEN ESCAPES

Golden Escapes for the 40-Plus Traveller is a Canadian tour operator that offers all-inclusive escorted tours in Canada, the U.S., and Europe as well as three-week tours of such exotic places as Greece, Egypt, Cyprus, Turkey, Tunisia, and South Africa. It also has long-stay programs where you lodge in an apartment or a hotel in a resort area—perhaps Portugal's Algarve, Newport Beach, Palm Springs, or the island of Crete—and take excursions by day, highlighted by parties, happy hours, entertainment, and other activities.

In addition, Golden Escapes is the representative in Canada for Back-Roads Touring Co., which takes you on minicoach tours of England, France, Scotland, or Ireland. *For information:* Golden Escapes, 75 The Donway West, Ste. 710, Toronto, ON M3C 2E9; 800-668-9125 or 416-447-7683; www.goldenescapes.com.

GRAND CIRCLE TRAVEL

Grand Circle Travel caters to people over 50 and plans all of its trips exclusively for them. The first U.S. company to market senior travel, it specializes in extended vacations, escorted tours, and cruises. On an extended vacation, you get round-trip airfare from your gateway city to a foreign country. Then you stay in one, two, or three destinations for as many weeks as you like, living in hotels or apartments with all meals, sight-seeing tours, social events, and an on-site program director included. Meanwhile you may spend your days as you wish, joining the rest of the group or exploring on your own.

Traditional escorted programs are also offered to a variety of destinations with experienced guides. Everything is included, from airfare to tours and many meals.

Traditional cruises are another choice, as are train tours and river cruises on small chartered boats on rivers such as the Danube, Rhine, Yangtze, and Nile.

Or look into the Discovery Series. These are educational travel trips designed to immerse you in the local culture, history, art, environment, and politics of a foreign country. You visit local families, take language lessons, learn to cook regional foods.

Grand Circle tries to match singles with appropriate roommates if they request them. If none is available, you'll get your own quarters for the price of a shared room. On many off-peak extended-stay packages, single supplements are waived.

For information: Grand Circle Travel, 347 Congress St., Boston, MA 02210; 800-248-3737 or 617-350-7500; www.gct.com.

GREAT ALASKA SAFARIS

The Silver Safaris, scheduled several times a summer, were created expressly for older travelers who want comfort as well as adventure. Mellower than trips planned for all ages, the seven-day safaris start at the Great Alaska Fish Camp on the Kenai Peninsula, where you stay in riverside cabins and take a trip to Homer, a remote artists' community. After hikes and other adventures, plus a glacier-and-wildlife cruise in Prince William Sound and a visit to Anchorage, you fly to a wilderness camp in Lake Clark National Park to see bears, moose, and other creatures of the wild.

For information: Great Alaska Safaris, 33881 Sterling Hwy., Sterling, AK 99672; 800-544-2261; www.greatalaska.com.

HOSTELLING INTERNATIONAL

This international organization, formerly known as American Youth Hostels, offers low-cost lodging all over the globe to people of all ages. Membership for adults costs $25 a year, but if you are 55 or older, you pay only $15. You get a membership card, a free guide to hostels in Canada and the U.S., and a free map of U.S. hostels. For an added fee, you may order guidebooks listing all 4,500 hostels in over 70 countries. In addition, you are entitled to hundreds of discounts on transportation, car rentals, restaurants, admissions, festivals, ski lifts, and more.

Lodgings are dormitory-style, women in one room, men in another, although some hostels also have private rooms for families, couples, and groups which may be reserved in advance. These include the Gateway City Hostels in seven of the country's major cities—New York, Los Angeles, San Francisco, Miami Beach, Washington, D.C., Chicago, and San Diego. All are centrally located and have program directors who arrange special activities—such as walking tours—for their guests. Although most hostels are located in basic structures, some are in castles, former dude ranches, convents, lighthouses, base camps, or other exotic locations.

You can book your space directly by phone, mail, or fax; or, for over 300 destinations throughout the world, you can reserve a prepaid bed by using HI's computerized international booking network via telephone or website.

For information: Hostelling International-AYH, 733 15th St. NW, Washington, DC 20005; 202-783-6161; www.hiayh .org.

HOSTELLING INTERNATIONAL–CANADA

A network of hostels throughout the Canadian provinces, HI-Canada offers members of all ages an inexpensive night's sleep in a wide variety of places ranging from modern facilities to historic homes, and refurbished jails to log cabins in the Rockies. Located in all major gateway cities and also in remote locations, your accommodations—private or shared—cost an average of $15 (Canadian) a night. Membership costs $25 (Canadian) per year or $35 for two years and allows you to use any HI facility worldwide.

For information: Hostelling International–Canada, 205 Catherine St., Ste. 400, Ottawa, ON K2P 1C3; 800-663-5777 (Canada only) or 613-237-7884; www.hostelling intl.ca.

IMMERSIA TRAVEL

Designed for adventurers over the age of 50, Immersia's trips take travelers to remote locales to explore local lifestyles and share other cultures in depth. They are divided into three categories—easy, moderate, and vigorous—so you may choose those that suit your abilities and tastes. The nine-day to three-week tours include Bali, Turkey, Irian Jaya, Thailand, Mexico, and Nepal. You'll spend time with the local inhabitants and spend nights in native villages, immersing yourself in the culture. Before you go, you'll receive substantial resource packets about the places you will visit.

On easy trips, you may travel by car, minivan, or leisurely walking and stay in local homes or guest houses. On moderate adventures, add treks, trains, and four-wheel-drive vehicles with stays in village homes, cottages, and guest houses. "Vigorous" may include travel in canoes, four-seater airplanes, and treks, while accommodations may be tents or village huts. Meals are always family style.

For information: Immersia Travel, 19 North King St., Leesburg, VA 20176; 800-207-5454 or 703-443-6939; www .immersiatravel.com.

MATURE TOURS

Mature Tours specializes in travel for "youthful spirits" over the age of 50 who wish to roam the world with other travelers in their own age group. A division of Solo Flights, which has a long history of catering to single voyagers of all ages, it welcomes both solo seniors and couples on its trips. Regular destinations include Costa Rica, Club Valtur in the Dominican Republic, Spain, and New York City. Also frequently on its schedule are steamboat cruises on the Mississippi River.

For information: Mature Tours, 10 Tait's Mill Rd., Trumbull, CT 06611; 800-266-1566 or 203-445-0107.

MAYFLOWER TOURS

Most of Mayflower's travelers are "55 or better," so the pace of its tours is leisurely and rest stops are scheduled every couple of hours. You travel by motor coach, stay in good hotels or motels, and eat many of your meals together. All trips are fully escorted by tour directors who make sure all goes well. If you are a single traveler and request a roommate at least 30 days before departure, you'll get one or a room to yourself with no single supplement to pay. Tours go almost everywhere in the U.S. and Canada, including national parks of the Southwest, the Canadian Rockies and Pacific Northwest, French Canada, Branson and the Ozarks, New England and Cape Cod, Hawaii, and New York. Cruises take you to the Caribbean, the Panama Canal, Alaska, Hawaii, or the New England coast.

For information: Mayflower Tours, 1225 Warren Ave., Downers Grove, IL 60515; 800-323-7604 or 630-960-3430; www.mayflowertours.com.

MOUNT ROBSON ADVENTURE HOLIDAYS

For people over 50 who crave action and the wilderness, this agency plans a couple of "gentle adventures" every summer in British Columbia's Mount Robson Provincial Park, just west of Jasper. Mount Robson is the highest mountain in the Canadian Rockies, and the park offers spectacular scenery. The Fifty Plus Adventure is a five-night package trip for up to 14 participants that includes a guided trek, a nature tour, a marshlands canoe trip, and a gentle rafting float trip, all led by local naturalists. You sleep at the base camp in heated log cabins with private bathrooms and eat three hearty meals a day.

For information: Mount Robson Adventure Holidays, PO Box 687, Valemount, BC V0E 2Z0; 800-882-9921 or 250-566-4386; www.mountrobson.com.

OUTWARD BOUND

Outward Bound is famous for its rugged wilderness survival trips for young people aimed at building self-confidence, self-esteem, and the ability to work as a team. But it also offers short adventure courses specifically designed for adults, a couple for those over the age of 50, who seek to examine their goals or gain personal insights. Among the recent one-week courses for these mature adventurers: a desert backpacking and canyon exploration trip in Big Bend National Park in Texas and canoeing down the Rio Grande.

For information: Outward Bound, 100 Mystery Point Rd., Garrison, NY 10524; 888-882-6863 or 914-424-4000; www.outwardbound.com.

MEXICAN PREVIEW

A California travel company, **Barvi Tours**, conducts a weekly five-night trip to Guadalajara, a popular retirement city in Mexico, for those who are contemplating retirement there. Here you tour the residential areas of Chapala and Ajijic on the shore of the largest lake in Mexico, explore the area, talk to residents, and learn from experts about cultural differences, personal finances, medical services, housing, immigration laws, cost of living, and shopping.

For information: Barvi Tours, 11658 Gateway Blvd., Los Angeles, CA 90064; 800-824-7102 or 310-474-4041.

OVERSEAS ADVENTURE TRAVEL

OAT's soft adventures, exclusively for travelers over 50, combine creature comforts with off-the-beaten-path experiences in exotic places all over the world, from the rain forests of Borneo to Botswana or the Galapagos Islands. Groups are small, with no more than 16 participants. The trips—rated from "easy" to "demanding"—move along at a leisurely pace and offer many optional side adventures. You'll travel by minivan and lodge in accommodations ranging from five-star hotels to jungle lodges, small inns, or spacious tents and sometimes use unconventional modes of transportation such as dugout canoes, camels, switchback trains, yachts, or your own two feet.

Among current tours, always including round-trip air, from this affiliate of Grand Circle Travel are excursions to such places as the Amazon, Peru, Morocco, Nepal, China, Tibet, Borneo, Tanzania, and Europe.

Solo travelers are not charged a single supplement if they

are willing to share accommodations, even if a roommate is not available.

For OAT's walking tours, see Chapter 13.

For information: Overseas Adventure Travel, 625 Mt. Auburn St., Cambridge, MA 02138; 800-873-5628; www .oattravel.com.

PETRABAX VACATIONS

An agency that specializes in affordable escorted tours to Spain, Portugal, and Morocco for mature travelers, Petrabax offers a 50 percent reduction for travel companions from November through March (except during the holiday season) on the cost of the land portion of many of its one- to three-week packages. For those who want to spend more time at resorts on the Costa del Sol or the Algarve, known for mild winter weather, additional weeks are available at low cost.

If you choose one of this company's self-drive vacation packages in Spain and Portugal (these include airfare, accommodations, and rental car) and wish to stay in the government-owned inns called paradores or pousadas, your rates will reflect the Golden Days Promotion. If you are over the age of 60, that means you can get a 35 percent discount on the room rates at certain times of the year and sometimes certain days of the week.

For information: Petrabax Vacations, 97–45 Queens Blvd., Ste. 600, Rego Park, NY 11374; 800-634-1188 or 718-897-7272; www.petrabax.com.

PLEASANT HAWAIIAN HOLIDAYS

To people at least 55 years old, many of Pleasant's hotels

and condos in the Hawaiian islands offer free room upgrades, car-rental upgrades, and discount certificates for activities and events. Called the *Makua Club*, the program is free and only one person per room needs to be the right age.

For information: Pleasant Hawaiian Holidays, 2404 Townsgate Rd., Westlake, CA 91361; 800-2-HAWAII (800-242-9244) or 818-991-3390; www.pleasantholidays.com.

RFD TOURS

Created many years ago to arrange visits between American and foreign farmers, and then to organize flower and garden tours, RFD Travel now plans a wide range of U.S. and international tours and cruises every year specifically for mature travelers. All hosted, the trips stress cultural heritage events, personal encounters with local residents, knowledgeable tour managers, and an easy pace.

For information: RFD Tours, 1225 Warren Ave., Downers Grove, IL 60515; 800-365-5359 or 630-435-8500; www.mayflowertours.com.

RIVER ODYSSEYS WEST

ROW reserves a couple of whitewater river trips each summer exclusively for adventurous people over 55 who like to travel with others their own age. These Prime Time trips take you down Idaho's Salmon River and the Snake River on the Oregon border for five days, passing through four spectacular volcanic canyons. You travel in rubber rafts by day and sleep in tents at the edge of the river by night.

Another choice for mature travelers is one of ROW's raft-supported walking trips in Hells Canyon or the Salmon River in Idaho. See Chapter 13 for details.

For its canoe trips on the wild and scenic upper Missouri River in Montana, ROW reserves a couple of departure dates for older adventurers. Following the trail of Lewis and Clark, you travel in comfortable 34-foot voyageur canoes carrying up to 14 passengers plus two guides. You'll float down the river for four or six days, stopping to explore many historic sites along the way. At the end of the day, you'll stop at luxury campsites with tents set up in advance, eat five-course meals, try your luck at fishing, and tell stories around the campfire.

For information: River Odysseys West, PO Box 579-UD, Coeur d'Alene, ID 83816; 800-451-6034 or 208-765-0841; www.rowinc.com.

SAGA HOLIDAYS

Saga caters exclusively to travelers over 50. It offers an astonishing variety of vacations, from fully escorted, all-inclusive tours of any place you've ever wanted to visit to cruises and safaris, educational travel, apartment stays, and winter resort stays. It also offers grand tours of Europe, holidays in Turkey or Greece, nature tours of Borneo, and river cruises down the Danube River or the Yangtze River in China.

All-inclusive resort holidays are designed to let you live a while in one place—in Portugal, Spain, Sicily, Costa Rica, Bali, Thailand, the Canary Islands, the French Riviera, or Greece—where you settle into your hotel for a relaxing stay-put vacation that includes entertainment, activities, and excursions.

In 1996, Saga introduced the *Saga Rose*, its own ship, and a variety of voyages including an annual around-the-world cruise. The only ship that caters exclusively to over-50s, its itineraries and amenities are tailored for mature customers.

Associated with Saga, too, are two educational travel programs. Smithsonian Odyssey Tours, in partnership with the famed Smithsonian Institution, gives you a wide choice of learning adventures guided by experts in their fields. Among recent choices: Egypt's ancient temples, Vikings and volcanoes in Iceland, Moorish castles in Spain and Portugal, U.S. and Canadian national parks, and the cultural treasures of Ireland.

The Road Scholar program offers travel-study itineraries each with a special theme, such as French impressionism, British mystery novels, the geology of Iceland, the archaeology of Newfoundland, and Dutch and Flemish art. Each trip includes lectures by experts from academic or cultural institutions, plus excursions and activities.

Saga schedules singles-only departures and tours with no single supplements on many of its itineraries, notably on its European tours, so that solo participants can usually pay the same amount per person as twosomes. Early birds on these itineraries get their own rooms; latecomers may have to bunk with a buddy. The company will also try to match travelers with roommates, if requested, for savings and companionship. For land vacations, a roommate is guaranteed or there is no extra charge if one is not available. If you can put together your own group of at least ten travelers, you can go free.

For information: Saga Holidays, 222 Berkeley St., Boston, MA 02116; 800-343-0273; www.sagaholidays.com. Road Scholar programs: 800-621-2151. Smithsonian Odysseys: 800-258-5885. *Saga Rose:* 800-952-9590.

SCI/NATIONAL RETIREES OF AMERICA

This agency, which began decades ago with trips to the Catskills resorts, now offers a long list of escorted group tours for seniors that range from 1-day outings to 45-day world cruises. The land tours—5-day jaunts by air to Las Vegas are its specialty—depart midweek, transport you by motor coach, and take you to such places as New Orleans, Quebec, Niagara Falls, the Poconos, Orlando, Nashville, or New York.

For information: SCI/National Retirees of America, 1186 Grand Ave., Baldwin, NY 11510; 800-698-1101 or 516-485-3200.

SOPHISTICATED VOYAGES

A sister company to Grandtravel, Sophisticated Voyages operates one or two upscale tours a year for older travelers who want a relaxed itinerary rich in cultural activities, outstanding meals, fine hotels, and plenty of free time. What they don't want are hassles, large groups, all-day bus rides, hurried breakfasts, and many events crammed into the day. Current trips include a 10-day Britain tour that combines five nights in London with three nights at Thornbury Castle in County Avon; and a two-week safari in Kenya where you are put up in elegant hotels, lodges, and tented camps.

For information: Sophisticated Voyages, 6900 Wisconsin Ave., Chevy Chase, MD 20815; 800-247-7651 or 301-986-0790; www.grandtrvl.com.

TRAFALGAR TOURS

After 50 years of taking Americans on tours of Europe, Trafalgar has now added a first-class tour program in the

U.S. and Canada with more than a dozen regional itineraries. Catering to older travelers who want to see the sights without worrying about logistics and details, these escorted motor coach tours include luxury coaches, first-class hotels or lodges, guided sight-seeing, gratuities, and most meals. Trafalgar also continues its overseas tours, both first-class and budget, to Europe, Britain, and South Africa. Traveling alone? You'll be matched with an appropriate roommate and won't be charged the single supplement.

For information: Trafalgar Tours USA, 11 East 16th St., New York, NY 10010; 800-854-0103 or 212-725-7776; www.trafalgartours.com.

VALUE WORLD TOURS

An agency that specializes in trips to central and eastern Europe, Value World Tours takes 10 to 20 percent off the cost of some of its tours and river cruises on some off-peak departure dates for travelers over the age of 50. River cruises include trips on inland waterways in Russia, Ukraine, central Europe, Egypt, and China, while the hosted or escorted motorcoach tours go to many destinations in the same parts of the world. The two-week programs may be extended before or after the trips.

For information: Value World Tours, 17220 Newhope St., Fountain Valley, CA 92708; 800-795-1633 or 714-556-8258; www.vwtours.com.

VANTAGE DELUXE WORLD TRAVEL

Vantage features upscale, fully escorted group travel packages for mature travelers. These all-inclusive packages include land tours, train trips, and both river and ocean cruises. Accommodations are always deluxe and explorations are leisurely and relaxed, so there is plenty of time to savor the sights. All trips are led by tour directors who see to it that everything—from ticketing and baggage handling to check-ins, meals, and tips—is taken care of for you. Among Vantage's most popular tours are a Danube River cruise, a trip through the Panama Canal, a visit to China and the Yangtze River, an exploration of Ireland, and the countries of Eastern Europe. There are also longer, more exotic trips including a deluxe around-the-world tour.

If you are traveling alone and want a roommate, a compatible companion will be found or you'll pay only half the single supplement on land programs.

For information: Vantage Deluxe World Travel, 90 Canal St., Boston, MA 02114; 800-322-6677; www.vantagetravel .com.

VISTA TOURS

Another agency providing escorted tours almost exclusively for the mature set, Vista Tours plans leisurely trips with plenty of stops and ample time to enjoy the points of interest and relax too. You travel on comfortable motor coaches with escorts who deal with the reservations, transfers, luggage, meal arrangements, and all other potentially problematic situations. Destinations, although mainly in the U.S., also include Canada, Europe, and Hawaii. A highlight every year is a five-day trip over the New Year's holiday to California for the Pasadena Rose Parade and a New Year's Eve party with a big band and a celebrity show. If you're a woman who doesn't have a dancing partner or wants a better one, you may take your turn whirling around the floor with one of the gentleman hosts who accompany the group.

For information: Vista Tours, 1923 N. Carson St., Ste. 105, Carson City, NV 89701; 800-248-4782 or 775-882-2100; www.frontiertours.com.

TIPS FOR FRUGAL TRAVELERS

A lively bimonthly 12-page newsletter packed with ways to stretch your travel dollars, **ThriftyTraveler.Com** includes tips, resources, tours, travel news, and a special section for readers over the age of 50. You have your choice of receiving it by mail or online.

For information: ThriftyTraveler.Com, PO Box 8168, Clearwater, FL 33758; 800-532-5731; www.thriftytraveler.com.

WARREN RIVER EXPEDITIONS

Warren River Expeditions offers many whitewater raft trips limited to adventurers over 50, plus two expeditions a year for grandparents and their grandchildren. All the trips take you down Idaho's Salmon River, the longest undammed river in the country—fast and wild in the spring, tame and gentle in late summer. You'll float through unique ecosystems, down the deep Salmon River Canyon, and through the Frank Church Wilderness Area, where you'll view the lush scenery and abundant wildlife. Planned as soft adventure trips for people who are not enthusiastic about sleeping on the ground, the six-day senior trips, limited to 16 guests, put you up each night in comfortable rustic backcountry lodges. There's a 10 percent discount on all trips for those over 55 or under 16.

For information: Warren River Expeditions, PO Box 1375, Salmon, ID 83467-1375; 800-765-0421 or 208-756-6387; www.raftidaho.com.

WEST COAST RAIL TOURS

For train buffs and anybody else who loves to ride the rails, the West Coast Railway Association is worth checking out. A nonprofit group dedicated to the collection and preservation of British Columbia's railway heritage, it runs many escorted rail tours all over the province as well as Washington state. Open to all comers, they range from one-day or weekend excursions to 12-day tours to historic and scenic locations escorted by experienced guides. On many you eat and sleep on board; on others there are stopovers for dining, sleeping, and seeing the sights along the way. Some transportation is by bus or ferry.

Seniors get a price break on almost all tours. Singles are matched with roommates if they wish and, if none are available, no single supplement is applied.

For information: West Coast Rail Tours, PO Box 2790 Stn. Main, Vancouver BC V6B 3X2; 800-722-1233 or 604-524-1011; www.wcra.org/tours.

CRUISING THE OCEANS, RIVERS, AND SEAS

Cruises have always appealed to the mature crowd. In fact, the majority of passengers on most sailings are over the age of 50, if not 60. So you are sure to find suitable companionship.

Whatever your age, never book a cruise without shopping around. Cruise rates have always been heavily discounted, but today anybody who pays the full sticker price (also called the brochure rate) should also be offered a chance to bid on the Brooklyn Bridge. Usually the best bargains come from travel agents who specialize in sea voyages or from cruise brokers who buy blocks of cabins and sell them at a discount. But the cruise lines offer special rates, too, on advance-purchase or last-minute bookings, introductory or off-season sailings, repositioning cruises, group bookings, and two-for-one deals. Occasionally they will have special senior rates too. All of this means you must do your homework before signing up for a cruise.

In the meantime, here are some opportunities specifically for you.

B&V WATERWAYS

Choose a cruise on a deluxe hotel barge on the canals and waterways of Europe and you will get a discount of 10 percent if you are a member of AARP. Take your pick of fully crewed and all-inclusive barge trips in Ireland, France, Holland, or England.

For information: B&V Waterways, 800-999-3636; www.bv associates.com.

CARNIVAL CRUISE LINES

The Senior Citizen Rates, recently introduced by Carnival Cruise Lines, can save you as much as 70 percent on the published brochure rates and are available on certain ships and voyages if you are at least 55 years of age. To inquire about them, call your travel agent or the toll-free number below and mention the code CPSE/CPSN.

In addition, you're entitled to savings on many of Carnival's cruises if you belong to AARP. You can save $200 per stateroom in categories 6 through 12 on Alaska cruises of seven days or more; $100 per stateroom on seven-day voyages to the Caribbean or the Mexican Riviera; $50 on shorter trips to the Bahamas or Baja, Mexico. Singles save half that much. If you are traveling alone, you may request a roommate and pay no single supplement even if no roommate is available.

For information: Carnival Cruise Lines, 800-CARNIVAL (800-227-6482); www.carnival.com.

COSTA CRUISES

Travelers over the age of 60 can get an additional discount of $50 per person when they book a cruise at least 120 days in advance of sailing using the early-booking Andiamo rate which is already discounted. Take children or grandchildren under 17 and they cruise for $199 each.

For information: Costa Cruises, 800-332-6782; www.costa cruises.com.

DELTA QUEEN STEAMBOAT CO.

Steamboating, always popular among mature travelers, is the specialty of this company, whose steam-powered overnight paddle wheelers ply the Mississippi River and other inland waterways on 3- to 14-night cruises. Among other offerings are big band cruises; culinary cruises; voyages for

Civil War buffs with lectures by historians and visits to bat-
tle sites; 1950s dance tours; Mark Twain cruises; a Kentucky
Derby cruise; a Cajun culture cruise; and veterans' reunions.
For information: Delta Queen Steamship Co., Robin Street
Wharf, 1380 Port of New Orleans Pl., New Orleans, LA
70130; 800-543-1949 or 504-586-0631; www.deltaqueen
.com.

ELDERHOSTEL'S ADVENTURES AFLOAT

One of Elderhostel's newest categories of learning vacations
for its 55-plus members is a group of programs on the
world's most spectacular waterways. Your education will
take place aboard river barges, yachts, cruise ships, or even
the *QE2*. Choices can be made from dozens of voyages all
over the world, from the Mississippi River to Scandinavia,
the Aegean Sea, the Yangtze River, the Texas Gulf Coast, the
Danube River, the Mediterraean, and across the Atlantic
Ocean. International programs include airfare, and all trips
include tuition, field trips, meals, and accommodations. For
more about Elderhostel, see Chapter 12.
For information: Elderhostel, 11 Avenue de Lafayette,
Boston, MA 02111; 877-426-8056 or 617-426-7788; www
.elderhostel.org.

HOLLAND AMERICA LINE

If you are a member of AARP and book an outside cabin on
a Holland America cruise or Alaska cruise tour of seven days
or longer, you can save $100 per stateroom. The saving is
$50 per stateroom on voyages of seven days or longer; $25
on shorter trips. Single travelers save half those amounts.

To get the discounts, your membership number must be provided when your trip is booked.

For information: Holland America Line, 800-887-3529; www.hollandamerica.com.

KD RIVER CRUISES OF EUROPE

Here you're in luck if you are celebrating a big anniversary. This company, the oldest and biggest river cruise line in Europe, takes 20 percent off of the bill for couples celebrating their 25th, 40th, 50th, or 60th anniversaries on most of its sailings on the Rhine, the Danube, or the Elbe Rivers in central Europe. The anniversary needn't coincide with the cruise departure date—it just has to take place some time in the same year. A marriage certificate or other proof of the wedding date is required.

For information: KD River Cruises of Europe, 800-346-6525 or 914-696-3600; www.rivercruises.com.

NORWEGIAN COASTAL VOYAGE

The 11-ship Norwegian Coastal Voyage fleet sails daily along the 1,250-mile west coast of Norway, calling at 34 ports between Bergen and Kirkenes. The voyage is a combination of a first-class cruise ship and a working ship that carries local passengers and cargo between remote coastal towns and villages. Passengers over the age of 67 get a small break on the rates—a reduction of $120 to $220 per person, one-way or round-trip, all year except between June 1 and July 15. And there's no single supplement in seven cabin categories on off-peak sailings.

AARP members are entitled to an additional discount of $70 to $100 per cabin one-way, and $150 on round-trip sailings.

For information: Norwegian Coastal Voyage, 405 Park Ave., New York, NY 10022; 800-323-7436 or 212-319-1300; www.coastalvoyage.com.

RENAISSANCE CRUISES

If you are at least 50 and a member of AARP, you can save $100 per member on all cabin categories on Renaissance "R-Series" cruises in the Mediterranean, Greek Isles, and South Pacific. This is, by the way, the first cruise line to ban smoking on board and limit passengers to those over the age of 18.

For information: Renaissance Cruises, 800-525-5350; www .renaissancecruises.com.

ROYAL CARIBBEAN INTERNATIONAL

Check with your travel agent to find out when this cruise line will be offering one of its special promotions for seniors, because the cost on these sailings, many of them scheduled in the off-peak seasons, is always less than the lowest standard discounted rates. If one passenger in your cabin is over the age of 55, your cabin mates each get the same deal. Because cruises have special appeal to the older population, RCI's brochures indicate the activity level and amount of walking on each shore excursion.

For information: Royal Caribbean International, 800-327-6700; www.royalcaribbean.com.

ROYAL HAWAIIAN CRUISES

These day trips—some of them are luncheon or dinner cruises—take you out on small ships (*Navatek I* or *Navatek II*), famous for their comfort and smooth ride; or adventure rafts (*Maui Nui Explorer* or *Na Pali Explorer*), more rugged and designed for ecotourism. You'll sail along exclusive routes for exploring, snorkeling, whale watching, and sightseeing in the Hawaiian Islands. If you are over 65, you'll get a 15 percent discount on all day trips. Mention your age when you make your reservations.

For information: Royal Hawaiian Cruises, 800-852-4183; www.royalhawaiiancruises.com.

SAGA ROSE

The voyages of the *Saga Rose*, the 580-passenger cruise ship now owned by Saga Holidays, caters exclusively to travelers over the age of 50. Based in England, the ship cruises to Iceland, Scandinavia, the Arctic Circle, Spain, the Canary Islands, and the Baltic cities. It also makes an annual 99-night trip around the world.

For information: Saga Holidays, 800-952-9590; www.saga holidays.com.

WORLD EXPLORER CRUISES

When the *S.S. Universe Explorer* is not serving as a floating university campus (see Chapter 12), it cruises to Alaska, the Caribbean, and Central and South America with on-board presentations on the history, wildlife, and culture of each of the ports visited. Members of AARP get a 20 percent discount on the brochure rates on selected Alaska and Panama Canal cruises. Single travelers qualify for a 5 percent discount off the single supplement on many voyages. Friends and family cruise free in third and fourth berths in some cabin categories.

By the way, this ship features a computer lab with instructors from SeniorNet (see Chapter 16) who teach passengers everything from basic word processing to the Internet. The classes are free to SeniorNet members who pay the annual membership fee.

For information: World Explorer Cruises, 800-854-3835 or 415-393-1565; www.wecruise.com.

GENTLEMEN HOSTS

Because single men of a certain age are scarce among the traveling population, especially on board ship, a growing number of cruise lines offer almost free travel to carefully chosen unattached men over 45—in some cases, over 65—with excellent social and dancing skills. These gentlemen hosts serve as dancing or dining partners, make a fourth for bridge, act as escorts for shore trips, and socialize—without favoritism—with the single women on board.

There are stringent screening procedures and many more applicants than positions, so don't be surprised if you are not encouraged to apply. Hosts must provide their own wardrobes and sometimes their own airfare as well as a fee to the placement agency for every week at sea.

Commodore Cruise Line's ship, *Enchanted Isle*, which sails every Saturday from the Port of New Orleans to Caribbean and Mexican ports, takes two or more male dance hosts on most cruises from August through April. Single, over-50, retired or semi-retired businessmen, their job is to attend all dance lessons and to dance with passengers to the music of an eight-piece orchestra each night of the seven-night voyage.

For information: Karp Enterprises, 1999 University Drive, Coral Springs, FL 33071; 954-341-9400.

Crystal Cruises, whose worldwide cruises carry three or four "ambassador hosts" per trip, look for personable social hosts over the age of 65 who are great dancers and enjoy keeping older single women passengers entertained both on board and ashore.

For information: Entertainment Dept., Crystal Cruises, 2049 Century Park East, Ste. 1400, Los Angeles, CA 90067.

Cunard Line's cruises aboard *Queen Elizabeth 2* and the *Caronia* carry along four to ten friendly gentleman hosts between the ages of 45 and 70. Their job is not only to whirl around the dance floor with women who need partners but to act as friendly diplomats who help passengers get to know one another. A knowledge of foreign languages is a plus.

For information: The Working Vacation, 12544 W. 159th St., Lockport, IL 60441; 708-301-7535; www.theworking vacation.com.

The Delta Queen Steamboat Co., which makes about 50 cruises a year up and down the Mississippi River, taking you back in time aboard huge paddle wheelers, employs mature and responsible male hosts, assigning two to each trip on the *Mississippi Queen* and four to each Big Band cruise. Their job is to dance with the single women aboard, organize activities, and help everyone enjoy the voyage.

For information: The Working Vacation, 12544 W. 159th St., Lockport, IL 60441; 708-301-7535; www.theworking vacation.com.

EuroCruises: Gentleman hosts, chosen for their dancing ability and social skills, now sail on every departure of the *Black Prince* and its sister ship *Black Watch* on their voyages in

Europe, South America, Africa, and the Caribbean. Their job is to ensure a friendly atmosphere for passengers traveling alone.
For information: EuroCruises, 33 Little West 12th St., New York, NY 10014; 800-661-1119; www.eurocruises.com.

Holland America Line recruits retired professionals with good social skills to act as hosts on its long cruises and Big Band Sailings. Usually four to six hosts go along on each trip. Eight are aboard the Rotterdam's 99-day world cruise.
For information: The Working Vacation, 12544 W. 159th St., Lockport, IL 60441; 708-301-7535; www.theworking vacation.com.

Merry Widows Dance Tours offers many cruises and land tours for single, widowed, or divorced women who were born to dance. Accompanying them on the trip are gentleman hosts (one for every four women) to serve as dance partners.
For information: Merry Widows Dance Tours, 1515 N. Westshore Blvd., Tampa, FL 33607; 800-313-7245 or 813-289-1444.

Orient Lines, whose ships, the *Marco Polo* and *The Crown Odyssey*, operate in the Far East, South Pacific, Indian Ocean, Mediterranean, and Antarctica, take three or four gentlemen hosts along on all voyages. The hosts act as dance and dinner partners for the women passengers who are traveling on their own.
For information: The Working Vacation, 12544 W. 159th St., Lockport, IL 60441; 708-301-7535; www.theworking vacation.com.

Radisson Seven Seas Cruises takes two male hosts along on all voyages of its vessels the *Navigator* and the *Mariner*, and on some sailings of the *Diamond*. Their job is to act as social liaison between the passengers and the staff.

For information: The Working Vacation, 12544 W. 159th St., Lockport, IL 60441; 708-301-7535; www.theworking vacation.com.

Royal Olympic Cruises takes two professional hosts on all of its longer winter cruises to Central and South America. Their assignment is to socialize and dance with the women who haven't brought partners along.
For information: Cruise Crafts International Inc., 411 Brandy Run, Blairsville, GA 30512; 706-781-1487.

Silversea Cruises has introduced gentlemen hosts aboard some of the sailings of the *Silver Cloud, Silver Wind, Shadow,* and *Silver Whisper.* The hosts' job is to dance, mingle, and mix, making sure all guests have an enjoyable voyage.
For information: The Working Vacation, 12544 W. 159th St., Lockport, IL 60441; 708-301-7535; www.theworking vacation.com.

World Explorer Cruises offers *The Universe Explorer,* whose summer ports are in Alaska and winter ports in the Caribbean and Central and South America. A couple of hosts are taken along on all sailings.
For information: The Working Vacation, 12544 W. 159th St., Lockport, IL 60441; 708-301-7535; www.theworking vacation.com.

WORLD OF KNOWLEDGE TOURS

This company's tours are exclusively for active people over the age of 50 who want to sail the earth's seas and oceans and learn at the same time. You'll travel with a small group of peers aboard a first-class cruise ship to such destinations as the Galapagos Islands, the Panama Canal, Alaska, the Mediterranean, and Northern Europe and Russia. Your group dines together every evening and is accompanied by two guides who conduct shipboard seminars about the history, culture, art, geology, and wildlife of the area.

For information: World of Knowledge Tours, 107 222nd St. SW, Bothell, WA 98021; 800-453-9283; www.knowledge tours.com.

10

Intergenerational Adventures

ould you like to get to know your grandchildren (or children, nieces, nephews, young friends) better? Take them on vacation. A trip with the kids or your adult children is a wonderful way to get close to them, especially for far-flung families who seldom have a chance to spend solid time together. Whether it's a one-day tour of a nearby city or two weeks on a dude ranch, this is the kind of family togetherness that works. You can plan your own itineraries, maybe visiting places you both want to see, renting a cottage at the beach, or choosing a resort or cruise that offers special activities for the youngsters.

Many grandparents, however, don't want the hassles and anxieties of traveling on their own with kids. If you are among them, do it the easy way by going with a tour company that specializes in intergenerational vacations. These are scheduled in the summer (and occasionally during winter breaks) when the children are out of school. The best of them are fully escorted by counselors, often schoolteachers on holiday. The tours, ranging from a visit to Washington, D.C., to a safari in Kenya, move at a leisurely pace suited to both generations with plenty of stops and time to relax and relate. Some are designed for children in a certain age range, while others accept all youngsters over 7 and up to 17 or 18.

By the way, consider taking a cruise together. Several cruise lines cater to children now, providing activities for all of them, from toddlers to teenagers. Besides, many ships have cabins that accommodate three or four passengers. These extra beds or bunks are often sold at very low rates, especially for children. And sometimes third and fourth passengers, children or otherwise, can go along absolutely free except for port taxes and extras.

Growing in popularity, too, are other multigenerational holidays, such as adventures for mothers and grown daughters, hostelers and adult children, and whole families including children, parents, and grandparents. Here are some of the current choices for a vacation with the family.

AFC TOURS

This group will take you and your grandchildren over the age of 7 to Washington, D.C., Boston, or San Antonio for a week of sight-seeing. Or you can visit Yellowstone National Park, Mount Rushmore, and other famous sites in the West. You and the grandkids can go to Hawaii for an eight-day cruise to all the Hawaiian Islands, complete with shore excursions and on-board activities. The supervised programs include activities for both age groups, a tour manager to lead the way, and a swimming pool at every hotel.

For information: AFC Tours, 11555 Sorrento Valley Rd., San Diego, CA 92121; 800-369-3693 or 858-481-8188; www.afctours.com.

COUNTRY COTTAGES

Choose from among more than 10,000 private homes— from cottages to castles—in England, Ireland, Scotland, or Wales, and take the kids along for a week or more. Country Cottages offers its Grandparents' Houseparty package that at certain times of the year costs about $100 a day per person, including round-trip air from New York and a rental car or minivan. In some seasons, it adds a small discount for grandparents and grandchildren. All of the properties are second homes equipped with linens, tableware, and cookware and have accessible caretakers to provide information or assistance.

For information: Country Cottages, Box 810997, Boca Raton, FL 33481; 800-674-8883; www.villacentral.com.

ELDERHOSTEL INTERGENERATIONAL PROGRAMS

Elderhostel offers many low-cost intergenerational vacations to its members, all of whom are over 55. Some of the packages are for Elderhostelers and their children and/or grandchildren (or nieces, nephews, or young friends) under the age of 25. Others are for members and their adult children. Recent adventures in the U.S. have included a five-night stay at Hampton University in Virginia to learn about aerospace, aircraft design, and navigation; a golfing vacation in Texas; and a geological exploration in Colorado. The program for intergenerational travelers has been expanded to include many overseas programs in Ireland, Scandinavia, Greece, and elsewhere.

For information: Elderhostel, 11 Avenue de Lafayette, Boston, MA 02111; 877-426-8056 or 617-426-7788; www .elderhostel.org.

EXPLORATIONS IN TRAVEL

Multigenerational trips for mothers, daughters, grandchildren, aunts, and other female friends or relatives are scheduled a couple of times a year by Explorations in Travel. This agency specializes in active vacations for women over 40 (see Chapter 13). A current offering is a weekend windjammer cruise for landlubbers or experienced sailors aboard a 67-foot schooner in Maine's Penobscot Bay. Another is a llama trek in the Berkshire Mountains. On these adventures, one participant must be over 40 and the other under 21.

For information: Explorations in Travel, 1922 River Rd., Guilford, VT 05301; 802-257-0152; www.exploretravel .com

FAMILYHOSTEL

Learning adventures in foreign countries have always been the specialty of FamilyHostel, a program sponsored by the University of New Hampshire Division of Continuing Education, but domestic vacations have recently been added. It takes families—perhaps you and your school-age children or grandchildren—on 10-day all-inclusive summer vacations to such places as Spain, Italy, England, Mexico, and the Netherlands. A few trips are exclusively for grandparents or parents over the age of 50 and children 8 to 15 years old.

Separately and together, you'll enjoy workshops, recreation, sight-seeing, and social events including visits with local residents. The groups are accompanied by university representatives and teachers from the U.S. and the host country. Lodging is in hotels or university apartments, and the cost is moderate for what you get.

Recently, FamilyHostel added family vacations in the U.S., starting with a tour of New England. Now destinations include Alaska, Hawaii, and California.

For information: FamilyHostel, University of New Hampshire, 6 Garrison Ave., Durham, NH 03824; 800-733-9753 or 603-862-1147; www.learn.unh.edu/interhostel.

GRANDTRAVEL

This company pioneered the notion of sending grandparents and their grandchildren off on vacations together. For grandparents of any age and children from 7 to 17, its tours include visits to London and Paris, New York, Western U.S. parks, or Alaska; barge trips in Alsace; tours of famous castles in England, Scotland, and Ireland; and safaris in Kenya. If you want to go on your own, the agency will also arrange a special tour just for your family group. You needn't be an authentic grandparent, either—aunts, uncles, cousins, godparents, and other surrogate grandparents are welcome. Its 5- to 15-day tours are deluxe, educational, and limited to groups of 20.

Tours, each designated for certain ages of children, are led by teacher-escorts and always include plenty of rest stops and opportunities for both generations to spend time alone with their own age groups. As part of the package, Grandtravel provides predeparture counseling to help you deal with any special concerns such as what to pack or how to deal with kids who miss their moms.

For information: Grandtravel, The Ticket Counter, 6900 Wisconsin Ave., Chevy Chase, MD 20815; 800-247-7651 or 301-986-0790; www.grandtravel.com.

GREAT CAMP SAGAMORE

Take your grandchild to camp with you for a week in the summer. The site is the Great Camp Sagamore, a former Vanderbilt wilderness retreat in New York State's Adirondack Park, and the purpose is to bring the two generations together to have fun and get to know one another better. In the mornings, the campers engage in joint activities such as walks, berry picking, games, and nature art. In the afternoons, the age groups are on their own, free to choose from options that include music, crafts, and swimming. Before dinner, grandparents meet for discussions of their own issues, and in the evenings everyone gets together for stories, campfires, sing-alongs, square dancing, and other activities.

For information: Great Camp Sagamore, PO Box 146, Raquette Lake, NY 13436; 315-354-5311; www.sagamore .org.

IRISH FESTIVAL TOURS

For a visit to your Irish roots, gather up your grandchildren (or nieces, nephews, or other young friends) this summer and take them on a 10-day tour that includes

Dublin, Avoca, Waterford, Killarney, the Ring of Kerry, and Galway. You'll learn about the folklore and traditions of the Irish people; visit castles, villages, farms, and museums; listen to storytellers; go pony trekking; see a working dairy farm; learn traditional dances; and otherwise enjoy a respite just for you and the youngsters. Most activities include both generations, but some separate events are planned as well.

For information: Irish Festival Tours, PO Box 169, Warminster, PA 18974; 800-441-4277; www.irishtours.com.

OVER THE HILL GANG

This club for people of action (see Chapter 13) offers an occasional grandparent-grandchild trip. Last year, the first such adventure was a week at Valley Guest Ranch in Colorado's Rocky Mountains for members and grandchildren age six and older. Activities include horseback riding, hiking, an overnight pack trip, barbecues, backcountry tours, campfires, fishing, hayrides, and a guest rodeo.

For information: Over the Hill Gang International, 1820 W. Colorado Ave., Dept. G, Colorado Springs, CO 80904; 719-389-0022; www.overthehillgangintl.com.

RASCALS IN PARADISE

Specializing in family vacations for parents and children, Rascals in Paradise also invites grandparents and grandchildren to go along on its adventure trips to such places as Mexico and the Caribbean, the Bahamas, Europe, New Zealand, Thailand, Australia, the Canadian Rockies, Africa, the Galapagos Islands, Hawaii, Alaska, and ranches in the West. All group trips, three to six families per group, include escorts who plan activities for the older children and arrange baby-sitters for the little ones. This agency will plan independent vacations, too, as well as family reunions and other multigenerational celebrations.

For information: Rascals in Paradise, 650 Fifth St., Ste. 505, San Francisco, CA 94107; 800-872-7225 or 415-978-9800; www.rascalsinparadise.com.

SIERRA CLUB

Among the Sierra Club's famous outings are a couple of remarkably affordable summertime vacations for grandparents and their grandchildren. One has long been an annual event, a six-day stay at the club's rustic lodge in California's Sierra Nevada Mountains. The laid-back holiday is designed for people between the ages of 5 and 95 who may pick and choose among the available activities that include short hikes, fishing, lake swimming, a beach picnic, and a tram ride at Squaw Valley. Lodging and meals are part of the package.

The second option is a week in Hawaii where the two generations spend five nights living in A-frame cabins near a beach—swimming, snorkeling, and learning about Hawaiian culture—before moving to Hawaii Volcanoes National Park to explore lava in its primal state.

For information: Sierra Club Outing Dept., 85 Second St., San Francisco, CA 94105; 415-977-5522; www.sierra club.org.

VISTA TOURS

The family tours offered by Vista are designed for children and their relatives, whether grandparents, parents, aunts and uncles, or otherwise. There are several different trips, ranging from 4 to 14 days, such as the Railroads of the Rockies, Southern California Art and Studio Tour, the Idaho and Oregon Trail, and the California National Parks. Activities are planned for the different generations separately and together.

For information: Vista Tours, 1923 N. Carson St., Ste. 105, Carson City, NV 89701; 800-248-4782 or 775-882-2100; www.frontiertours.com.

WARREN RIVER EXPEDITIONS

Take the grandkids down the Salmon River in Idaho on a raft trip run by Warren River Expeditions. On special summer trips reserved for grandparents and grandchildren, you'll float through canyons and forests, taking time to swim and kayak. You'll sleep in comfortable backcountry lodges, some quite rustic, along the river's edge and have plenty of exciting adventures on the big rubber rafts powered by expert oarspeople. At least two midsummer departures, with a 10 percent discount for those over 55 or under 16, are reserved each summer for the two generations.

For information: Warren River Expeditions, PO Box 1375, Salmon, ID 83467-1375; 800-765-0421 or 208-756-6387; www.raftidaho.com.

11

Singles on the Road

f you're single or on your own again, have a partner who isn't the traveling kind and couldn't care less about seeing Venice, or simply like to travel independently, you can do it your own way. Many people love to be on their own, never having to cater to anyone else's whims or demands about where to go, when to eat, how long to stay at the museum, or what time to go to bed. Others, however, find traveling solo to be a rather lonely business and would prefer not to wander around the world by themselves.

To encourage and accommodate the growing numbers of mature single travelers, there are increasing numbers of tour companies, cruise lines, and clubs now catering to them. Some plan itineraries for the independents while others organize singles group tours or schedule special departure dates specifically for solo travelers. Most mix them with everyone else but try to match you up with a roommate so you can avoid paying a single's supplement, the extra charge for the privilege of sole occupancy of a room or cabin. Another way to avoid paying more than paired people is to watch for the special deals when single supplements are waived altogether. These are usually offered on off-peak packages with space that may otherwise go unclaimed.

Going with a group provides ready-made companions and an organized travel plan. But if you don't want to go places by yourself even in a group, consider joining a match-maker club that helps you find a fellow traveler who is also looking for someone with whom to share adventures and expenses.

Finally, one of the surest ways to enjoy a vacation on your own is to sign up for a trip that features activities that especially intrigue you, because you'll meet people who like the same things you do. Consider, for example, art tours, bike trips, golf schools, gourmet tours, tennis camps, language programs, volunteer vacations.

TRAVEL COMPANION EXCHANGE

TCE specializes in helping single travelers find compatible travel partners. Managed by veteran travel expert Jens Jurgen, Travel Companion Exchange is the largest, most enduring, and most successful matchmaking service, with close to 3,000 active members whose ages range from 20 to 85.

Members of TCE receive bulky fact-filled bimonthly newsletters packed with travel tips and helpful advice plus long listings of people who are seeking new friends and/or travel partners of the same or opposite sex. For more information about those who seem to be good possibilities, you can send for full profiles and photographs so you may judge their suitability for yourself. You do your own matchmaking. Jurgen suggests you talk by telephone, correspond, meet, and, even better, take a short trip together before setting out on a major adventure.

You may join TCE for a year at an introductory fee of $159, using a credit card if you wish. Membership includes their award-winning newsletter. By the way, you don't have to join TCE to subscribe to the *TCE Newsletter* (without the listings) for $48 per year. It is a gold mine of detailed travel news, tips, and bargains for all enthusiastic travelers, single or not.

For information: Travel Companion Exchange, Inc., PO Box 833, Amityville, NY 11701; 800-392-1256 or 631-454-0880. Send for a free brochure or enclose $6 for a sample newsletter.

CONNECTING: SOLO TRAVEL NETWORK

A club based in Canada, Connecting is a "solo travel network" that aims to keep its 1,500-or-so single members—almost half of them over 50—in touch with each other, advising them on where to go, what to do, and how to enjoy their travel alone or with friends. Members, who pay an annual fee of $40 (Canadian) or $28 (U.S.), receive an informative bimonthly newsletter and supplementary Singles-Friendly Travel Directory. The newsletter, which devotes a section to mature travelers, includes unlimited free listings for members looking for compatible travel companions, reader recommendations and comments, and a directory of travel companies that offer special accommodations or programs for singles. An added benefit: you may participate in the Hospitality Program, which recruits volunteers to spend time—talking, sight-seeing, hiking, sharing a meal, whatever—with visiting members from elsewhere. Other volunteers share their personal travel tips and tales.

For information: Connecting: Solo Travel Network, 689 Park Rd., Gibsons, BC V0N 1V7, Canada; 800-557-1757 or 604-886-9099; www.cstn.org.

TOURS FOR SOLO TRAVELERS

Most tour operators and agencies specializing in escorted trips for people in their prime will try to find you a same-sex roommate to share your room or cabin so you do not have to pay a single supplement. And, if they can't manage to find a suitable roommate for you, they will usually reduce the supplement or even cancel it. Some run singles-only trips, too. In any case, keep in mind that you'll hardly have time or opportunity to be lonely on the typical escorted tour run by these agencies. If you are planning an extended stay in just one location, however, you may have more need for company.

GO SOLO TRAVEL CLUB

This club for "the mature and discriminating traveler without a partner" guarantees private rooms on all trips, domestic and overseas, and no single supplements for those traveling alone. And its guided group tours travel in their own private buses. A newsletter issued three times a year offers travel tips and announcements of upcoming tours that have recently included Ireland, Branson, Paris, San Francisco, Santa Fe, and Alaska. The annual fee of $35 is deducted from the cost of your first trip of the year.

For information: Go Solo Travel Club, Tallyho Travel, 92 E. Main St., Elmsford, NY 10523; 914-592-4316; www.go solotravelclub.com.

MERRY WIDOWS DANCE TOURS

Designed for solo women from 50 to 90 who love to dance but don't have partners, **Merry Widows Dance Tours** runs many cruises every year to such places as the Caribbean, Southeast Asia, Alaska, Greece and the Mediterranean, and the Panama Canal. The trips range from seven days to eighteen. Sponsored by the AAA Auto Club South, the cruises take along their own gentleman hosts, one professional dancer for every four women. Each woman receives a dance card that rotates her partners every night throughout the cruise, whether she's a beginner or a polished dancer. The men are also rotated at the dinner tables so everyone gets the pleasure of their company. You don't have to be a widow and you don't even have to know the cha-cha or the macarena to enjoy these trips. If you are traveling alone and wish to avoid paying a single supplement, you will be assigned a roommate.

Merry Widows also operates tours to major resorts, in such settings as the Cloister in Georgia's Sea Islands. Out-of-the-country resort destinations include European capitals, the Greek Isles and Turkey, Tahiti, Hawaii, and the Caribbean.

For information: Merry Widows Dance Tours, 1515 N. Westshore Blvd., Tampa, FL 33607; 800-313-7245 or 813-289-1444.

GOING SOLO TRAVEL CLUB

A singles-only travel and social club, Going Solo caters to unattached travelers ranging in age from 23 to 80, with an average age of 50. Located in Calgary, Alberta, in Canada, it has many U.S. members and welcomes them all on its worldwide tours to places like the British Isles, Africa, Belize, Guatemala, Mexico, Turkey, and Greece.

The club also offers day trips, local social activities, and weekend getaways. Members, who pay an annual fee of $66.34 (Canadian) or $45 (U.S.), travel at group rates and because they are matched with roommates are charged no single supplement fees.

For more information: Going Solo Travel Club, 629 11th Ave. SW, Calgary, AB T2R OE1; 888-446-7656 (outside Alberta) or 403-256-7871; www.goingsolotravel.com.

SPECIAL FOR SOLO DINERS

Check out SoloDining.com if you often eat meals alone for pleasure or business whether in your own hometown or on the road. It publishes a bimonthly newsletter (mailed) and maintains a website, both of them full of tips and strategies to increase your options and comfort as a solo diner.

For information: SoloDining.com, PO Box 1025, S. Pasadena, CA 91031; 800-299-1079 or 323-257-0026; www.Solo Dining.com.

O SOLO MIO SINGLES TOURS

A travel club for singles who like to travel in groups, O Solo Mio welcomes members of all ages but designs some of its tours specifically for those over 60 who prefer traveling with other singles their own age. Members who pay a fee of $20 a year receive a quarterly newsletter announcing upcoming plans and may ask to be matched with a roommate to avoid paying a single supplement fee. The 60-plus tours vary every year but recent destinations have included Nova Scotia and Prince Edward Island, Switzerland with a Rhine cruise, Branson, and Mexico.

For information: O Solo Mio Singles Tours, 636 Los Altos Rancho, Los Altos, CA 94024; 800-959-8568 or 650-917-0817; www.osolomio.com.

SENIOR WOMEN'S TRAVEL

Solo women travelers over the age of 50 are invited to join the special one-week tours offered by Senior Women's Travel. Planned for "women who want it all," the upscale guided tours of no more than 10 participants concentrate on food, history, art, music, and literature. They take you to Paris, Venice, Provence, Malta, Bilbao, New York, or London where you unpack once, settle down, and then set forth to explore the destination in depth.

For information: Senior Women's Travel, 136 E. 56th St., New York, NY 10022; 212-838-4740; www.poshmosh.com.

SOLO FLIGHTS

This 26-year-old company makes it its business to know about the best tours, cruises, packages, and groups for single travelers of all ages. It represents major tour operators and cruise lines and also offers its own exclusive trips, some marketed by its division, Mature Tours, for "youthful spirits" over 50. Regularly featured tours go to Costa Rica four times a year and also to New York City, Ireland, Spain, and Morocco. Get in touch to discuss your best options.

For information: Solo Flights, 10 Taits Mill Rd., Trumbull, CT 06611; 800-266-1566 (outside Connecticut) or 203-445-0107; hometown.aol.com/SoloFlights.

SOLO'S HOLIDAYS

The U.K.'s largest singles tour operator, Solo's Holidays offers hosted group vacations for unattached people. Although it is based in England, it will happily take Americans and Canadians on tour all over the world, giving them a chance to talk, dine, dance, and share experiences with other lone travelers. All trips are divided into two groups, the first exclusively for ages 28 to 55, and the second for ages 45 to 69, although sometimes the ages are mixed.

For information: Solo's Holidays, 54-58 High St., Edgware, Middlesex HA8 7EJ, England; 011-44-181-951-2800; www .solosholiday.co.uk.

TGIF VANCOUVER

A travel club for singles over 35, TGIF is based in Vancouver, B.C., but welcomes solo travelers—most members are 50-plus— from everywhere on its getaway weekends and tours all over the world. Membership fee for one year is $50 (U.S.) or $75 (Canadian). Almost all of the club activities occur in or around Vancouver and include dances, hikes, picnics, parties, weekend excursions, sailing trips, and theater nights. Recent tours and cruises have taken members to Mexico, Bali and Hong Kong, Alaska, the Caribbean, Greece, and California's west coast.

For information: TGIF Vancouver, 977 Wellington Dr., North Vancouver, BC V7K 1L1; 800-661-7151 or 604-988-5231; www.tgif.bc.com.

WANDER WOMEN

"On your own but not alone" is the motto of Wander Women, a new travel club exclusively for active women over 50. Affiliated with AFC Tours, the club, which charges no membership fees, schedules several women-only trips each year for its 500-or-so members who receive quarterly newsletters announcing new adventures. Recent outings have been a six-day tour of the northern California coast and a seven-day stay in San Antonio, Texas. Members who live in southern California are invited to get-acquainted lunches, teas, travel shows, and seminars. Benefits include the security of traveling with a group and a way to avoid paying single supplements. List yourself and your preferences in the Share Finder program if you're looking for a compatible travel companion.

For information: Wander Women Travel Club, AFC Tours, 11771 Sorrento Valley, San Diego, CA 92121; 800-369-3693 or 858-481-8188; www.afctours.com.

HOOK-UPS FOR SOLO RVers

RVers who travel alone in their motor homes or vans can hook up with others in the same circumstances when they join one of the groups mentioned below. All of the clubs provide opportunities to travel together or to meet at campgrounds on the road, making friends with fellow travelers and having a fine time.

LONERS OF AMERICA

LOA is a club for single campers who enjoy traveling together. Established in 1987, it currently has 29 chapters throughout the country and well over 500 active members from their 40s to their 90s, almost all retired and widowed, divorced, or otherwise single. Many of them live year-round in their motor homes or vans, and others hit the road only occasionally. They camp together, rally together, caravan together, often meeting at special campgrounds that cater to solo campers.

A not-for-profit member-operated organization, the club publishes a biannual membership directory and a lively monthly newsletter that keeps its members in touch and informs them about campouts and rallies all over the country. The chapters organize their own events as well. Currently, dues are $40 a year plus a $5 registration fee for new members.

For information: Loners of America, PO Box 3314, Napa, CA 94558; 888-805-4562; www.napanet.net/~mbost.

LONERS ON WHEELS

A camping and travel club for mature single campers, Loners on Wheels is not a lonely hearts club or a matchmaking service, but simply an association of friends and extended family. With 68 chapters located throughout the U.S. and Canada, LOW now has a membership of about 2,400 unpartnered travelers. The club schedules hundreds of camping events during the year at campgrounds, some of which are remote and cost little.

The club's newly acquired RV Ranch in Deming, New Mexico (which also serves as its headquarters), offers special rates for club members, two rallies a year, dances and games in the clubhouse, and occasional forays into Mexico. A monthly newsletter and an annual directory keep everyone up-to-date and in touch.

Annual dues at this writing are $45 U.S. and $54 Canadian, plus a one-time enrollment fee of $5.

For information: Loners on Wheels, PO Box 1355, Poplar Bluff, MO 63902; 888-569-4478; www.lonersonwheels .com. Ask for a free sample newsletter.

FRIENDLY ROAMERS

Founded by former members of Loners on Wheels, Friendly Roamers is open to everyone, couples as well as singles, so friendships and RV activities can be continued despite a change of marital status or travel arrangements. Membership gets you admission to all club events, such as rallies and campouts, a newsletter, and a membership directory. Annual dues are $10 plus a one-time registration fee of $5 for new members. Local chapters hold their own events and join the others as well.

For information: Friendly Roamers, c/o Herbert Ott, PO Box 95967; 530-872-8702.

S*M*A*R*T

An RV club for retired members of the U.S. and Canadian armed forces, Special Military Active Retired Travel Club (S*M*A*R*T) sponsors caravans and gatherings for its 3,700 members in 54 chapters around the country and helps military bases improve their family campgrounds. Caravans have recently traveled to many destinations in the U.S., including Arkansas, Tennessee, and several Western states.

The club also tours such places as Australia, New Zealand, Tahiti, Great Britain, and Scandinavia, flying overseas and then touring on land in fully equipped rented RVs. To join, U.S. residents pay an initiation fee of $10 and then $30 a year per family; Canadian residents pay a $15 initiation fee and $30 dues per family, while associate members (disabled, former POWs, Medal of Honor recipients, widows or widowers of eligible members) pay a $10 initiation fee, then $15 a year.

For information: S*M*A*R*T, Inc., 600 University Office Blvd., Pensacola, FL 32504; 800-354-7681 or 850-478-1986; www.smartrvclub.org.

RVing WOMEN

Women travelers who take to the highways in recreational vehicles can get advice and support from RVing Women, a club with over 4,000 female members. The group sponsors rallies, caravans, and other events across the U.S., Canada, and Mexico, plus weekend RV maintenance and RV driving classes in many locations around the country. Members pay an annual membership fee of $42 and receive a bimonthly magazine that covers topics such as safety, scams on the road, vehicle maintenance, and announcements of upcoming events and includes an annual directory of members.

For information: RVing Women, PO Box 1940, Apache Junction, AZ 85217; 888-55-RVING (888-557-8464) or 602-983-4678; www.rvingwomen.com.

12

Learning After 50

ave you always wanted to speak French, study African birds, examine Eskimo culture, learn to paddle a canoe or ski down a mountain, or delve into archaeology, international finance, horticulture, the language of whales, or great literature of the 19th century? Now is the time to do it. If you're a typical member of the over-50 generation, you're in good shape, healthy, and alert, with the energy and the time to pursue new interests. So why not go back to school and learn all those things you've always wished you knew?

You are welcome as a regular student at just about any institution in the U.S. and Canada, especially in the continuing-education programs, but many colleges and universities have set up special programs designed to lure older people back to the classroom. Some offer good reductions in tuition (so good indeed that often you may attend regular classes at half price or even free) and give credits for life experience. Others have designed programs and, sometimes, whole schools specifically for mature scholars. And almost every state college and university in the U.S. is now mandated to permit seniors to audit courses for free.

Going back to class is an excellent way to generate feelings of accomplishment and to exercise the mind—and one of the best ways to make new friends. It doesn't necessarily mean you'll have to turn in term papers or take excruciatingly difficult exams. Sign up for one class a week on flower arranging or Spanish conversation or a once-a-month lecture series on managing your money. Or register as a part-time or full-time student in a traditional university program. Or take a learning vacation on a college campus. Do it *your* way.

You don't even have to attend classes to learn on vacation. You can go on archaeological digs, count butterflies, help save turtles from extinction, brush up on your bassoon playing, listen to opera, search for Roman remains in Europe, study dancing or French cuisine, or go on safari in Africa.

CHAUTAUQUA INSTITUTION

For over a century people have been traveling up to the shores of Lake Chautauqua, in southwestern New York State, to a cultural summer center set in a Victorian village. The 856-acre hilltop complex offers a wide variety of educational programs, including summer weeks and off-season weekends designed for people over the age of 55. The 55-Plus Weekends and the Residential Week for Older Adults are filled up far in advance, so if you are interested, don't waste a moment before signing up.

Each 55-Plus Weekend has a specific focus, such as the U.S. Constitution, natural history, national politics, music appreciation, or trade relations with Japan. They include discussions, workshops, lectures, films, recreational activities, and evening entertainment, all led by professionals. Housing and meals are available in a residence hall with double rooms and shared baths.

The Residential Week for Older Adults is similar but longer and includes lodging and meals as well as admittance to other happenings at the center.

It's all quite cheap. The cost of tuition, room, meals, and planned activities for a Residential Week is currently $475, while a 55-Plus Weekend costs $40 for commuters or $150 with accommodations and meals.

For information: Program Center for Older Adults, Chautauqua, NY 14722; 800-836-2787 or 716-357-6200; www .chautauqua-inst.org.

CLOSE UP WASHINGTON

For a behind-the-scenes view of Washington, D.C., and the democratic process, you can attend classes on current events, study the presidents, exchange views with national political leaders, and gain insights on public policy, all in a tightly packed five- or six-night program of on-site seminars organized for older adults by the Close Up Foundation's Lifelong Learning Series. What's more, there's time for relaxation, conversation, social events, and theater in and around the nation's capital.

For your stay in the nation's capital, your lodging will be at a comfortable hotel, all meals will be provided, and activities and in-town transportation are included in the modest fee.

There are three ways to participate. First, you can sign up with Elderhotel for a five-night program by calling 877-426-8056. Or, if you have a group of 35 or more participants, you can arrange for your own six-night Lifelong Learning Series program in the nation's capital by calling the Close Up Foundation. And last, you may join the Close Up Congressional Senior Citizen Intern Program for which you must be at least 60 years old and in good health. During your six-night program in Washington, you will attend briefings and seminars on the inside workings of the government.

For information: Close Up Foundation, 44 Canal Center Plaza, Alexandria, VA 22314; 800-363-4762 or E-mail lifelong@closeup.org; www.closeup.org/lifelong.htm. For the Congressional Senior Citizen Intern Program, call 703-706-3692.

THE COLLEGE AT 60

At Fordham University's The College at 60, you're welcome at a mere 50, despite its name. You are entitled to a discount on courses in liberal arts at Fordham's Lincoln Center Campus. You pay half the regular university tuition to take the courses for credit, and only half of that to audit. The 13-week courses are taught by university faculty. Included are a lecture series and the use of all college facilities. After taking four courses, students receive a certificate and are encouraged to enter the regular Fordham University program for a degree.

For information: The College at 60, Fordham University at Lincoln Center, 113 W. 60th St., Room 301, New York, NY 10023; 212-636-6372; www.fordham.edu/collegeat60.

COLLEGE FOR SENIORS

A membership program for those 50 or older, the College for Seniors is a component of the North Carolina Center for Creative Retirement at the University of North Carolina at Asheville. The courses, most of them taught by peer seniors, range from Chaucer to computers, foreign affairs to opera, and chemistry to tap dancing. The per-term fee is currently $52 to $105, depending on the number of weeks involved. Added benefits include social events, travel programs, wellness clinics, exploration weekends, library privileges, parking decals, and access to the fitness center.

For information: College for Seniors, 104 Carmichael Hall, CPO #1660, UNCA, 1 University Heights, Asheville, NC 28804; 828-251-6384; www.unca.edu/ncccr.

ELDERFOLK

Each of Elderfolk's two- to five-week courses in Nepal, India, Tibet, Bhutan, China, and Pakistan focuses on Himalayan culture, history, natural history, religion, native cuisine, and arts and crafts. Exclusively for adventurers over the age of 55, they are offered by the Folkways Institute, a small international school without walls "whose projects are designed to permit cross-cultural understanding," which plans study courses for students and professors.

Some of the courses, combining education and exotic travel, are cultural treks on which you'll be put up at night in roomy tents or lodges. Others are residential or overland trips where you lodge in small hotels or guest houses, such as the Ancient Silk Road trip from Xian to Lahore.

No expertise or training is required, but some stamina definitely is.

For information: Elderfolk, Folkways Institute, 14600 SE Aldridge Rd., Portland, OR 97236-6518; 800-225-4666 or 503-658-6600; www.www.folkwaystravel.com.

ELDERHOSTEL

Elderhostel, the vast campus study program of learning vacations for mature Americans that was initiated 25 years ago, offers some of the world's best bargains. Its remarkabley affordable and infinitely varied short-term noncredit programs number in the thousands. All are hosted by a network of over 2,000 educational and cultural sites including colleges and universities, conference centers, state and national parks, museums, outdoor educational centers, and many others, in all 50 states and over 90 countries.

The only requirement for participation is that you must be 55 or older. An accompanying spouse or adult companion may be younger. No previous educational background is required and there are no exams or grades and only occasional homework. The one- to four-week programs with classes on every conceivable topic are taught by the host institutions' faculty, staff, and local experts and include excursions and social activities.

Accommodations range from college dormitories or motels to conference centers, cruise ships, barges, rustic cabins, hotels, and even resorts. Meals are included. Domestic programs last for a week, while the overseas programs are

HOSTELSHIPS

Elderhostel offers a limited number of full or partial scholarships, to be used only in the U.S., for people who find the tuition costs of the programs beyond their means. Funds to cover travel costs are not included and eligibility is determined upon completion of an application that includes a confidential questionnaire. Scholarship programs in Alaska and Hawaii are available only to residents of those states.

For information: Write to Elderhostel, 11 Avenue de Lafayette, Boston, MA 02111. Attention: Hostelships.

planned for one to four weeks and include transportation.

The myriad course offerings are listed in voluminous seasonal catalogs. You may also view them 24 hours a day, seven days a week, on the Web at www.elderhostel.org, where you may search by subject, date, or location.

Many of the programs include sports and other outdoor activities such as canoeing, skiing, biking, rafting, and walking (see Chapter 13). The homestay program (Chapter 5) sets you up in the home of a foreign family for a few days of a two- or three-week program. The service programs (see Chapter 18) connect you to a wide variety of volunteer organizations that provide significant services all over the world. Train Trek programs use trains both as a way to cover territory and as a moving classroom. Adventures Afloat uses ships as a chance to study remote places. Intergenerational programs for members and their children or grandchildren are another option, along with many others.

For information: Elderhostel, 11 Avenue de Lafayette, Boston, MA 02111; 877-426-8056 or 617-426-7788; www.elderhostel.org.

ELDERTREKS

The exotic adventures planned by ElderTreks to places such as Lapland, Honduras, China, Nepal, Tibet, Thailand, Vietnam, and Borneo qualify as travel/study trips because they immerse you in the cultures you visit. See Chapter 9 for more.

For information: ElderTreks, 597 Markham St., Toronto, ON M6G 2L7; 800-741-7956 or 416-588-5000; www.elder treks.com.

GOLDEN ID STUDENT PROGRAM

You can get an education for free when you join the University of Maryland's Golden ID Student Program. State residents who are over 60 and employed no more than 20 hours a week may take up to seven credits per semester— and pay nothing for the privilege. The only charge is an admission fee of $30 and the only hitch is that your acceptance into the program is contingent on space availability in the courses you have chosen.

For information: Golden ID Program, University of Maryland, Mitchell Building, Room 1101, College Park, MD; 301-314-8219. At the University College Campus, 301-985-7930; www.umuc.edu.

INTERHOSTEL

Interhostel is an international study/travel program for adults over the age of 50 and travel mates over 40. Sponsored by the University of New Hampshire Continuing Education, it offers several weeklong travel programs in the U.S. and more than 75 two-week adventures packed with activities in other countries from Italy and New Zealand to Belize.

Each program combines lectures and presentations with field trips, sight-seeing, museum visits, and excursions.

On the foreign trips, you will live in modest hotels or university accommodations, eat the local food, and learn about the land you're in. The moderate cost includes airfare, room, meals, tuition, ground transportation, and all activities.

Each program is sponsored by host-country educational institutions whose faculty lecture on culture and history and lead field trips. Good physical shape is a requisite for participation because you will be expected to climb stairs, tote your own baggage, and walk comfortably at a moderate pace for at least a mile at a time. See Chapter 13 for Interhostel's walking trips abroad.

Recent Interhostel-USA programs have taken place in the Southwest, New Orleans, Bryce Canyon and Zion National Park, Portsmouth, New Hampshire, Alaska, and more. They cost remarkably little, include all meals, accommodations, and activities, and are led by UNH faculty and representatives.

For information: Interhostel, 6 Garrison Ave., Durham, NH 03824; 800-733-9753 or 603-862-1147; www.learn.unh .edu/interhostel.

NATIONAL ACADEMY OF OLDER CANADIANS

Based in Vancouver, the NAOC's mission is to involve Canadians over the age of 45 in lifelong learning and to work in partnership with other nonprofit organizations to develop programs to promote its membership's contribution to society. These programs currently include computer classes, periodic workshops, and discussion groups on issues of special interest. Annual membership fee is $17 (Canadian) or about $11 (U.S.).

For information: National Academy of Older Canadians, 411 Dunsmuir St., Vancouver, BC V6B 1X4; 604-681-3767; www.vcn.bc.ca/naoc.

OASIS

OASIS (Older Adult Service and Information System) is a nonprofit organization sponsored by the May Department Stores Company in collaboration with local hospitals, medical centers, government agencies, and other participants in about 52 locations in 25 cities across the nation. Its purpose is to enrich the lives of people over 55 by providing educational and wellness programs and volunteer opportunities to its members. At its centers, OASIS offers classes ranging from French conversation and the visual arts to dance, bridge, creative writing, history, exercise, classical music, points of law, and prevention of osteoporosis. Also featured are special events such as concerts, plays, and museum exhibits; lectures; and even trips and cruises. If you live in an OASIS city, sign up—this is a good deal. Membership is free.

For information: The OASIS Institute, 7710 Carondelet Ave., Ste. 125, St. Louis, MO 63105; 314-862-2933; www.oasisnet.org.

PLUS PROGRAM, NYU

All students over 65 who register for at least one regular course for which they pay half tuition in the School of Continuing Education and Professional Studies at New York

University are eligible to become members of PLUS, a Program of Lifelong Learning for University Seniors, for an additional fee of $85 per semester. Membership includes a choice of two specially designed, five-session minicourses on a broad range of subjects. Topics for the courses, scheduled on Monday, Tuesday, and Thursday afternoons, have recently included Great Decisions in Foreign Policy, Russian Cinema, and the Creative World of Leonard Bernstein. PLUS members may also attend five weekly luncheon/discussion lectures with prominent speakers.

For information: PLUS, NYU School of Continuing Education, 11 W. 42nd St., New York, NY 10036; 212-790-1352 or 212-998-7130.

SAGA HOLIDAYS

Saga Holidays, marketing travel only for people over 50, offers travel/study programs as well as myriad escorted tours and cruises. One is its own series of Smithsonian Odyssey Tours and another is the Road Scholar program, with itineraries that feature educational themes. The programs include expert lecturers, selected literature, and predeparture educational materials. See Chapter 9 for more.

For information: Saga Holidays, 222 Berkeley St., Boston, MA 02116; 800-343-0273; Smithsonian Odyssey Tours: 800-258-5885. Road Scholar program: 800-621-2151; www.sagaholidays.com.

SEMESTER AT SEA

A 100-day educational voyage around the world, Semester at Sea, academically sponsored by the University of Pittsburgh and administered by the Institute for Shipboard Education, takes more than 600 college students and about 60 "senior scholars" on a unique learning experience that is designed to advance the exchange of understanding and knowledge between cultures. The S.S. *Universe Explorer*, a former passenger ship refitted as a floating campus, circumnavigates the earth twice a year, visiting countries that have included Japan, China, India, Malaysia, Kenya, Brazil, Venezuela, Egypt, Israel, South Africa, Greece, Turkey, Vietnam, and Morocco.

While the college students earn credit hours toward an undergraduate degree, the older participants may audit classes or enroll for full credit, choosing from among 60 courses taught by faculty from various universities. Onboard courses range from anthropology and biological sciences to economics, fine arts, philosophy, political science, and religion. Lengthy stays in each port of call give students a chance to experience the peoples and cultures firsthand.

Amenities include an adult coordinator, entertainment, buffet-style meals, lectures, discussion groups, guest scholars with expertise in local cultures, films, art shows, sports, and more.

In addition to the long voyage scheduled during the spring and fall, there's a new, condensed 65-day summertime Semester at Sea which combines a smaller number of college students and seniors. Beginning and ending in Greece, the group travels aboard the *MTS Odysseus* to Spain, Norway, Russia, Belgium, Portugal, Italy, Egypt, and Israel, learning all the way.

For information: Semester at Sea, 811 William Pitt Union, University of Pittsburgh, Pittsburgh, PA 15260; 800-854-0195 or 412-648-7490; www.semesteratsea.com.

SENIOR SUMMER SCHOOL

In this program, you can spend 2 to 10 weeks in the summer taking classes at your choice of 10 college campuses in vacation locations: San Diego State University, University of Wisconsin, University of California at Santa Barbara, University of California at La Jolla, West Virginia University at Morgantown, University of Judaism in Los Angeles, Marymount-Manhattan College in New York, University of Illinois at Champaign-Urbana, Appalachian State University in Boone, North Carolina, and Mount Allison University in New Brunswick, Canada.

The courses are college level but there are no grades, compulsory papers, or mandatory attendance. Accommodations and meals are in student residence halls. Sightseeing trips, excursions, classes, weekly housekeeping, and social activities are all part of the deal. While most students are in their mid-60s, people of any age are welcome to enroll. There are no previous educational requirements.
For information: Senior Summer School, PO Box 4424, Deerfield Beach, FL 33442; 800-847-2466; www.senior summerschool.com.

SENIOR U NETWORK

Senior U offers inexpensive five-day learning vacations on three different campuses on the East Coast. These are Boardwalk U at the Port-O-Call Hotel in Ocean City on the New Jersey shore; Hilton Head U at the Hilton Oceanfront Resort in North Carolina; and Pocmont U at the Pocmont Resort and Conference Center in Bushkill, Pennsylvania. At each location, the program includes lodging for four nights, all meals, the use of the hotel facilities, a gala graduation lunch, and two two-hour classes a day. Course subjects, taught by university professors and expert lecturers, range from the opera to Shakespeare, the Bible, basic bridge, Chinese culture, legal guidance, Spanish conversation, and computers. Evenings are open for socializing and entertainment.

For information: Senior U Network, PO Box 1104, Bala Cynwyd, PA 19004; 800-334-4546 or 610-771-1111. Boardwalk U: 800-334-4546. Hilton Head U: 800-845-8001. Pocmont U: 800-762-6668; www.pocmont.com.

SENIOR VENTURES IN OREGON

Southern Oregon University in Ashland offers inexpensive one- or two-week educational theater programs for people at least 50 years of age (and companions who may be younger). The summer programs coincide with the university's famous annual Oregon Shakespeare Festival. Classes are taught by actors, backstage professionals, and Shakespearean scholars. You stay on campus and eat your meals there. Added bonus: theater tickets to current productions.

Alternative residential programs for over-50s in the fall combine theater programs with intermediate-level bridge classes or theater with hiking. A few travel adventures, such as a Canadian theater expedition, are also offered.

For information: Senior Ventures, Southern Oregon University, 1250 Siskiyu Blvd., Ashland, OR 97520; 800-257-0577 or 541-552-6285; www.sou.edu/ecp/senior/srvtrs.htm.

SENIOR VENTURES IN WASHINGTON

Senior Ventures at Central Washington University in Ellensburg, Washington, is a summer residential program for older adults that offers over 50 courses—with no tests, papers, or grades—taught by university faculty. Students,

LEARNING COMPUTER TECHNOLOGY

SeniorNet is a national nonprofit organization dedicated to teaching older adults how to use computers and to understand computer technologies. It sponsors almost 200 community-based SeniorNet Learning Centers all across the country where members may take classes and use the facilities. Independent members participate through the organization's electronic community, SeniorNet Online.

To take the classes at a learning center, you must join SeniorNet for $30 a year, which gives you other benefits as well: a quarterly newsletter; discounts on computer-related books, software, and hardware; and invitations to national conferences and regional meetings.

Without cost, you can access SeniorNet Online, where you may join any of about 600 discussion groups and share information and opinions about everything from computers to politics, finance, news, social concerns, the arts, leisure, and health.

For information: SeniorNet, 121 Second St., San Francisco, CA 94105; 800-747-6848 or 415-495-4990; www.senior net.org.

who may sign up for two-week sessions and take up to six classes a day, are housed in residence-hall suites with private bathrooms and eat in their own cafeteria-style dining hall. Courses range from personal computers and the Internet to baroque art, Chinese customs, modern art, music, tennis, golf, jewelry-making, and psychology. Excursions and weekend field trips are included, as are evening activities.

For information: Senior Ventures, CWU, 400 E. 8th Ave., Ellensburg, WA 98926; 800-752-4380 or 509-963-1526; www.cwu.edu/~contedhp/senprog.html.

TRAVELEARN

The upscale learning vacations by TraveLearn take small groups of adults all over the world, putting you up in first-class or deluxe accommodations and providing local lecturers and escorts chosen from a network of more than 300 cooperating universities and colleges in each place you visit. You'll learn through on-site lectures, seminars, meals with local families, visits to homes and workplaces, and field trips. Destinations include Ireland, Egypt, Kenya, Indonesia, China, Morocco, Greece, Israel, Italy, Turkey, South Africa, Costa Rica, Peru, Belize, and Spain. If you are traveling alone and wish to share a room with another single traveler, you are guaranteed the double rate if you register 90 days in advance, even if a roommate is not found for you.

For information: TraveLearn, PO Box 315, Lakeville, PA 18438; 800-235-9114 or 570-226-9114; www.travelearn .com.

UNIVERSITY VACATIONS

Summer scholars may attend a range of 6- to 12-day study programs at such prestigious institutions as the Sorbonne in Paris, the University of Bologna in Italy, Trinity College in Dublin, Harvard University in the U.S., and Cambridge and Oxford Universities in England. In-depth classroom lectures by university faculty are augmented by field trips, walking tours, excursions, and notable meals. Students live on campus or in nearby hotels and eat in fine restaurants. The programs are open to all ages but are largely attended by older students.

For information: University Vacations, 3660 Bougainvillea Rd., Coconut Grove, FL 33133; 800-792-0100 or 305-567-2904.

WORLD OF KNOWLEDGE TOURS

Board a cruise ship with a small group of 50-plus fellow travelers, bound for the Galapagos Islands, Antarctica, Alaska, Sweden, or other exotic places and you'll not only see the sights but learn all about your destinations through shipboard seminars conducted by experienced and knowledgeable guides.

For information: World of Knowledge Tours, 107 222nd St. SW, Bothell, WA 98021; 800-453-9283; www.knowledge tours.com.

INSTITUTES FOR LEARNING IN RETIREMENT

Another way to learn with a group of contemporaries is to join an Institute for Learning in Retirement (ILR), a community-based organization of retirement-age learners for local people who commute to the program. Located in over 260 communities across the U.S., most of these institutes are member-run under the auspices of a host college or university and each is independent and unique, providing non-credit academic programs developed and often led by the members themselves. The institutes have an open membership for retirement-age students regardless of previous education and charge modest membership fees.

For a directory of current ILRs, or information about starting a new program in your community, contact the Elderhostel Institute Network (EIN) which helps community groups set up their own learning programs.

For information: Elderhostel Institute Network, 11 Avenue de Lafayette, Boston, MA 02111; 617-422-0784; www.elder-hostel.org/ehin.

13

Good Deals for Good Sports

Real sports never give up their sneakers. If you've been a physically active person all your life, you're certainly not going to become a couch potato now—especially since you've probably got more time, energy, and maybe funds, than you ever had before to enjoy athletic activities. Besides, you can now take advantage of some interesting special privileges and adventures offered exclusively to people over the age of 49.

ELDERHOSTEL

Many Elderhostel programs (see Chapter 12) include a wide selection of outdoor and sports activities for beginners as well as experienced athletes. Among the choices are golf, birding, walking and trekking, tennis, hiking, biking, sea kayaking, sailing, whitewater rafting, wilderness canoeing, skiing, snowshoeing, and trail biking.

For information: Elderhostel, 11 Avenue de Lafayette, Boston, MA 02111; 877-426-8056 or 617-426-7788; www.elderhostel.org.

EXPLORATIONS IN TRAVEL

Specializing in outdoor and cultural vacations for women over 40, Explorations in Travel features action-filled itineraries geared for energetic women who love the outdoors and like to travel with contemporaries. Trips include inn-to-inn hiking and canoeing in Vermont, wildlife-watching in Ecuador, walking in the French Pyrenees, rafting down the Salmon River in Idaho, and exploring New Zealand or the Georgia coast. At least one multigenerational trip is planned each year for mothers and daughters, grandmothers, aunts, and other female friends and relatives (one participant must be over 40, another under 21). Brand new: weekend walking trips, most of them in New England, with your dog.

For information: Explorations in Travel, 1922 River Rd., Guilford, VT 05301; 802-257-0152; www.exploretravel .com.

THE OVER THE HILL GANG

This is a club that welcomes fun-loving, adventurous people from 50 to 90-plus (and younger spouses) who are looking for action and contemporaries to pursue it with. No naps, no rockers, no sitting by the pool sipping planter's punch. The Over the Hill Gang started as a ski club many years ago but its members can now be found participating in all kinds of activities when the ski season ends. Recent trips have included skiing at many ski areas in the West, Europe, and South America. Other options include white-water rafting in Idaho; biking in Holland, Argentina, and Nova Scotia; hiking in North Carolina; rafting in the Grand Canyon; and golfing in the Canadian Rockies. A recent addition to the roster are trips for grandparents and their grandchildren. See Chapter 10.

The club currently has over 6,000 members in 50 states and 14 countries and 12 regional "gangs" (chapters). Each local gang decides on its own activities. If there's no chapter in your vicinity, you may become a member-at-large and participate in any of the happenings.

The annual membership fee ($40 single, $65 for a couple) brings you a quarterly magazine, discounts, information about national and chapter events, and a chance to join the fun. The local gangs charge small additional yearly dues.

For information: Over the Hill Gang International, 1820 W. Colorado Ave., Dept. G, Colorado Springs, CO 80904; 719-389-0022; www.overthehillgangintl.com.

ADVENTURES FOR BIKERS

Biking has become one of America's most popular sports, and people who never dreamed they could go much farther than around the block are now pedaling up to 50 miles in a day. That includes over-the-hill bikers as well as youngsters of 16, 39, or 49. In fact, some tours and clubs are designated specifically for over-50s.

CANADIAN TRAILS ADVENTURE TOURS

Canadian Trails, a company that's been around for many years, has recently introduced several tours for bikers over the age of 50. All tours take place in areas popular with the older population, such as Vancouver Island, the Okanagan wine region in British Columbia, and the Bay of Fundy in New Brunswick, and sometimes take advantage of the gentle routes provided by the new rail trails. On some trips you stay in country inns and on others at elegant campgrounds. *For information:* Canadian Trails Adventure Tours, 162-2025 Corydon Ave., Ste. 153, Winnipeg, MB R3P 0N5; 800-668-2453; www.canadiantrails.com.

CAPE COD BICYCLE ADVENTURES

A few of this company's many bicycle tours on Cape Cod during the warm months are planned exclusively for 50-plus bikers, covering about 30 miles a day on leisurely pedals through the cape's towns and dunes. You bike in a group with a guide to three different elegant inns in your five-night tour. Included are your bicycle, four dinners, all breakfasts, a boat tour, and a few lunches, plus a support vehicle that carries your luggage and stands ready to give you a lift if you want one. *For information:* Cape Cod Bicycle Adventures, PO Box 649, S. Chatham, MA 02659; 888-644-4566 or 781-641-2714; www.capecodbybike.com.

COMPASS HOLIDAYS

For a "cycling break" in the heart of England—the Cotswolds, Thames Valley, Oxford, Stratford, Cirencester—look into the guided or self-planned biking tours from Compass Holidays. With a guide you can ride for three days, for example, around Bourton-on-the-Water, or seven days in the Cotswolds, starting and ending in Cheltenham. You can also ride on your own with maps and planned accommodations on circular routes along quiet country roads from village to village near Bath or Malmesbury. Your luggage is transported for you. For bikers over 50, this tour company—which also schedules walking tours—offers a 10 percent discount if you take a tour of at least two nights and mention this book. Take your own bike or rent one there.

For information: Compass Holidays, 48 Shurdington Rd., Cheltenham, Gloucestershire GL53 OJE, UK; www.compass -holidays.com; E-mail: info@compass-holidays.com.

THE CROSS CANADA CYCLE TOUR SOCIETY

This is a bicycling club for retired people who love to jump on their bikes and take off across the countryside. Most of the club's members are over 60, with many in their 70s and 80s and only a few under 50. Says the society, "Our aim is to stay alive as long as possible." Now there's a worthwhile goal.

Based in Vancouver, B.C., with members—both men and women, skilled and novice—mostly in B.C., Ontario, and Alberta, it organizes many trips a year, all led by volunteer tour guides. Membership costs $25 single or $35 per couple per year and includes a monthly newsletter to keep you up to date on happenings. Several times a week, local members gather for day rides, and several times a year there are longer club trips to such far-ranging locations as the San Juan Islands, Waterton Park in Canada and Glacier National Park in the U.S., Australia, Hawaii's Big Island, Arizona, New Zealand, and Denmark. Every few years a group of intrepid bikers pedals clear across Canada, an adventure that takes a few weeks to accomplish, with some members dropping in and out along the way. Many of the longer trips are tenting or camping tours, while others put you up in hostels, motels, or hotels.

For information: Cross Canada Cycle Tour Society, 6943 Antrim Ave., Burnaby, BC V5J 4M5; 604-433-7710; www .vcn.bc.ca/cccts.

ELDERHOSTEL BICYCLE TOURS

Elderhostel's famous educational travel programs include both domestic and foreign bicycle tours among its many offerings. These vary by the season and the year and are all listed in the organization's frequent and voluminous catalogs. Recent tours in the U.S. have included six-day inn-to-inn pedals along the Erie Canal in New York State, the northwest corner of Arizona, and the rolling hills of Texas. Lectures and sight-seeing are included.

Bike tours in foreign lands are scheduled weekly from April through September in Bermuda, Denmark, England, Italy, Germany, Austria, France, and the Netherlands. Led by a guide and riding as a group, you cover 25 to 35 miles a day and learn about the culture and history from local educators and other specialists. Three-speed bikes are provided, as are breakfast and dinner and accommodations in small hotels. The support van that travels with the group to carry the luggage and repair equipment will carry you as well if you decide that you can't possibly make it up another hill.

For information: Elderhostel, 11 Avenue de Lafayette, Boston, MA 02111; 877-426-8056 or 617-426-7788; www.elderhostel.org.

INTERNATIONAL BICYCLE TOURS

The Fifty Plus Tour run by IBT is planned for people over 50 who are not into pedaling up mountains but love to cycle. The trip goes to Holland in May and takes you on a leisurely trip along bicycle paths and quiet country roads on flat terrain through farmland and quaint villages. You'll cover only about 30 miles a day, so there is plenty of time for sightseeing, snacking, shopping, and relaxing. You lodge in small hotels and dine on local specialties.

Although this is the only tour designated specifically for over-50s, many older bikers are found on IBT's other bike tours to Holland, Denmark, England, Ireland, Italy, France, Bermuda, Austria, Cape Cod, Charleston, the Chesapeake and Ohio Canal, Nantucket, and Florida.

For information: International Bicycle Tours, PO Box 754, Essex, CT 06426; 860-767-7005; www.gorp.com/intlbike.

SIERRA CLUB OUTINGS

A few of the inexpensive bike tours led by volunteers for the Sierra Club target over-50 bikers. These include an inn-to-inn tour in the Berkshires that takes you to Tanglewood Music Center among other places, and a couple of camping trips, one that explores famous Civil War sites in Virginia

and another the forests and rocky shores of Acadia National Park in Maine. All include most meals and a sag wagon.
For information: Sierra Club Outings Dept., 85 Second St., San Francisco, CA 94105; 415-977-5522; www.sierraclub .org.

VBT BICYCLING VACATIONS

This venerable bike company has recently been acquired by Grand Circle Travel—a specialist in cultural, educational, and adventure vacations around the world for adventurers over the age of 50—and plans to tailor some of VBT's trips for this fast-growing age group. Although challenging routes will remain for those who want them, many of the itineraries in the U.S. and overseas will be less demanding and their schedules more relaxed. As a start, VBT's biking vacations currently include a number of trips eminently suitable for older bikers who seek adventure without all that much physical stress. One is the Salzburg Sojourn, which takes participants on flat bicycle paths and easy descents in the Austrian Alps. Another option is a tour of County Galway and the Connemara Coast in Ireland, visiting small villages, castles and pubs, lush forests, islands, and rocky ocean shores.
For information: VBT, PO Box 711, Bristol, VT 05443; 800-245-3868 or 802-453-4811; www.vbt.com.

WANDERING WHEELS

A program with a Christian perspective and "a strong biblical orientation," Wandering Wheels operates long-distance bike tours for all ages in the U.S. and abroad, including a six-week, 2,600-mile Breakaway Coast-to-Coast every spring that's geared specifically for people who are "middle age or older." So are the one-week fall specials that take you to a different locale every year.

For information: Wandering Wheels, PO Box 207, Upland, IN 46989; 765-998-7490; www.wanderwheels.com.

WOMANTOURS

Bicycle trips for women are the specialty of this group which schedules at least three trips a year exclusively for women over the age of 50. These trips are selected for their moderate terrain and for mileage that's suitable for both beginning cyclists and more experienced riders. Each a week long, the 50-plus trips this year take you to the Teton Mountains, the Canadian Rockies from Banff to Jasper, or the Vermont Champlain Valley. A van goes along with every group to carry the luggage and repair equipment and give weary riders a lift. Also for women over 50 is a much more ambitious 83-day, 4,250-mile trip across the entire country, from Yorktown, Virginia, to Florence, Oregon. Mileage averages 50 to 70 miles a day, mostly on fairly flat terrain, with one rest day per week. For this trip, you'd better be in shape.

For information: WomanTours, PO Box 68, Coleman Falls, VA 24536; 800-247-1444 or 804-384-7328; www.info @womantours.com.

TENNIS, ANYONE?

An estimated three million of the nation's tennis players are over 50, with the number increasing every year as more of us decide to forego rocking chairs for a few fast sets on the courts. You need only a court, a racquet, a can of balls, and an opponent to play tennis, but, if you'd like to be competitive or sociable, you may want to get into some senior tournaments.

UNITED STATES TENNIS ASSOCIATION

The USTA offers a wide variety of tournaments for players over the advanced age of 35, at both local and national levels. To participate, you must be a member ($25 per year). When you join, you will become a member of a regional section, receive periodic schedules of USTA-sponsored tournaments and events in your area for which you can sign up, get a discount on tennis books and publications, and receive a monthly magazine and a free subscription to *Tennis* magazine.

In the schedule of tournaments, you'll find competitions listed for specific five-year age groups: for men from 35 to 90-plus and for women from 35 to 80-plus. There are also self-rated tournaments that match you up with people of all ages who play at your level. If you feel you're good enough to compete, send for an application and sign up. There is usually a modest fee.

For information: USTA, 70 W. Red Oak Ln., White Plains, NY 10604; 914-696-7000; www.usta.com.

USA LEAGUE TENNIS, SENIOR DIVISION

If you want to compete with other 50-plus tennis players in local, area, and sectional competitions on four different surfaces, culminating in a national championship, join the Senior Division of the USA League Tennis program. Your level of play will be rated in a specific skill category ranging from beginner to advanced, and you'll compete only with people on your own ability level. Sign up in your community or write to the USTA for details.

For information: USTA, 70 W. Red Oak Ln., White Plains, NY 10604; 914-696-7000; www.usta.com.

VAN DER MEER TENNIS UNIVERSITY

Van der Meer Tennis University offers five-day Seniors Clinics from September to May every year at its Van der Meer Shipyard Tennis Resort on Hilton Head Island. Specifically for 50-plus players, beginning or experienced, the clinics provide more than 16 hours of instruction, including video analysis, tactics and strategies for singles and doubles, match play drills, plus round robins, social activities, and free court time. The goal is to improve your strokes and game strategy so you'll get more enjoyment out of your game. Discounted accommodations are available for participants.

For information: Van der Meer Tennis University, PO Box 5902, Hilton Head Island, SC 29938; 800-845-6138 or 843-785-8388; www.vandermeertennis.com.

WALKING TOURS

There are so many walking/hiking trips designed for or eminently suited to mature travelers that we can't list them all here. The following, however, specialize in travel on foot for older participants. Get yourself in shape for the hikes by walking 10 miles or more every week for at least a month.

APPALACHIAN MOUNTAIN CLUB

Every year this famous hiking club, the oldest conservation and recreation organization in the U.S., schedules a few inexpensive two- to five-day treks especially for people over the age of 50. You'll hike two to eight miles a day at an easy pace in these lush mountains and valleys and sleep in a comfortable lodge at night, with plenty of time to savor the scenery and glimpse the wildlife. Routes vary from year to year and sometimes include trips for women only. Check out the 50+ Silver Sneakers Walking or Hiking/Biking Weekends in New Hampshire every year and the spring hiking in the White Mountains.

For information: Appalachian Mountain Club, 5 Joy St., Boston, MA 02108; 800-411-5776 or 617-523-0636; www .outdoors.org.

COMPASS HOLIDAYS

This company specializes in walking and cycling tours through "the heart of the English countryside," the area roughly encompassing the Cotswolds, Bath, Oxford, Cirencester, Tetbury, Stratford, and the Thames Valley. Compass Holidays offers short holidays with or without the presence of a guide. You'll walk through quiet villages, bustling towns, and pastoral countrysides for three to eight days, covering only a few or many miles, stopping each evening at a small family hotel for local food and a comfortable night's sleep. If you are over the age of 50 and sign up for a minimum of a two-night break, you'll get a 10 percent discount if you mention this book.

For information: Compass Holidays, 48 Shurdington Rd.,

Cheltenham, Gloucestershire GL53 OJE, UK; www.compass
-holidays.com; E-mail: info@compass-holidays.com.

COUNTRY INNS ALONG THE TRAIL

If you choose this company to take you walking, you have
your choice of many destinations both in the U.S. and
abroad, especially for adventurers over 50. Groups are small,
with a maximum of 12 guests. The terrain is gentle and the
mileage is within reason—most days you'll walk five to nine
miles. Accommodations in small country inns or beds-and-
breakfasts, most meals, and admissions to historic sites are
included.

Current trips include a hike along the Pembrokeshire
coast of Wales with a bird-watching trip to Skomer Island,
or a walk along the coast of Maine or in the White Mountains of Vermont. There's a walking tour of Cornwall in
England including coastline and moors, castles and cottages.
And take another hiking trip in the Cotswolds and Dorset
through Shakespeare and Hardy country.
For information: Country Inns Along the Trail, RR#3, Box
3115, Brandon, VT 05733; 802-247-3300; www.inntoinn
.com.

ELDERHOSTEL WALKING
& HIKING PROGRAMS

Elderhostel's special international programs include two-
or three-week walking and hiking tours for which participants must be regular walkers or hikers in good health.
Accompanied by guides, lecturers, and local specialists, the
walkers, carrying small day packs, cover 4 to 12 miles a day,

rain or shine. You'll stay and dine mostly in small hotels, while lunch is taken en route. Some of the current destinations are Bermuda, Australia, Austria, Italy, Greece, Norway, South Africa, Wales, England, and Switzerland. Trekking trips are also on Elderhostel's menu, taking you up to eight miles a day on footpaths in Nepal or Argentina. For these you must be in even better physical shape and accustomed to vigorous exercise.

For information: Elderhostel, 11 Avenue de Lafayette, Boston, MA 02111; 877-426-8056 or 617-426-7788; www.elderhostel.org.

ELDERTREKS

On these trekking trips in exotic lands, most of them in the Far East, you will hike overland on foot and, in many cases, sleep on an air mattress in a tribal village house or a tent. The trips are rated for difficulty so you may choose one that matches your abilities. For more, see Chapter 9.

For information: ElderTreks, 597 Markham St., Toronto, ON M6G 2L7; 800-741-7956 or 416-588-5000; www.elder treks.com.

50+ MOUNTAIN TOURS

Fully catered and guided camping and hiking tours of the Canadian Rocky Mountains for adventurers over 50 are the specialty of this Canadian company. Starting and ending in Calgary, the 10-day tours are scheduled in the summer months and take groups of no more than 10 participants accompanied by two staff members to campsites in Kananaskis and Lake Louise, where they settle down in large stand-up tents furnished with comfortable cots. Meals, served up by the cook, are eaten in a dining tent. Each day, there's a choice of graded hikes, from easy strolls to strenuous all-day hikes deep into the mountains.

For information: 50+ Mountain Tours, Ltd., PO Box 1709, Cochrane, AB T4C 1B6; 888-932-8333 or 403-931-2208.

INTERHOSTEL

If you love to amble along taking a good look at the world, sign on for one of Interhostel's educational walking tours for people over 50. Foreign itineraries currently include vacations around Galway and Killarney in Ireland, Stirling and Edinburgh in Scotland, the Dordogne Valley in France, and Tuscany in Italy. Itineraries in the U.S. include California, Colorado, Alaska, and more. Traveling from place to place by van, you explore on foot and cover perhaps three to five miles a day on gentle terrain that includes some hills and lodging in small hotels or student residences. See Chapter 12 for more about Interhostel's programs.

For information: Interhostel, 6 Garrison Ave., Durham, NH 03824; 800-733-9753 or 603-862-1147; www.learn.unh .edu/interhostel.

NIFTY OVER FIFTY TOURS

From Pacific Pathways, these wildlife, horticultural, and botanical tours specifically for energetic people over 50 take small groups—or just two of you—to less-traveled scenic and perhaps remote areas of New Zealand or Australia. You'll observe the bird life, view the animals, study the plants, learn about local culture and customs, meet the people through farmstays, home visits, shared meals, private garden tours, birding trips, and hikes in a variety of forest, alpine, bush, and coastal locations.

For information: Nifty Over Fifty Tours, Pacific Pathways, 1919 Chula Vista Dr., Belmont, CA 94002; 650-595-2090; www.pacificpathways.com.

OVERSEAS ADVENTURE TRAVEL

OAT, which runs soft adventure trips all over the globe, has introduced European walking tours designed for the active mature traveler. Everything's included, even airfare, on these leisurely 12- to 14-day guided strolls through Tuscany, the Cotswolds, Ireland, Provence, Scotland, Switzerland, or other wonderful places. Rated from easy to challenging, the walks cover three or four miles a day and never exceed seven. Included are extras such as cooking classes, market excursions, painting classes, wine-tasting sessions, and meals in the homes of local residents. See Chapter 4 for more about OAT.

For information: Overseas Adventure Travel, 625 Mt. Auburn St., Cambridge, MA 02138; 800-873-5628 or 617-876-0533; www.oattravel.com.

RIVER ODYSSEYS WEST

If you love wilderness rivers but aren't into whitewater rafting (see Chapter 9), consider ROW's raft-supported walking tours along trails that follow the course of the Middle Fork of the Salmon River in Idaho or the Snake River in Hells Canyon on the Oregon border. Carrying only a day pack and led by a guide, you hike six or eight miles a day with plenty of time to smell the flowers and spot the wildlife. A cargo raft carries all the camping gear and your luggage as well as the food and other supplies, and a smaller support raft floats along at the group's pace to act as a sag wagon for tired walkers. When you arrive at camp each afternoon, the staff has already set up the roomy tents and the kitchen and has started cooking dinner, giving you time to relax, fish, or explore.

For information: River Odysseys West, PO Box 579-UD, Coeur d'Alene, ID 83816; 800-451-6034 or 208-765-0841; www.rowinc.com.

SILVER SNEAKER EXCURSIONS

Silver Sneaker walking tours, many of them exclusively for people over 50, are guided by a couple of experienced Appalachian Mountain Club leaders. In the U.S., their trips vary from weekends to 18-day adventures, including hikes from inn to inn in Vermont as well as walks on Rhode Island's beaches, in Sedona and the Grand Canyon in Arizona, on the coast of Maine, and around the famous resort city of Newport, Rhode Island. Abroad, they offer hiking trips in Wales or England's Cornwall as well as the Copper Canyon in Mexico, Bolivia and Peru, Ecuador and the Galapagos Islands, and Costa Rica.

See Chapter 14 for this company's ski adventures.

For information: Silver Sneaker Excursions, 100 Worsley Ave., N. Kingstown, RI 02852; 401-295-0367.

WALK YOUR WAY

Walk Your Way Into the Heart of England tours always include a few trips per year just for older walkers. These are 12-day tours off the beaten path in quaint and picturesque places on the Isle of Wight, the Lake District, the Dales of Yorkshire, or the Cotswolds. Some walks are circular, beginning and ending in the same village, averaging five miles a day. Others are linear, covering 8 to 10 miles a day. The group is never larger than 10, lodging is in family guest houses or bed-and-breakfasts, and evening meals are eaten in a local pub.

For information: Walk Your Way, PO Box 231, Red Feather Lakes, CO 80545; 970-881-2709.

WALKING THE WORLD

Anyone over 50 who loves adventure and is in good physical shape is invited to participate in Walking the World's explorations. These are 8- to 19-day backcountry treks, covering 6 to 10 miles a day, that focus on natural and cultural history. On some trips, you'll camp out and, carrying only a day pack, hike to each new destination. On others, you will lodge in small country inns, hotels, or bed-and-breakfasts, setting forth on daily walks into the countryside. Groups are small, from 12 to 18 participants plus two local guides, and there's no upper age limit. No previous hiking experience is necessary.

Destinations include Arches and Canyonlands National Parks in Utah; Banff and Jasper National Parks in the Canadian Rockies; plus trips in Maine, Arizona, Scotland, England, Norway, Wales, Switzerland, Ireland, Portugal, New Zealand, Hawaii, Tahiti, Peru, Ecuador, Costa Rica, and Italy.

For information: Walking the World, PO Box 1186, Fort Collins, CO 80522; 800-340-9255 or 498-225-0500; www.walkingtheworld.com.

NATURAL HISTORY TOURS
ELDERHOSTEL BIRDING PROGRAMS
Among Elderhostel's many outdoor programs are trips specifically designed for bird-watching in the field in Australia, Costa Rica, Ecuador, and Norway. Here in the U.S. there are many Elderhostel programs that include this popular activity among their courses.

For information: Elderhostel, 11 Avenue de Lafayette, Boston, MA 02111; 877-426-8056 or 617-426-7788; www.elderhostel.org.

NATURE VENTURE TOURS
On these trips, all exclusively for energetic people over the age of 55, the emphasis is on plants, animals, birds, geology, ecology, and archaeology as you explore fascinating areas. Among current tours is a hiking trip that takes you to several national parks in Utah, such as Canyonlands and Arches, Bryce, Zion, and Capital Reef. Another adventure is an archaeological tour by bus out of Phoenix to Sedona, the Grand Canyon, Monument Valley, Mesa Verde, Chaco Canyon, Canyon de Chelly, and the Petrified Forest.

For information: Nature Venture Tours, 2241 Park Crescent, Coquitlam, BC, V3J 6T1; 888-817-8417 or 604-461-7770.

SNOWMOBILE TOURS
SENIOR WORLD TOURS
Explore the winter wonders of the Tetons and Yellowstone National Park aboard your own snowmobile on a seniors-only six- or seven-day adventure trip planned by Senior

World Tours. All tours travel on roadways already groomed for the use of park personnel—and never off-road, where snowmobiles can damage the environment. Included in the package are driving lessons, snowmobiles, fuel, boots, gloves, helmets, cross-country skis, meals, and trusty guides. No experience is necessary, but don't even think of going unless you enjoy the snow and are in good physical condition.

On the Yellowstone trip, you start at Togwatee, 50 miles out of Jackson, Wyoming, then ride through Yellowstone and Gros Ventre River Valley to view the wildlife, geysers, hot springs, and splendid scenery. Every year, by the way, there are a couple of seven-day tours for "ladies only," a seven-day Alumni Special Tour for experienced snowmobilers, and a 10-day seniors-only tour to Alaska.

For information: Senior World Tours, 2205 N. River Rd., Fremont, OH 43420; 888-355-1686; www.seniorworld tours.com.

SNOWSHOEING/CROSS-COUNTRY SKIING

APPALACHIAN MOUNTAIN CLUB

Famous for its hiking programs in New England (see Chapter 13), AMC also schedules several affordable cross-country skiing and snowshoeing courses for grownups every winter. The 50+ Cross Country Skiing for Beginners gives you a chance to join a small group of peers for two nights at an inn in the Berkshires or an AMC lodge in the White Mountains where you'll get accommodations, meals, and lessons on groomed trails. The 50+ Snowshoe Adventure is a similar program for beginners who want to learn the basics about navigating on top of the snow. To participate, you need to be in good shape and be able to carry a full day pack. Members of the club are entitled to a 10 percent discount on the cost of these adventures.

For information: Appalachian Mountain Club, 5 Joy St., Boston, MA 02108; 800-411-5776 or 617-523-0636; www .outdoors.org.

MOTORCYCLE HEAVEN
BEACH'S MOTORCYCLE ADVENTURES

If motorcycling is your passion and adventure is in your blood, look into the motorcycle tours offered by the Beach family who have been conducting cycling tours since 1972. All ages, including yours, may choose trips in "the world's best motorcycling areas" in the Alps, Norway, and New Zealand. You must, of course, have a valid motorcycle license. Motorcycles are provided in your choice of available models and there is no mileage charge. A guide goes along with you, and your luggage is carried by a van. By the way, both bikes and automobiles are welcome on these tours, so if friends or family want to join you they may go along in a car.

You're on your own during the day, following a tour book that gives daily itineraries, road maps, distances, estimated en route times, business hours, sight-seeing ideas, good (and bad) roads, suggestions for activities, driving tips, and directions to the hotel of the night. The daily routing, pace, and stops are up to you. There are several riding options for each day, so you may decide to cruise along or ride long and hard. Every evening, you'll meet the group and your guide at a hotel or family farm where you'll eat dinner that night and have breakfast the next morning.

For information: Beach's Motorcycle Adventures, 2763 W. River Pkwy., Grand Island, NY 14072; 716-773-4960; www .beachs-mca.com.

RETREADS MOTORCYCLE CLUB

Retreads, an association of motorcycle enthusiasts with an average age of 60 and a few members in their 80s, get together for state, regional, and international rallies to talk cycling and ride together. Each state association and local chapter (there are more than 40 in Florida) also has regular get-togethers for short jaunts and socializing. Started as a correspondence club in 1969, Retreads has grown to over 15,000 members—men and women—in the U.S., Canada, and several other countries including Japan, England, New Zealand, and Australia. Annual contribution is $15 a year per person or $20 per couple. A club newsletter keeps members informed of the activities.

For information: Retreads Motorcycle Club International, 528 North Main St., Albany, IN 47320; 765-789-4070. From November 1 to May 31: 4504 Pittenger Dr., Sarasota, FL 34234; 941-351-7199.

KAYAKING TOURS
NEW ZEALAND ADVENTURES

Here's your chance to take a five-day sea kayak tour among the six main islands in the Bay of Islands in New Zealand. This is a relaxed tour specifically for 50-plus adventurers who are looking for an active vacation. You'll stay in tents at campsites, eat home-cooked meals, and travel with a knowledgeable local kayak guide your own age. You'll paddle two to four miles a day by kayak exploring the volcanic rock formations and sea caves, take day hikes on island trails, swim, snorkel, sail, and become acquainted with the Maori culture. Trips are scheduled year-round. For more vigorous tent camping adventures, join a tour "for all ages."

For information: New Zealand Adventures, HCR 56, Box 575, John Day, OR 97845; 541-932-4925; www.teraki.co.nz/seakayak.

GOLFING VACATIONS

GREENS FEES

Most municipal and many private golf courses offer senior golfers (usually those over 65) a discount off the regular greens fees, at least on certain days of the week. Take along identification and always make inquiries before you play.

GOLF ACADEMY OF HILTON HEAD ISLAND

Golfers over 50 will get a 15 percent discount on the three-day golf schools at the Golf Academy of Hilton Island at Sea Pines if they mention this book when they make their reservations. The school includes five hours of daily instruction from Class A PGA professionals each morning, followed by 18 holes of golf in the afternoon. Also included are on-course instruction, video analysis with a take-home tape, a personalized improvement manual, plus breakfast and lunch all three days.

For information: Golf Academy of Hilton Head Island, PO Box 5580, Hilton Head Island, SC 29938; 800-925-0467 or 803-785-4540; www.golfacademy.net.

THE GOLF CARD

Designed especially for senior golfers, the Golf Card entitles members to two complimentary rounds of golf per year per course at over 1,600 courses in the country, up to half off the player's fees at 1,800 additional courses, and savings at 300 stay-and-play golf resorts in the U.S., Canada, the Bahamas, Jamaica, and the Dominican Republic. Current membership fees are $75 the first year for a single or $120 for a couple, thereafter $70 a year for a single and $110 for a couple. A subscription to *Golf Traveler*, a magazine that serves as a guide to the participating courses and resorts, is part of the package.

For information: The Golf Card, PO Box 7020, Englewood, CO 80155; 800-321-8269 or 303-790-2267; www.golfcard .com.

NATIONAL SENIOR GOLF ASSOCIATION (NSGA)

More than 1,500 golfers over 50—average age 63—belong to NSGA, which sponsors recreational and competitive four-day midweek golf holidays once or twice a month at highly rated courses all over the country. The holidays include accommodations, golf (including a 54-hole medal-play tournament), breakfasts, at least two dinners, and -activities for nonplaying companions. Recent locations have included Pebble Beach Resorts in California; Kiawah Island, South Carolina; Banff Springs in Canada; and The

Equinox in Vermont. Longer golf holidays are scheduled once a year to more far-flung locations such as Scotland and Portugal.

Membership in NSGA costs $35 a year or $75 for three years, includes your spouse, entitles you to participate in the trips, and gets you a voluminous monthly newsletter. The three-year membership includes discounts at selected golf courses around the country.

For information: NSGA, 10 Manners Rd., Ringoes, NJ 08551; 800-282-6772 or 609-466-0022; www.amgolftour .com.

JOHN JACOBS GOLF SCHOOLS

Golfers over the age of 62 get a discount of 10 percent on the cost of golf vacations offered July through December at any John Jacobs Golf School. You'll learn how to improve your game while you play at some of the finest courses in the country. Most packages include lodging, breakfast and dinner, instruction, course time, greens fees, and cart. Commuter packages are available, too, at all 45 schools.

For information: John Jacobs Golf Schools, 800-472-5007; www.jacobsgolf.com.

SENIORS GOLF TOURNAMENT

Golfers over the age of 50 with a maximum handicap of 24 for men and 36 for women can sign up for the Annual Seniors Golf Tournament held every winter at the Port Royal Golf Course on Bermuda's southwest coast. A special package includes six nights at the Pompano Beach Club, breakfasts and dinners, four rounds of golf, parties, and more.

For information: Pompano Beach Club, 800-343-4155.

EVENTS FOR RAPID RUNNERS
FIFTY-PLUS FITNESS ASSOCIATION

This is not a club, although it occasionally sponsors athletic events for its over-50 members. It is an organization formed by eminent exercise researchers at Stanford University for the exchange of information about physical exercise and its known benefits (and hazards) among the older population. Its members, from almost every state and several foreign countries, also serve as volunteers for ongoing studies of such activities as running, swimming, biking, and racewalking. Each is asked to contribute $35 a year, tax-deductible, to defray costs. The association sponsors many events throughout the U.S. but mostly in northern California. These include walks, runs, swims, bike rides, and seminars and conferences on aging.

For information: Fifty-Plus Fitness Association, PO Box D, Stanford, CA 94309; 650-323-6160; www.50plus.org.

OVER-50 SOFTBALL
INTERNATIONAL SENIOR SOFTBALL ASSOCIATION

ISSA, an association that was founded to promote softball for men and women over the age of 50, conducts the World Championship Tournaments for over 300 senior teams every year in northern Virginia. Players who are members of senior leagues and local softball associations all over the U.S. may join, and so may individuals without affiliation. Members receive a master nationwide tournament schedule, the results of all national tournaments, and the rankings of all senior softball teams.

For information: ISSA, 9401 East St., Manassas, VA 20110; 703-368-1188; www.seniorsoftball.org.

NATIONAL ASSOCIATION OF SENIOR CITIZEN SOFTBALL

The NASCS is an association of several thousand softball players and hundreds of teams in the U.S. and Canada, with a goal of promoting a worldwide interest in senior softball. To play ball on one of its teams, you must be at least 50 years old. There's no upper age limit, and both men and women are welcomed. NASCS runs 16 qualifying tournaments for the annual Senior Softball World Series, when more than 125 teams from the U.S. and Canada compete in a major ballpark. A quarterly magazine keeps members up to date on happenings here and abroad.

For information: NASCS, PO Box 1085, Mt. Clemens, MI 48046; 810-792-2110.

SENIOR SOFTBALL-USA

This organization, the largest senior softball group in the world, conducts softball tournaments all over the country and organizes international tournaments as well, including the Senior Softball World Championship Games held in September. Anyone over 50, man or woman, in the U.S. and Canada may join for a $15 registration fee, and many thousands have. Members get assistance finding teams in their areas and may subscribe to the *Senior Softball-USA News*, which keeps them up to date on tournaments and other news. They are eligible to take part in an annual international tour that takes teams to play ball in foreign lands.

For information: Senior Softball-USA, 7052 Riverside Blvd., Sacramento, CA 95831; 916-393-8566; www.seniorsoftball .com.

SOFTBALL WINTER CAMP

Softball Winter Camp is an annual event held every winter in Altamonte Springs, Florida (10 miles from Orlando). Older amateur players gather for five days to train, get batting and fielding practice, play eight umpired games, compete in a mini-tournament, join an exercise program, and socialize. Men of all ages and abilities participate, with wives invited to come along to enjoy the fun. Lunch every day, a couple of breakfasts, an awards banquet, an equipment bag, a team shirt, and a cap are included in the fee as are special hotel rates and a Superbowl Party.

For information: Softball Winter Camp, Active Life Styles, 11465 Kanapali Lane, Boynton Beach, FL 33437; 888-335- 3828; www.softballcamp.com.

SENIOR GAMES

NATIONAL SENIOR GAMES ASSOCIATION

The NSGA sponsors the Summer National Senior Games/ The Senior Olympics every two years, attracting about 12,000 athletes over the age of 50 who compete in 18 sports. The Winter National Senior Games/The Senior Olympics, also held every other year, features competitions in alpine skiing, cross-country, curling, figure skating, ice hockey, and snowshoeing.

To compete in the national games, you must first qualify in authorized state competitions, which means you must be a medal winner in your age group or meet minimum performance standards in time and distance events.

For a free Qualifying State Games Directory, write to NSGA at the address below or download it from its website. You'll find a representative sample of the games in the following pages.

For information: National Senior Games Association, 3032 Old Forge Dr., Baton Rouge, LA 70808; 225-925-5678; www.nsga.com.

HUNTSMAN WORLD SENIOR GAMES

Every October, about 6,000 athletes—men and women, 50 and over, from the U.S. and many other countries—gather in St. George, Utah, for two weeks of competition in up to 32 events from basketball, mountain biking, golf, swimming, and tennis to track and field and triathlon. The registration fee (currently $69) includes participation in any of the athletic events and additional perks such as free health screenings, seminars on healthy living, and receptions, band concerts, and ceremonial dinners.

For information: Huntsman World Senior Games, 82 W. 700 South, St. George, UT 84770; 800-562-1268 or 435-674-0550; www.seniorgames.net.

STATE AND LOCAL SENIOR GAMES

Most states hold their own senior games once or twice a year and send their best competitors to national events. If you don't find your state among those listed here, that doesn't mean there's no program in your area—many are sponsored by counties, cities, even local agencies and colleges. Check with your local city, county, or state recreation departments to see what's going on near you or contact the NSGA for a free list. You don't have to be a serious competitor to enter these games but merely prepared to enjoy yourself. So what if you don't go home with a medal? At the very least, you'll meet other energetic people and have a lot of laughs.

ARIZONA

If you are over 50, male or female, you are eligible to participate in the Flagstaff Senior Olympics held over four days every year in September. You may compete in events that include bowling, cycling, golf, handball, racewalking, swimming, tennis, track and field, powerlifting, and more. Sign up for the festivities, which include an evening social and tickets to a Northern Arizona University football game. Medals are awarded for each event.

For information: Flagstaff Senior Olympics, PO Box 5063, Flagstaff, AZ 86011; 520-523-3560.

CALIFORNIA

On the last weekend in February each year, the Running Springs Senior Winter Games are held at a resort in the San Bernardino National Forest. Open to anyone over the age of 50, the competitions include skiing, ice skating, ice fishing, snowball throwing, snowshoe racing, and a few indoor games such as billiards, bridge, and table tennis. Social events are included. There is a modest registration fee plus a small additional fee for each event entered.

For information: Running Springs Senior Winter Games, PO Box 3333, Running Springs, CA 92382; 909-867-3176.

COLORADO

The Senior Winter Games at the Summit take place each year during three days in the second week of February in the quaint Victorian village of Breckenridge. Anyone from anywhere who's over 55 and wants to compete against peers is welcome. Events include cross-country skiing, downhill slalom, speed skating, snowshoe races, biathlon, figure skating, and more, plus social activities. Age categories for the competitions begin at 55 to 59 and increase in five-year increments to 90-plus. A registration fee that allows you to participate in as many events as you wish currently stands at $25.

The summer Rocky Mountain Senior Games are held in Greeley the first week in August and include over 20 competitions in sports ranging from basketball and racquetball to golf, softball, bowling, cycling, and tennis. A registration fee of $41 includes admission to eight different events, continental breakfast, and snacks. To participate, you must be at least 50 and you can compete no matter where you're from.

For information: Senior Winter Games at the Summit, PO Box 442, Breckenridge, CO 80424; 970-453-2461; or Rocky Mountain Senior Games, 1010 6th St., Greeley, CO 80631; 970-350-9433.

CONNECTICUT

The Connecticut Senior Summer Olympics include not only competitive sport events but also a mini–health fair and many physical fitness activities. Residents of Connecticut and neighboring states who are 50-plus converge on the town of Southington on the first weekend in June for three days of events such as the 5,000-meter run, the 100-yard dash, the mile run, the long jump, swimming, bocci, and tennis. These summer games require a small entrance fee.

The one-day Connecticut Senior Winter Olympics, held in February, are open to anyone from anywhere who's at least 50 and an amateur. The games feature downhill, giant slalom, cross-country, and snowshoe races, and take place at Ski Sundown.

For information: Connecticut Senior Olympics, 26 N. Main St., Southington, CT 06489; 860-621-4661; www.ctsenior games.org.

FLORIDA

The Golden Age Games in Sanford have taken place every November since 1974. Today they host over 1,500 athletes for a week of 40 different competitions, plus ceremonies, social events, and entertainment. If you are over 50, you are eligible to participate regardless of residency. In other words, you needn't be a Florida resident to compete for the gold, silver, and bronze medals in such sports as basketball, biking, bowling, canoeing, checkers, dance, swimming, tennis, triathlon, track and field, canasta, and croquet. There is an entry fee of $6 for the first event and $2 for each additional event.

For information: Golden Age Games, PO Box 1298, Sanford, FL 32772; 407-330-5697.

MISSOURI

The St. Louis Senior Olympics have become an institution in Missouri by now. A five-day event in May that is open to anyone who lives anywhere and is at least 50 years old, it costs a nominal amount and is action-oriented. No knitting contests here—only more than 70 energetic events such as bicycle races, 200-meter races, standing long jumps, golf, basketball, free throw, sprints, tennis singles and doubles, and swimming.

For information: St. Louis Senior Olympics, JCC, 2 Millstone Campus Dr., St. Louis, MO 63146; 314-432-5700, ext. 3188; stlouisseniorolympics.org.

MONTANA

Men and women over the age of 50, from Montana or otherwise, are invited to participate in the Montana Senior Olympics, held every year in June. Events range from archery, badminton, bowling, and basketball to swimming, tennis, softball, and track.

For information: Montana Senior Olympics, 465 Freedom Ave., Billings, MT 59105; 406-252-2795.

NEW HAMPSHIRE

For three days in August, you can compete with your peers in the Granite State Senior Summer Games in Manchester, where you can choose from 15 sports events ranging from swimming to tennis, track and field, shuffleboard, and table tennis. In alternate odd-number years, these are qualifying games for the National Senior Games. Sign up if you are a man or a woman who is at least 50 and in good operating condition. The cost is minimal.

The Granite State Senior Winter Games, held in Waterville Valley for three days in February, are open to men and women 50 and over who compete in groups of five-year increments. They get a chance to challenge their peers in dual slalom, giant slalom, and cross-country races. Other events include speed skating, snowball throw, hockey goal shoot, and snowshoe races. Costs for entry, lift tickets, fees, rentals, and social affairs are low.

For information: Granite State Senior Games, 610 Front St., Ste. B, Manchester, NH 03102; 603-622-9041.

NEW JERSEY

Held once a year, the New Jersey Senior Sports Classic games feature more than 1,000 seniors competing in 21 competitive sports such as archery, golf, tennis, and track and field.

For information: Senior Citizens Activities Network, Monmouth Mall, Eatontown, NJ 07724; 732-542-1326; www .scannj.com.

NEW YORK

The Empire State Senior Games, open to all New York residents who are 50 or over, are held in Syracuse over three days in June. Winners may qualify for the National Senior Olympics. For a small registration fee, amateur athletes may compete in many events—swimming, bridge, basketball, softball, croquet, track and field, tennis, racewalking, cycling, and more. There are additional fees for golf and bowling. Participants are invited to social events each of the three nights.

For information: Empire State Senior Games, NYS Parks, 6105 E. Seneca Turnpike, Jamesville, NY 13078; 315-492-9654; www.empirestategames.org.

NORTH CAROLINA

After local games are held statewide, the winners travel to Raleigh for the North Carolina Senior Games State Finals and, perhaps, on to the national games. Most sports are on the agenda, plus an arts competition that celebrates artists in heritage, literary, performing, and visual arts. The state also sponsors the SilverStriders, a walking club for those 50 or better that gives its members logbooks for tracking progress, gifts and awards, and an annual report of their accomplishments.

For information: North Carolina Senior Games, PO Box 33590, Raleigh, NC 27636; 919-851-5456; www.ncsenior games.org.

PENNSYLVANIA

The Keystone Senior Games "combine sports, recreation, and entertainment with fellowship." You can get some of each if you are a Pennsylvania resident who is 50 or older. The games are held over five days in July at a university campus where you can get lodging and three meals a day at low cost. If you prefer to stay in a motel, you'll get a senior discount.

For information: Keystone Senior Games, PO Box 3131, Wilkes Barre, PA 18773; 570-823-3164; www.keystone games.com.

UTAH

The Utah Winter Games, open to everyone whatever age, abilities, or home address, schedules over 100 free clinics and events all over the state from November to January in a variety of winter sports. It includes a free Senior Ski clinic at Brighton Ski Resort in late November, where skiers over 50 are invited for a day of instruction and fun.

The Utah Summer Games Foundation holds annual Olympic-style competitions every June in 41 events from archery to track and field, all of them open to amateur athletes of all ages and skill levels.

For information: Utah Winter Games, 801-975-4515; www.utahwintergames.org. Utah Summer Games, 351 W. Center St., Cedar City, UT 84720; 435-865-8421; www.utah summergames.org.

VERMONT

If you are over 50 years old and an amateur in your sport, you are invited to become a member of the Green Mountain Senior Games (GMSG) for $10 a year per person or $15 per couple. At the summer games held throughout the summer months at several locations and at the three-day games at Green Mountain College in Poultney every fall, you may compete in sports ranging from golf and tennis to swimming, darts, walking, running, bowling, softball, and more. The winter games are usually held in January at two sites— cross-country and snowshoeing events take place at Blueberry Hill, and the downhill skiing events are held at Stratton Mountain.

For Information: Green Mountain Senior Games, 89 Trombley Rd., Andover, VT 05143; 802-875-4508.

VIRGINIA

The Virginia Senior Games are an annual four-day event held each spring on a college campus, where older athletes compete to qualify for the U.S. National Senior Olympics— or just for the fun of it. It is a combination of social events and entertainment with sports competitions, open to Virginia residents over the age of 50. Spouses are invited to come along and enjoy the hospitality, which includes parties, dances, tours of local sites, and other festivities. The fees are low, lodging and meals are cheap, and the sporting events are many, ranging from rope jumping, miniature golf, and riflery to swimming, running, and tennis for age groups from 55 upwards.

For information: Virginia Senior Games, Virginia Recreation and Park Society, 6038 Cold Harbor Rd., Mechanicsville, VA 23111; 804-730-9447; www.vrps.com.

14

Adventures on Skis

VER THE TOP

Downhill skiing is one sport you'd think would appeal only to less mature, less wise, less breakable people. On the contrary, there is an astounding number of ardent over-50 skiers who would much rather glide down mountains than sit around waiting for springtime. In fact, many of us ski more than ever now that we're older because we can often go midweek when the crowds are thinner and we get impressive discounts on lift tickets, especially after the age of 65 or so. A lot of us, too, are taking up the sport for the first time. Ski schools all over the U.S. and Canada are reporting an increase of older students in beginner classes.

The truth is, you're never too old to learn how to ski or to improve your technique. Once you get the hang of it, you can ski at your own speed, choosing the terrain, the difficulty level, and the challenge. You can slide down cliffs through narrow icy passes or wend your way on gentle slopes in a more leisurely fashion, aided by the new improved skis and boots. You'll find clearly marked and carefully groomed trails and sophisticated lifts that take all the work out of getting up the mountain.

Besides, ski resorts are falling all over themselves catering to older skiers, offering discounts on lift tickets, cheaper season passes, and other engaging incentives. In fact, it is a rare ski area that does not give a substantial break to skiers over a certain age.

CLUBS FOR MATURE SKIERS
OVER THE HILL GANG

OTHG is a club for energetic men, women, singles, and couples over 50 (the average age of members is 63) that schedules a wide assortment of escorted ski trips every year in this country and abroad. Members—about 6,000 to date—are entitled to reduced rates for lift tickets, lessons, rentals, services, equipment, lodging, and transportation at many of the top ski areas.

The club's 12 regional "gangs," or chapters, in the U.S. run their own ski trips as well, and all members everywhere are invited to go along. At some ski areas, local and visiting members meet regularly to ski with their own guides. At Steamboat, for example, they gather four days a week during the season. At Vail, they ski together on Mondays; at Breckenridge on Tuesdays; at Winter Park on Wednesdays; and at Keystone on Thursday mornings. Out-of-town members and anyone else over 50 are invited to come along.

Members who reach their 70th birthday (and are willing to admit it) are part of the "Over 70 Gang," and members who have turned 80 are included in the "Over 80 Gang." They receive special shoulder patches and a discount on their next membership renewal or their next trip with the club.

When ski season ends, you may join OTHG for other activities including biking, rafting, hiking, and golfing (see Chapter 13).

Annual membership fee: $40 single, $65 per couple, plus chapter dues if you join a local gang.

For information: Over the Hill Gang International, 1820 W. Colorado Ave., Dept. G., Colorado Springs, CO 80904; 719-389-0022; www.overthehillgangintl.com.

70+ SKI CLUB

Once you hit 70, you're eligible to join the 70+ Ski Club for an annual fee of $10 ($15 for couples)—until you're 90, when you pay only a one-time $10 fee. Don't laugh. Among the approximately 16,000 registered members worldwide, 174 are over the age of 90 and almost 4,000 are between 80 and 90. Members get a selection of ski trips and special events every year at ski resorts in the Northeast and the West; at least one in Europe; and the others in New Zealand, Chile, or Argentina. Hunter Mountain in New York hosts the club's annual meeting each March. Here the 70+ Ski Races have become such a popular event that contestants are divided into three age groups: men 70 to 80, women 70 to 80, and anyone over 80. Awards are presented at a gala party at the lodge.

Founded in 1977, the club has always promoted the interests of senior skiers, especially those on limited incomes. Today, largely as a result of its efforts, most ski areas give seniors free or half-price lift tickets.

Proof of age is required with your application to join the club, and you may not apply earlier than two weeks before your 70th birthday. Members receive a patch, a membership card, a periodic newsletter, and a directory of areas around the country that offer discounts or free skiing.

For information: 70+ Ski Club, 1633 Albany St., Schenectady, NY 12304; 518-346-5505; e-mail: rtl70plus@aol.com.

SILVER SNEAKER EXCURSIONS

Anybody over 50 is invited to join Silver Sneaker Excursions for a weekend or longer of downhill skiing, cross-country, and/or snowshoeing in New Hampshire or Vermont. Featured are small groups, instruction if you need it, all kinds of terrain, sometimes skiing door-to-door from inn to inn. See Chapter 13 for information on this company's walking tours.

For information: Silver Sneaker Excursions, 100 Worsley Ave., N. Kingstown, RI 02852; 401-295-0367.

THE WILD OLD BUNCH

Skiers who frequent Alta in Utah are advised to search out members of the Wild Old Bunch, an informal group of long-time skiers who hang out together on the mountain and welcome anyone who wants to join them. There are no rules, no regulations, no meetings. The only requirement is that you must be over 55. The group grows haphazardly as members pick up stray mature skiers on the slopes. Lunch is usually on the deck of the mid-mountain Alpenglow Inn.

For information: Look for the Wild Old Bunch on the slopes.

GOOD DEALS EVERYWHERE FOR SKIERS

The older you are, the less it costs to ski. There's hardly a ski area in North America today that doesn't give mature skiers a break. Many cut the price of lift tickets in half for skiers at age 65, and most stop charging altogether at 70, although a couple—Alta in Utah and Mt. Tom in Massachusetts— make you wait until you're 80 to ski free. A few areas charge anybody over the age of 65 only $5 a day for lift tickets, and most make offers on season passes that are hard to refuse. Others plan special senior programs specifically for mature skiers.

To give you an idea of what's out there, here is a sampling of the special senior programs, workshops, and clubs in the states where skiing is big business. This list does not include all areas, of course, so be sure to check out others in locations that interest you. Remember to carry proof of age with you at all times. The ski areas change their programs every year, so while you can use the following information as a guide, you must do your own research, too.

CALIFORNIA

Ski in California and you'll get good deals on lift tickets and season passes almost everywhere. Plus, there are some special programs designed especially for mature skiers, such as the following.

Tahoe Donner Downhill Ski Area schedules ski clinics for skiers over the age of 50 every Tuesday morning. The inexpensive package for beginners and experienced skiers includes a lift ticket, continental breakfast, three hours of ski lessons, and a videotape review of your skiing technique.

At Northstar-at-Tahoe, the three-day Golden Stars Clinic has been tailored for skiers over 60 of intermediate or better ability who want to improve their skills on the slopes. Offered several times a winter, the clinic provides daily three-hour lessons and all-day lift tickets.

Adults, intermediate through expert, can take advantage of the Vertical Improvement Clinic, free with the purchase of a lift ticket morning and afternoon, any day you choose at Sierra-at-Tahoe. Although the clinic is not strictly for over-50 skiers, it attracts plenty of them.

At Heavenly Ski Resort, there are free four-hour workshops for skiers over 55. And Mammoth Mountain offers three-day senior ski clinics.

The senior program at Bear Valley, in the Sierra Nevada Mountains between Lake Tahoe and Yosemite, is even better. At 65, you may ski free any day, anytime. If you prefer a season pass, you can get one for just $10.

COLORADO

Every ski area in Colorado offers discounted lift tickets to seniors, some starting at 60, others at 65, and almost every ski area charges nothing at all to ski after 70. And there are many special programs, lessons, and clubs especially designed for mature skiers.

Aspen offers skiers over 70 a Silver Pass for $99. It allows unlimited skiing there and also at Snowmass, Ajax, Buttermilk, and Highlands.

At Breckenridge, two-day Silver Skiing Seminars for skiers over 50 of all abilities, taught by seniors, include lift tickets, lessons, video analysis, and a group dinner.

Breckenridge is the place where members of the local Over the Hill Gang, plus any other visitors 50 and over, get together on Tuesdays for a day on the slopes with their own guide. It also cohosts with Keystone the Senior Winter Games at the Summit for three days in February.

It's Thursday mornings at Keystone for Gang members and visitors to ski with volunteer guides.

At Vail, any skier over 50 is welcome to meet on Mondays and ski with OTHG members.

At Steamboat, led by local guides, they gang up on the slopes every day from Sunday through Thursday.

Silver Creek Resort offers Never-Ever 50+, a learn-to-ski program exclusively for mature people who have never been on skis before. Scheduled on Wednesday and Saturday mornings, it includes lesson, equipment, and lift ticket.

Sunlight Mountain Resort in Glenwood Springs has its 100 Club, open to couples whose combined ages total 100 years or more, and singles who are 50 or older. Club members, beginners to experts, meet here each Wednesday and sometimes at other areas on weekends during the season to ski in the morning and stay for lunch. They often plan trips to other area resorts as well and after the ski season get together for tennis, golf, hiking, and mountain biking. Cost for membership is currently $8 a year and includes a monthly newsletter.

Powderhorn's New Tricks for Old Dogs is a program that meets on four Thursdays a year during ski season to help older skiers improve their techniques and learn how to use the new-shaped skis. Included are a personal video analysis and a farewell party.

At Eldora, skiers and snowboarders 65 and older can participate in Senior Ski every Tuesday. Senior Days at Ski Cooper gives you a day lift ticket, free racing, and an après-ski party.

Every winter, Purgatory Resort in Durango schedules two one-week skiing and social events for skiers over 50. Called the Snowmasters Classic, each session, which currently costs $75, includes daily continental breakfast, two wine and cheese parties, and three half-day clinics. The clinics are chosen from the following subjects: shaped skis, powder skiing, racing, mogul skiing, and ski improvement. Participants get discounts on lift tickets, rentals, accommodations, food, and more.

The Ski Meisters, a group of 55-plus skiers based in Denver, ski together in small groups led by volunteer guides. They ski every Wednesday, Thursday, and Sunday from November to April. With 400 members and a waiting list, the club charges a one-time fee of $100, then $50 a year. Guests are permitted, but they may ski with the club only twice during the season. To keep themselves busy when ski season is over, members get together for biking, hiking, tennis, and golf.

The two Ski Forever Weeks held at Telluride each winter cater to mature skiers, intermediate to expert. The five-day sessions, which currently cost $575, include five hours a day of on-snow instruction, an alignment session, a welcome reception, professional speakers, video analysis, races, social gatherings, and a farewell party.

IDAHO

Sun Valley's Prime Time, a week reserved for older skiers, is scheduled twice each winter. It includes seven nights' lodging, five days of lift tickets or a Nordic trail package, discount coupons, races, parties, special events, and a Big Band Buffet Dinner Dance. Skiers over 60 pay less for the package than those under 60.

Schweitzer Mountain's Prime Timers Club for skiers 55 and over is an informal club whose members ski together almost every day and get together for social gatherings on Thursday afternoons. In addition, there's a bargain senior ski week in March, the Snowmaster's Classic, a week of workshops, clinics, social activities, and race training for older skiers who are seeking to improve their technical abilities.

MAINE

At Sunday River Ski Resort, those who purchase the Perfect Turn Gold Card or Platinum Card and are over 50 may become members of the Prime Time Club. Members ski together weekday mornings and, for a discounted fee, have the option of participating in twice-a-week 50-plus clinics.

At Sugarloaf/USA, a Perfect Turn Gold or Platinum Card is what you need to participate free in the Prime Time Club for skiers over 50. This card is good for group skiing and coaching once a week.

MASSACHUSETTS

Jiminy Peak in Hancock holds Senior Day every Thursday, when, if you already have a season pass or are over 70, the cost is only $20 for a lift ticket and a two-hour ski clinic. For others, the day costs twice as much.

At Catamount, members of the 70+ Club ski for $7 any time.

Butternut's season pass for skiers over 70 costs $99.

MICHIGAN

The Silver Streakers program at Crystal Mountain Resort, for skiers 55 or older, provides an inexpensive midweek package three times each winter. It includes lodging and lift tickets for two. Other privileges for mature skiers include half price on lift tickets, cross-country trail passes, rental equipment, and group lessons, except during the winter holidays.

At Caberfae Peaks Ski Resort in Cadillac, every Tuesday, Wednesday, and Thursday (except during the major holiday weeks) are Silver Streak Days, when anybody over the age of 50 may ski all day for $12. In addition to the lift ticket, you get free rental skis and, if you want one, a one-hour lesson.

NEW HAMPSHIRE

It's a rare ski area in this state that does not offer older skiers an impressive break on lift tickets at age 65 or older and a free pass at 70. Many also have special programs for senior skiers.

If you're 55 or older you can join the Silver Streaks at Waterville Valley, paying very little to ski the slopes with a guide four mornings a week. Cross-country skiers who join Silver Streaks may ski with a guide at the Nordic Center on Wednesdays.

At Attitash Bear Peak, TGIF (Thank Goodness I'm Fifty) is a midweek adult ski group that meets every nonholiday Thursday morning throughout the season for coffee and doughnuts plus two hours of skiing. Other perks include workshops and a party, all for only $5 a day and the cost of midweek lift tickets.

At Loon Mountain, Flying 50s Plus meets every Thursday and Friday morning except on holidays for two-hour group skiing with instruction. Members who pay $99 for the season also get discounts on lift tickets, lodging, and special activities.

At Cannon Mountain, the Cannon Cruisers, for skiers over 50, meet Monday mornings to ski for two hours with instructors at $10 per session or $79 for 10 sessions.

At Temple Mountain, the Morning Birds, a six-week program for seniors, runs Monday through Friday with lessons on skiing or snowboarding.

Ragged Mountain offers its Mountain Ramblers ski club for skiers over 50, who meet on Tuesday mornings for group lessons.

For skiers 55-plus, Wildcat offers Tuesday Aristocrat Day on nonholiday Tuesdays. It includes a lift ticket and lesson for $34.

And at Mount Sunapee, the Senior Cruisers program for skiers and boarders age 65 and over meets on nonholiday Wednesdays throughout the season for skiing and socializing.

NEW MEXICO

Sign up for a Masters Ski Week at Taos Ski Valley if you are 50-plus and you get six mornings of instruction, all-day lift tickets for the week, and après-ski seminars.

NEW YORK

Skiers over 50 are invited to join the Senior Skier Program at Ski Windham for eight weeks of Tuesdays in January and February. The purpose is to strengthen skiing skills, socialize, and meet new people. Join for all eight weeks or by the day, if you prefer. What you get is morning coffee, guest speakers, two-hour morning and afternoon on-snow lessons, and a midweek nonholiday season pass to Ski Windham. For information, call 518-734-5070.

UTAH

Virtually all of Utah's ski areas give senior skiers reduced rates on lift tickets at 60 or 65, with Sundance and Elk Meadows offering free rides to those over 65. Most others stop charging at 70—except Alta, where you must wait until you are 80!

At Snowbird, any skier who's 62 or more can ski for free with a group of peers for three hours on Tuesday mornings with well-known ski instructor Junior Bounous. For $20 plus the cost of a lift ticket, you can ski with him again in the afternoon for some instruction. Also at Snowbird: the Silverwings program for skiers over 50 that lets you ski all day on Wednesdays and Thursdays with a senior instructor. This one currently costs $72 plus a lift ticket.

The seniors program at Sundance sets aside four afternoon sessions a month for group skiing with a guide.

As for Brighton Ski Resort, the Senior Workshop, a three-day program for "seasoned" skiers over 50, includes lessons, a lift pass, breakfast, and a social hour.

VERMONT

Vermont's ski areas were the first to cater to older skiers. It is highly unlikely that there are any resorts there that don't give seniors a decent break on lift tickets and season passes. Along with special rates, several areas offer special senior programs as well. Here's a sample.

Stratton Mountain's Trailblazers Ski Club, open to skiers or snowboarders over 50 (and their partners), schedules activities for its 600 members almost every day of the week, starting with bridge or canasta on Mondays, snowshoe and cross-country activities on Wednesdays, recreational racing on Fridays, and après-ski parties whenever. Members may also participate in a special 50-plus ski clinic program that comes in two versions. The first, for full-time residents of the area, meets Monday, Wednesday, and Friday mornings (except on holidays) to ski in small groups with an instructor; the second is a weekend program that meets on Saturday mornings for 14 weeks. Basic membership fee is $25 a year per person, with an extra charge for participation in the ski clinics.

At Jay Peak any skier over the age of 55 is invited to join the Silver Peaks Club, a group that skis together every Tuesday. For a nominal fee, you are entitled to a day that includes your lift ticket, guide, coffee and doughnuts, and après-ski activities. If you're over 65, you may ski here any time for $10 a day.

The Prime Time Club at Sugarbush offers skiers age 50 years and up, levels five to eight, a chance to meet, ski, and learn with a group of their peers. The club meets Tuesday and Thursday mornings for skiing on a variety of terrains.

Mount Snow's Prime-Time Seniors program, also for skiers and snowboarders 50 and over, meets once a week in February and March and offers clinics and a specialized video as well as resort savings.

The Silver Griffins Senior Program at Bromley Mountain meets every nonholiday Monday and Tuesday for group skiing, fun races, picnics, and parties. Members of the group get preferred parking midweek and discounts on food, equipment, and lessons.

Okemo's Mountaineers Program for intermediate and advanced skiers over 65 runs for six consecutive Wednesdays. Members, who may purchase the program one session at a time or buy all six, meet in the morning for coffee and then ski with others of similar ability and pace with the guidance of one of the mountain's older teaching pros.

For a fee of $10 for the season, Smuggler's Notch offers its Smuggler's 55-Plus Club, which meets on Wednesdays for breakfast, morning skiing with a guide, and afternoon activities such as movies, demonstrations, and guest speakers. Members also get half off the cost of lift tickets, rentals, and group lessons.

WISCONSIN

Monday through Friday, anybody over 55 may purchase a lift ticket, day or night, for $10 at Cascade Mountain Ski Area in Portage.

15

Perks in Parks and Other Good News

Here and there throughout the U.S. and Canada, enterprising officials in states, provinces, and cities have initiated some enticing programs designed to capture the imagination of the mature population. Often they are expressing their appreciation of our many contributions to society and simply want to do something nice for us. And sometimes they are trying to attract us and our vacation dollars to their neighborhood, having discovered that we're always ready to enjoy ourselves and know a good deal when we see one.

But, first, keep in mind:

- Before you set off for a new place, write ahead for free maps, calendars of events, booklets describing sites and scenes of interest, accommodation guides, and perhaps even a list of special discounts or other good things that are available to you as a person over 50.

■ Many states offer passes for admission to their state parks and recreation facilities free or at reduced prices to people who are old enough to have learned how to treat those areas respectfully.

■ After the section on national parks, you'll find information about state park passes and special events in many states. There may be other good deals that have escaped our attention, but those in this chapter are probably the cream of the crop.

NATIONAL PARKS
GOLDEN AGE PASSPORT

Available for $10 to U.S. citizens or permanent residents who are at least 62, the Golden Age Passport is good for a lifetime and admits you free of charge to most national parks, forests, refuges, monuments, and recreation areas. Your family and friends, whatever their ages, also get free admission when you enter in a private car, so one pass is enough if you are a couple or a group traveling together. Turn up at the gate in a commercial vehicle such as a bus, and the passport admits you, your spouse, and your children without cost.

It also gives you a 50 percent discount on fees charged for facilities and services such as camping, swimming, boat launching, parking, and cave tours. It does not, however, cover or reduce special recreation permit fees charged by concessioners.

The passport is not available by mail but must be purchased in person at any federal area where entrance fees are charged or at regional offices of the National Park Service, the U.S. Forest Service, or the Fish and Wildlife Service. You must provide proof of age. Your driver's license will do just fine.

The free Golden Access Passport provides the same benefits for the disabled of any age.

If you are not yet 62, you can buy a National Parks Pass that costs $50 and is good for a year. When a per-vehicle fee is charged at a national park, the pass admits you and your

---

ESCAPEES CLUB

Escapees is a club dedicated to providing a support network for RVers, full-time or part-time, most of whom are on the far side of 50. It publishes a bimonthly magazine filled with useful information for travelers who carry their homes with them; organizes rallies in the U.S., Canada, and Mexico; and hosts five-day seminars on RV living. Its almost 50 regional chapters also coordinate rallies and host get-togethers, and its Birds of a Feather (BOF) groups connect members who have common interests. Benefits include discounted RV parks and campgrounds, emergency road service, mail service, calling card service, vehicle insurance, and voice message service. After a $10 enrollment fee, the annual membership fee is $50 a year per family.

The club has established its own CARE Center (Continuing Assistance for Retired Escapees), a separate RV campground where retired members can live independently in their own RVs while receiving medical and living assistance, housekeeping, and transportation services as needed.

For information: Escapees, Inc., 100 Rainbow Dr., Livingston, TX 77351; 888-757-2582 or 409-327-8873; www.escapees .com.

passengers in a private vehicle; when a per-person fee is charged, it admits you, your spouse, your children, and even your parents. It may be purchased on-line or by telephone. *For information:* National Park Service, Office of Public Inquiries, U.S. Dept. of Interior, 1849 C St. NW, Washington, DC 20013. For National Parks Pass only: 888-GO-PARKS; www.nationalparks.org.

CANADIAN NATIONAL PARKS

The national parks and national historic sites throughout Canada charge modest entry fees for adults and take about 20 percent off those for visitors over 65. The same is generally true for provincial parks.

OFFERINGS FROM THE STATES

Virtually every state has a special senior rate for hunting and fishing licenses for people over a certain age (usually 65). Some states require no license at all for seniors, while others give you a reduced fee (usually half). Most require that you are a resident of the state in order to get these privileges. Most states also offer state park discounts to seniors, usually only residents, reducing or eliminating entrance fees and marking down camping rates. To check out the regulations in your state or a state you are visiting, call the state or local parks department or the state tourism office.

For a free listing of all the state tourism offices and their toll-free numbers, send a self-addressed, stamped envelope to Discover America, Travel Industry Association of America, 1100 New York Ave. NW, Ste. 450, Washington, DC 20005.

CALIFORNIA

Anybody who's 62 or older gets $2 taken off admissions and overnight camping fees in all state parks. Just show your ID at the gate.

For information: California State Parks, 916-653-6995; www.calparks.ca.gov. For campsite reservations, call 800-444-7275.

COLORADO

The Aspen Leaf Pass entitles Colorado residents 62 and over to free entrance to state parks any day and camping Sundays through Thursdays. The pass costs $10 per year.

For information: Colorado Division of State Parks, 1313 Sherman St., Room 618, Denver CO 80203; 303-866-3437; www.colorado.parks.org.

CONNECTICUT

Residents of Connecticut who are over 65 get a free lifetime Charter Oak Pass that gets them into state parks and forests plus Gillette Castle, Dinosaur Park, and Quinebaug Valley Hatchery for free. To get your pass, write to the address below and send along a copy of your current Connecticut driver's license.

For information: DEP, Charter Oak Pass, State Parks Division, 79 Elm St., Hartford, CT 06106; 860-424-3200; www.dep.state.ct.us.

FLORIDA

Orlando, one of the most popular destinations in the U.S. today, is visited by over seven million mature travelers a year. To accommodate them, the city offers a free vacation planning kit that includes the *Mature Travelers Guide*. It lists senior savings, most of them valid for anyone over the age of 50 or 55, at many hotels, tourist attractions, water parks, dinner shows, museums, and more. The city also offers a free Orlando Magicard for all ages with even more discounts.

For information: Pick up the free packet at the Official Visitor Center, 8723 International Dr., Ste. 101, Orlando, FL 32821. To get it in advance, call 800-972-3308 or access the website at www.go2orlando.com.

Visit Marathon in the Florida Keys in the month of November and you will get special savings when some hotels, diving facilities, fishing charters, and restaurants offer seniors 15 to 50 percent off their rates. There are special events planned for you during the month as well. Send for the free Senior Discount Card and a brochure describing other offers and discounts in the Keys.

For information: Call 800-262-7284 or 305-743-5417; www.floridakeysmarathon.com.

The thick little booklet, *$500 Worth of the Palm Beaches*, is not exclusively for visitors over 50 but it is included here because it offers many ways to save money, such as discounts, two-for-one deals, and complimentary offers on shopping, dining, sporting activities; and attractions including restaurants, airboat tours, museums and galleries, bicycle shops, haircuts, boat rentals, and campgrounds. To order, call the toll-free number.

For information: Palm Beach County Convention and Visitors Bureau; 800-554-PALM.

HAWAII

Hawaii caters to the over-50 crowd and there are discounts for almost everything, including hotels, golf courses, rental cars, and movies. If you live in Oahu and are 65-plus, take advantage of an offer from TheBus, Honolulu's municipal bus system. This is a pass good for two years of unlimited travel on the island for only $20 or a four-year half-fare discount for $6 plus 50¢ per trip. Yet another choice is the Visitor Pass, which is available for all ages and costs $10 for four days of unlimited travel.

For information: TheBus Customer Service, 811 Middle St., Honolulu, HI 96819; 808-848-5555; www.thebus.org.

INDIANA

The Golden Hoosier Passport admits Indiana residents over the age of 60 and fellow passengers in a private vehicle to all state parks and natural resources without charge. An application for the passport, which costs $9 a year, is available at all state parks or from the Indiana State Parks Department.

For information: Indiana State Parks Dept., 402 W. Washington St., Indianapolis, IN 46204; 317-232-4124; www.state.in.us/dnr.

KANSAS

If you're over 65 and a Kansas resident, show proof of age at the gate and you'll pay only half of the usual adult entry fee at all state parks. In addition, at the same age you no longer require a hunting and fishing license, although you must pay for special permits to hunt certain game.

For information: Kansas Department of Wildlife and Parks, 900 SW Jackson, Topeka, KS 66612; 785-296-2281; www.kdwp.state.ks.us.

MAINE

Pick up your free Senior Citizen Pass and you will not have to pay any day-use fees at Maine state parks and historic sites. The pass is available at any state park or by writing to the Bureau of Parks and Lands; be sure to include proof of your age.

For information: Maine Bureau of Parks and Lands, State House Station 22, Augusta, ME 04333; 207-287-3821.

MICHIGAN

You can get some good deals in Michigan if you are a resident who's reached the age of 65. These include a motor-vehicle permit that gets you into all state parks for $5 a year, a fishing license with an annual fee of $3 a year, and a hunting license that costs $5.20 a year.

For information: Call the Department of Natural Resources at 517-373-9900; www.dnr.state.mi.us.

MISSOURI

Missouri residents over the age of 60 are entitled to a free Silver Citizen Discount Card that gives discounts at restaurants, stores, pharmacies, and other businesses throughout the state. To get a card, call the toll-free number below.

For information: Missouri Dept. of Social Services, PO Box 1337, Jefferson City, MO 65102; 800-235-5503.

MONTANA

You need pay only half the usual camping fee in Montana's state parks if you are over the age of 62.

For information: Montana Fish, Wildlife, and Parks Dept., 1420 E. 6th Ave., Helena, MT 59620; 406-444-4041.

NEVADA

In Carson City, you will strike silver without doing any digging—if you are over 50 and join the free Seniors Strike Silver Club. You'll get a list of discounts in town, plus a membership card to present as identification to participating merchants.

For information: Carson City Convention & Visitors Bureau, 1900 S. Carson St., Carson City, NV 89701; 800-NEVADA-1 (800-638-2321) or 775-687-7410; www.carson-city.org.

NEW MEXICO

For a brochure listing senior discounts at attractions, stores, hotels, restaurants, and transportation in Albuquerque, call the toll-free number below.

For information: Albuquerque Convention & Visitors Bureau; 800-733-9918, ext. 3340.

NEW YORK

Simply by presenting your current valid New York driver's license or a New York nondriver's identification card, you will be entitled to all of the privileges of the Golden Park Program for residents over the age of 62. The program offers, any weekday except holidays, free vehicle access to

state parks and arboretums, free entrance to state historic sites, and reduced fees for state-operated swimming, golf, tennis, and boat rentals. Just show your driver's license or ID card to the guard at each facility as you enter.
For information: State Parks, Albany, NY 12238; 518-474-0456.

Send for the free booklet, *Fifty Plus Diner's Guide*, from New York City's Department of Consumer Affairs. It lists hundreds of eateries, from bistros, diners, and delicatessens to elegant restaurants, in all five boroughs of the Big Apple that offer good deals to customers 50 and over. Some give discounts to 10 to 20 percent while others feature early-bird and pre-theater specials.
For information: New York City Department of Consumer Affairs; 212-487-4270; www.ci.nyc.ny.us/consumers.

OHIO
When residents of Ohio turn 60 they may sign up for a free Golden Buckeye Card, which entitles them to discounts, typically about 10 percent, on goods and services at thousands of participating businesses throughout the state.
For information: and the sign-up site nearest your home: Golden Buckeye Unit, Ohio Dept. of Aging, 50 W. Broad St., 9th floor, Columbus, OH 43215; 800-422-1976 (in Ohio) or 614-466-5500; www.state.oh.us/age.

PENNSYLVANIA
In Pennsylvania, the Lottery Fund pays for many good things for seniors. Among them is free statewide transportation. Anyone over the age of 65, resident of the state or not, can acquire a special identification card that gets him or

her aboard scheduled commuter railways, buses, trolleys, and subways without paying a cent. They must, however, travel off-peak: before 7 A.M., between 8 A.M. and 4:30 P.M., or after 5:30 P.M. on weekdays, and all day on weekends and holidays.

On the SEPTA (Southeastern Pennsylvania Transportation Authority) regional rail lines in the Philadelphia area, those with a valid ID pay only $1 to ride the trains during the same nonpeak hours as above, any day of the week, no matter the distance.

GOOD SAM CLUB

The **Good Sam Club** is an international organization of people who travel in recreational vehicles, mentioned here because the vast majority of those in rolling homes are over 50. Its goal is to make RVing safer, more enjoyable, and less expensive. Among the benefits are 10 percent discounts on nightly fees at over 2,000 RV parks and campgrounds, plus more discounts on propane, parts, and accessories at hundreds of service centers.

The club offers a toll-free hotline, a lost-key service, lost-pet service, trip routing, mail forwarding, telephone message service, insurance, a magazine, and campground directories. Most important, it provides low-cost emergency road service anywhere in the U.S. and Canada, including Alaska. Social activities include Good Sam rallies and travel tours and cruises all over the world. And about 2,100 local chapters in the U.S. and Canada hold campouts and meetings and participate in local volunteer projects. Membership is $25 a year per family, $44 for two years, $59 for three.

For information: The Good Sam Club, PO Box 6885, Englewood, CO 80155; 800-234-3450; www.goodsamclub.com.

Another perk is the Shared Ride Program, also funded by the state lottery, which provides door-to-door transportation, usually by van, at a discount of up to 85 percent to anybody over 65 who requests it and makes an advance reservation.

For information: Call your local transit agency or the Bureau of Public Transportation, Pennsylvania Department of Transportation, 555 Walnut St., Harrisburg, PA 17101; 717-783-8025. SEPTA: 215-280-7852.

SOUTH CAROLINA

Residents of South Carolina who are 65 or older must merely show their driver's licenses to get free admission at all state parks, plus half off on both the camping fees at all parks and the greens fees at Hickory Knob and Cheraw State Parks.

For information: South Carolina Department of Parks, Recreation, and Tourism, 1205 Pendleton St., Columbia, SC 29201; 803-734-0166.

TENNESSEE

Anyone over the age of 62, state resident or not, gets a 10 percent discount on food at park restaurants, cabins, and rooms at the Resort Park Inns. Tennessee residents over 62 pay no greens fees at state golf courses on Mondays. Besides, they are charged only 50 percent of the regular camping fees, while out-of-state campers are entitled to a 25 percent reduction. Admission to all state parks is free, regardless of your age.

For information: Tennessee Parks and Wildlife, 401 Church St., LC Tower, Nashville, TN 37243; 800-421-6683.

TEXAS

The Blue Bonnet Passport is free to all comers, residents of Texas or not, who are over the age of 65. If you turned 65 before September 1, 1995, the pass gives you free admission to state parks. If your 65th birthday was after that date, it admits you to the parks at half price. Pick up the pass at any park.

For information: Texas Parks and Wildlife, 4200 Smith School Rd., Austin, TX 78744; 800-792-1112.

If you are a winter snowbird in Galveston, stop at the Galveston Island Visitor Information Center and sign up for a free Special Winter Texan ID card. It gives you discounts or specials at over 100 businesses on the island, including accommodations, attractions, auto services, banking services, retail stores, restaurants, medical services, fishing charters, and golf courses.

For information: Galveston Island Visitor Information Center, 2428 Seawall Blvd., Galveston, TX 77550; 888-425-4753 or 409-763-4311; www.galvestontourism.com.

UTAH

The Silver Card issued by Park City, an old mining town known for its great ski mountains, is a summer program of discounts that gives you 10 percent or more off on merchandise, tickets, and meals. Pick up your free ID card and an information packet for seniors at a participating hotel or the Park City Visitors Bureau.

For information: Park City Convention and Visitors Bureau, 1910 Prospector Ave., Park City, UT 84060; 800-453-1360 or 801-649-6100; www.parkcityinfo.com.

VERMONT

Vermont's residents over 60 may purchase a Green Mountain Passport for $2 from their own town clerk. It is good for a lifetime and entitles them to free or reduced day-use admission at any Vermont State Park and its programs. Other benefits include discounts on concerts, restaurant meals, prescriptions, and more.

For information: Vermont Dept. of Aging, 103 S. Main St., Waterbury, VT 05676; 802-241-2400.

VIRGINIA

In this state that abounds with historical sites, you'll find senior discounts almost everywhere you go. You'll get them, for example, at Colonial Williamsburg, Busch Gardens, Berkeley Plantation, Mount Vernon, Woodlawn Plantation, Gunston Hall Plantation, the Edgar Allan Poe Museum in Richmond, and the Virginia Air and Space Center.

For information: Virginia Division of Tourism, 1021 E. Cary St., Richmond, VA 23219; 800-786-4484.

WEST VIRGINIA

Everybody who turns 60 in West Virginia gets a Golden Mountaineer Discount Card, which entitles the bearer to discounts from more than 3,500 participating merchants and professionals in the state and a few outside of it. If you don't receive a card from the state soon after your 60th birthday, you may apply for one at your local senior center or by calling the number below. Flash it wherever you go and save a few dollars.

Furthermore, when you're 65, you can get into all the state parks that charge admission at half price simply by showing your driver's license or other ID with proof of age.

For information: West Virginia Department of Parks, 1900 Kanawha Blvd., Charleston, WV 25305; 304-558-2764. Tourism hotline: 800-CALL-WVA.

WISCONSIN

This state's residents who are over the age of 65 pay only half the annual fee for fishing and hunting licenses, and for the annual admission sticker that gets them into state parks. On a daily park pass, they save a dollar.

For information: For hunting and fishing licenses: Wisconsin Department of Natural Resources, PO Box 7924, Madison, WI 53707; 877-945-4236. Or download the applications from www.dnr.state.wi.us. For state parks admission stickers: DNR Parks & Recreation, PO Box 7921, Madison, WI 53707; 608-266-2181. Or buy the stickers at the entrance to parking areas.

16

Back to Summer Camp

aybe you thought camp was just for kids, but if you are a grown-up person who likes the outdoors, swimming, boating, birds, and arts and crafts; and if you appreciate fields and forests and star-filled skies, you too can pack your bags and go off on a sleepaway. Throughout the country, many camps set aside weeks for adult sessions, while others offer adult programs all season long. More and more adults are getting hooked on summer camp, and many wouldn't miss a year.

ASSOCIATION OF JEWISH SPONSORED CAMPS

You can renew your spirits by spending a week or two during the summer with other 55- or 60-plus Jewish men and women at one of the six adult camping centers operated by this association. All are inexpensive, all but one serve kosher meals, put you up in heated lodges, and are located within a few hours of New York City. You'll be kept busy morning till night with activities and entertainment.

For information: Association of Jewish Sponsored Camps, 130 E. 59th St., New York, NY 10022; 212-751-0477; www.jewishcamps.org.

RV ELDERHOSTELS

On these Elderhostels, you take along your own housing—a recreational vehicle, travel trailer, or tent—and stay on the host campus or at a nearby campgrounds. Classes, usually held on the campus, are included, as are meals and excursions. On most RV tours you join the group for classes, meals, and excursions but sleep on your own premises. On others, a group of RVers form a moving field trip, moving along like a wagon train, listening to lectures over their CB radios as they travel and making stops along the way.

For information: Elderhostel, 11 Avenue de Lafayette, Boston, MA 02111; 877-426-8056 or 617-426-7788; www.elderhostel.org.

ELDERHOSTEL

Many of Elderhostel's programs are a combination of camping and college. In this wildly successful low-cost educational program (see Chapter 12 for details), you can spend a week or two camping in remote scenic areas, enjoying all the activities from horseback riding to crafts, boating, campfires, and sleeping in a cabin or under the stars.

For information: Elderhostel, 11 Avenue de Lafayette, Boston, MA 02111; 877-426-8056 or 617-426-7788; www.elderhostel.org.

GRANDPARENTS/GRANDCHILDREN CAMP

See Chapter 10 for information about summer camps and other vacations designed to give grandparents and grandchildren some special time together.

THE SALVATION ARMY

The Salvation Army operates scores of rural camps across the country, most of which have year-round adult sessions. The camps are run by regional divisional headquarters of the army; thus each is different from the others. Open to anyone, they cost very little.

For information: Contact a local unit of the Salvation Army.

VOLUNTARY ASSOCIATION FOR SENIOR CITIZEN ACTIVITIES (VASCA)

VASCA is a nonprofit organization that will provide you with detailed information about camps in the New York area for people over the age of 55. The agency represents 11 vacation lodges scattered about New York, New Jersey, Connecticut, and Pennsylvania, all of them amazingly affordable. Some are small rustic country retreats, most are lakeside resorts, others are huge sprawling complexes with endless activities. Several are designed to accommodate the disabled and the blind as well as the very elderly. The camps are sponsored by various nonprofit organizations and foundations, some with religious affiliations but nonsectarian.

For information: VASCA, 151 W. 30th St., New York, NY 10001; 212-216-9137; www.vasca.org.

YMCA/YWCA

The Y runs many camps, most of them for children, but some also offer inexpensive weeks for adults. For example, the YMCA of the Rockies operates a resort, Snow Mountain Ranch, with a special program in mid-August for active adults over the age of 50 at its Camp Chief Ouray in Granby, Colorado. The High Point YMCA's Camp Cheerio, in the Blue Ridge Mountains of North Carolina, sets aside three weeks a year for campers over 50, who live in the same cabins and pursue the same activities as the kids do the rest of the summer.

For information: Call your local YMCA or YWCA for information about camps in your area.

CAMPS SPONSORED BY CHURCH GROUPS

There are many adult camps and summer workshops sponsored by religious organizations—too many and too diverse to list here. One source of information is the website of Christian Camping International, where you can find camps for "senior adults" in its membership directory of about 1,000 camps and conferences in the U.S.

For information: Christian Camping International/USA, PO Box 62189, Colorado Springs, CO 80962; 719-260-9400; www.cciusa.org.

17

Shopping Breaks, Taxes, Insurance, and Other Practical Matters

In this chapter you won't find suggestions for interesting vacation possibilities or unusual places to explore. Instead, you'll get useful information about benefits and services that could be coming to you simply because you are now sufficiently mature to take advantage of them.

SAVE MONEY IN THE STORES

All over the U.S. and Canada today, retail stores offer discounts to seniors, usually over the age of 60 or 65, because they realize that mature people tend to be cautious consumers who know the value of a dollar, are extremely fond of bargains, and have the potential of becoming loyal customers. In fact, the older population has now started to expect reduced prices when they shop.

Stores vary on the age at which you may take advantage of their special offers, but most start you off at 60. Some give you 10 or 15 percent off every day, while others reserve one day a week for their senior discounts. Grocery stores, too, are getting into the act and so are many specialty food stores. Major department stores, such as Bloomingdale's and Lord and Taylor, occasionally feature senior savings days, when everything costs 10 or 15 percent less for customers over 60. Banana Republic gives customers 62 and older 10 percent off every day. Sears has a club that entitles you to discounts and other services.

What all this means is that it never hurts to ask wherever you shop whether any good deals are available to you.

SEARS MATURE OUTLOOK PLUS

Mature Outlook Plus, a membership program for Sears cardholders age 45 and over, provides a variety of benefits and savings, including money coupons to be used for the store's products and services. Coupons are included in the club's magazine and in the annual membership kit and may be used in all Sears stores in the country. See Chapter 19 for details.

For information: Mature Outlook Plus, PO Box 9390, Des Moines, IA 50306; 800-688-5665.

GETTING HELP ON YOUR TAX RETURNS

Assistance in preparing your tax returns is available free from both the Internal Revenue Service and AARP.

The IRS offers Tax Counseling for the Elderly (TCE) for people over 60 and Voluntary Income Tax Assistants (VITA) for younger people who need help. Trained volunteers pro-

HELP FROM THE IRS

The IRS publishes a useful free booklet, *Tax Information for Older Americans* (Publication No. 554). Get it from your local IRS office or call 800-TAX-FORM. You can also read it or download it—along with all tax forms, reports, and other useful publications—from the IRS website: www.ira.gov.

vide information and will prepare returns at thousands of sites throughout the country. Watch your local newspaper for a list of sites in your area or call 800-TAX-1040 during the tax season, January 2 to April 15.

Or you may enlist the help of AARP's Tax-Aide Service at more than 10,000 sites nationwide where, in the ten-week period before April 15, volunteers help low- and moderate-income members of AARP to prepare their tax returns. Volunteers will even go to your home, when necessary, if you are physically unable to get to a site. To locate a site in your community, call 800-227-7669. Or call your regional or state AARP offices. Or check the website: www.aarp.org/taxaide. Have your membership number and zip code handy and also your calendar, as an appointment is required.

SAVE ON AUTO AND HOMEOWNER'S INSURANCE

Among the nice surprises waiting for you on your 50th or 55th birthday is the possibility of paying less for your automobile and homeowner's insurance because of lower claims costs. So see if you can take advantage of your age when you shop for a new policy or renew an existing one.

Mature drivers get breaks because, as a group, they tend to be cautious drivers, much more careful than the younger crowd, having shed their bad habits such as speeding and reckless driving. And, although older drivers total more accidents per mile, they drive fewer miles, have fewer serious accidents, use their seat belts, usually don't use their cars for daily commuting in rush-hour traffic, and tend to stay off the roads at night and in bad weather. Therefore, statistically, they have fewer accidents per driver than other risk categories do, at least until they are over the age of 75.

In addition, you may get a discount—usually 10 percent—on some of your automobile coverage in most states when you successfully complete a state-approved defensive-driving course. Among the programs is AARP's 55 Alive/ Mature Driving (call 888-227-7669 for information), an eight-hour classroom refresher that specifically addresses the needs of older drivers with physical and perceptual changes that affect their driving. Open to both AARP members and nonmembers at a current cost of $8 per person, and taught by volunteers, the course is offered locally all over the country. Defensive-driving courses are offered by other groups, including local high schools and the AAA.

Homeowners over a certain age are also considered better risks for insurance claims than younger people because they spend more time at home where they can keep an eye on things and take care of their property. So some companies offer them reductions on premiums.

Although discounts are wonderful and we all love to get them, they aren't everything. Always shop the bottom line when you buy insurance. In other words, know what you are getting for what you are paying. You may be able to save hundreds of dollars just by shopping around. If one company charges higher premiums for comparable coverage and then gives you a discount, you have not profited. Get quotes from at least three insurers, going over your list of drivers, vehicles, and specific coverage needs.

Insurance regulations differ from state to state, but here are some of the offerings made in some states to older drivers and homeowners by some major insurance companies.

Be sure to ask for the discounts that may be coming to you because agents don't always volunteer this information. In addition to your age-related discount, ask about others. Some insurers offer discounts for insuring more than one car on the same policy, clean driving records, antitheft devices, low mileage, more than one policy with the same company, and longtime coverage. And watch out for policies that bump up your costs again when you turn 70.

ALLSTATE

Allstate gives a discount of 10 percent off the premiums across the board—liability, comprehensive, and collision coverage—on automobile insurance in almost every state for those who are 55 and retired. It chops an additional 5 or 10 percent off for completing an approved defensive-driving course.

As for property coverage, Allstate offers 10 to 25 percent off the premiums in most states to homeowners and renters who are at least 55 and retired.

AMERICAN FAMILY

If you are between the ages of 50 and 69, American Family gives you 10 percent off on almost all auto coverages. Preferred customers—those with good driving records—who buy both auto and homeowner insurance from this company get another discount of about 10 percent. Not only that, but taking a defensive-driving course nets you an additional 5 to 10 percent discount in some states.

CHUBB GROUP
From age 51 through 64, Chubb policyholders in many states get approximately 20 percent off on automobile coverage. From age 65 through 78, it's about 15 percent. Then at 79, you revert to the base rate you paid at age 50. Inquire about a defensive-driving discount and a rate reduction for pleasure driving only.

COLONIAL PENN
Homeowners age 55 or more who work fewer than 24 hours a week get a credit of 10 to 30 percent from this subsidiary of GE Auto Insurance Program on policies covering their principal residences. Both husband and wife must be at least semi-retired and live in the insured home.

FARMERS
At age 50, you get a discount of 2 to 15 percent in some states on your automobile liability coverage, plus another 5 to 10 percent at age 55 for completing a defensive-driving course. As a homeowner, your credit ranges from 2 to 14 percent starting at age 50 and usually increases each year.

GE AUTO INSURANCE PROGRAM
Drivers over the age of 55 who commute by car no more than two days a week and work fewer than 24 hours a week get a credit in many states of about 5 to 10 percent on lia-

bility coverage and 10 to 15 percent on coverage for physical damage to their vehicles. A defensive-driving course adds another break of about 10 percent.

GEICO

As a general rule, GEICO applies a lower rate on all automobile coverages for good drivers ages 50 to 74, retired or not, if the cars they principally operate are only used for pleasure. A certificate from an approved driving course takes off another 10 percent. In many states, GEICO offers a Prime Time contract for households in which the principal operator is over 50, no one on the policy is under 25, and drivers have had no accidents or driving convictions within the

FOR MEDICAL EMERGENCIES

If you have a chronic medical condition, drug or food allergies, special needs such as a surgical implant, or take medications on which your life depends, consider joining MedicAlert, an emergency medical information service that is especially useful when you're traveling. Members wear metal bracelets or pendants inscribed with their condition, membership number, and a collect-call telephone number accessible 24 hours a day from anywhere in the world. In an emergency, attending medical personnel can call for essential medical information, as well as names and phone numbers of personal physicians and family members.

The cost is $35 to enroll, then $15 a year thereafter. Members may update their records as often as necessary at no extra charge.

For information: MedicAlert; 800-825-3785 or 209-668-3333; www.medicalert.org.

past three years. Once issued, this policy is guaranteed to be renewable, regardless of age, accidents, or driving convictions.

Homeowners over 50 and retired in some states can get 5 to 20 percent off on coverage of their homes.

THE HARTFORD

This company underwrites the auto and homeowners insurance designed for AARP members, all of whom are over 50. It gives credits or discounts up to 15 percent for clean driving records, combined policies, safety devices, completion of an accredited driving course, and even for driving only in daylight. Renewal is guaranteed regardless of age or driving record.

As a homeowner or renter, you'll get a discount ranging from 1 to 15 percent when you and your spouse retire, insure new homes, or install fire and burglary systems.

LIBERTY MUTUAL

When you reach the age of 40, this company lowers its base rate in some states by about 10 percent on automobile insurance across the board. At 65 or older, you get the same 10 percent reduction only if you retire or commute less than three miles each way. More miles a day than that and the credit is decreased depending on the mileage. An additional 5 to 10 percent is taken off at age 55 if you complete an approved driving course.

NATIONWIDE

In most states, this company reduces premiums by 5 percent on all coverage from ages 50 to 54. From 55 to 69, you'll get

HOW TO FIND ELDER SERVICES

For information about community services for older adults such as senior centers, home health services, housing, transportation, legal assistance, or adult day care centers, call the **Eldercare Locator** at 800-677-1116. This nationwide governmental resource will help you find the appropriate state or local agencies in your area. Call between 9 A.M. and 8 P.M. (Eastern Time) Monday through Friday and explain the problem. Be prepared to provide the name, address, and zip code of the person needing help, as well as a brief description of the assistance you are seeking.

a 10 percent break; at age 70, the credit drops back to 5 percent. Take a defensive-driving course at age 55 and you'll be entitled to an additional 5 to 15 percent off.

PRUDENTIAL

Prudential gives drivers ages 50 through 54 a discount of about 10 percent in most states, 15 percent for ages 55 through 64, 10 percent for ages 65 through 74. You'll get an additional discount of 5 to 10 percent when you complete a defensive-driving course.

On homeowner insurance, there's a 5 percent Mature Homeowner Credit if one owner on the policy is 55 or more.

STATE FARM

State Farm lowers the rates by about 15 percent in most states for principal drivers of insured cars who are over 50 and do not allow anyone in the household under 25 to drive them. At age 55, policyholders who take a driving course get an additional 5 percent in the states that require it.

TRAVELERS PROPERTY CASUALTY

Here the average discount for drivers 54 through 74 is 11 percent in many states. At 75, it drops to about 6 percent. In some states, a driving course at age 55 adds another 5 percent reduction. As for homeowners insurance, policy-holders are offered discounts up to 20 percent if they are over 50 and retired.

BENEFITS FROM BANKS

Almost all banks today offer special incentives and services to their older customers, often starting at age 50. These include privileges such as a low minimum-balance require-ment; free safe-deposit boxes; and elimination of monthly service charges, per-check charges, fees for traveler's checks, cashier's checks, or money orders. Some banks even throw in discount eyewear and pharmacy service, accidental-death insurance, social activities, group excursions, seminars, and newsletters.

Bank and state regulations differ, so it pays to be a com-parison shopper to make sure you're getting the best deals available in your community.

LEGAL ASSISTANCE

Call upon your local area senior agency, which is required by law to provide some legal assistance to older citizens. Yours may help you untangle some puzzling legal problems or, at least, tell you what services are available to you. Or contact your local bar association for information about referrals or pro bono programs; or the National Academy of Elder Law Attorneys (520-881-4005 or www.naela.org), which sells directories that list its members by region.

FREE LEGAL SERVICES

Members of AARP who need the services of an attorney or have a legal question can get a free 30-minute consultation with a lawyer associated with the AARP Legal Services Network. They can also have simple wills and powers of attorney drawn up for them at fixed fees and take advantage of a 20 percent reduction in the attorney's usual rates for other legal services.

For information: Call 800-424-3410; www.AARP.org/lsn.

For a list of LSN attorneys, write LSN Fulfillment, PO Box 100084, Pittsburgh, PA 15290; or look in the Yellow Pages in the Associations, Attorneys, or Lawyers sections under the heading AARP-Legal Services Network. Another alternative is to visit the LSN website at www.aarp.org/lsn.

18

Volunteer for Great Experiences

If, perhaps for the first time in your life, you have time, expertise, talent, and energy to spare, consider volunteering your services to organizations that could use your help. There is plenty of significant work waiting for you, and more and more older Americans are volunteering as a way of finding fulfillment both before and after retirement. If you are looking for a good match between your abilities and an organization that needs them, take a look at the programs described here, all of them specifically seeking the experience and enthusiasm of older adults.

But, first, keep in mind:

When you file your federal income tax, you may be allowed to deduct unreimbursed expenses incurred while volunteering your services to a charitable organization. You may be able to deduct program fees and reasonable costs for transportation, parking, tolls, meals, lodging, and uniforms. You may not be able to take off all of your travel expenses, meals, and lodging, however, when you spend a significant amount of personal or vacation time before, during, or after a service program, or if you get benefit from your service, such as academic credit.

AARP VOLUNTEER CENTER

VTB is a nationwide computerized volunteer-reference service that matches the interests and skills of AARP members who wish to volunteer their services with programs, projects, and organizations that can use their help in their own neighborhoods. The volunteer programs range from AARP community programs, such as Tax Aide, 55 Alive/Mature Driving, and Health Advocacy, to well-known national organizations such as the American Red Cross, Habitat for Humanity, Recording for the Blind, March of Dimes, and the U.S. National Fish and Wildlife Service.

For information: AARP Volunteer Center, 601 E St. NW, Washington, DC 20049; 800-424-3410 or 202-434-3200; www.aarp.org.

ELDERHOSTEL SERVICE PROGRAMS

Elderhostel Service Programs tap the experience and expertise of older adults (55 or over) in short-term volunteer projects in the U.S., in Canada, and throughout the world. Teams of hostelers are paired with nonprofit organizations for a wide variety of service activities, from historical preservation to teaching English to natural-resources conservation, working with children with special needs, archaeological research, and even helping to build affordable housing. No special skill or experience is required, and training is provided on the job. A 55-plus volunteer may be accompanied by an adult who is younger.

Currently about 90 institutions and organizations—far too many to list here—are collaborating with Elderhostel to put mature Americans, retired or not, to work for one to three weeks per session in the U.S. or in other countries of the world. These are hosted by such diverse groups as Habitat for Humanity, Oceanic Society Expeditions, the U.S. Forest Service, Global Volunteers, Cross-Cultural Solutions, Appalachian Mountain Club, Hole in the Woods Ranch, the Center for Bioacoustics, the Museum of Science and Industry in Chicago, Grand Canyon National Park, and many more.

The fee you must pay to participate varies with each program and includes full room and board, equipment, social and cultural events, and, in most cases, airfare.

For information: Elderhostel, 11 Avenue de Lafayette, Boston, MA 02111; 877-426-8056 or 617-426-7788; www.elderhostel.org.

FAMILY FRIENDS

A national program sponsored by the National Council on Aging, Family Friends recruits volunteers over the age of 55 to work with children with disabilities, chronic illnesses, or other problems in many locations around the country. The volunteers act as caring grandparents, helping the families in whatever ways they can, mostly dealing with children at home but occasionally in hospitals. They are asked to serve at least four hours a week and to commit themselves to the program for at least a year. Volunteers are reimbursed for expenses incurred.

The local projects are funded by the federal government, corporations, foundations, and local, county, city, or state governments.

For information: Family Friends Resource Center, 409 Third St. SW, Washington, DC 20024; 202-479-6675; www .ncoa.org.

HOW TO HELP THE ENVIRONMENT

Environmental Alliance for Senior Involvement (EASI) is designed to tap the talents, knowledge, experience, and enthusiasm of older people interested in the environment. Together with local and national senior and environmental organizations such as AARP, RSVP, the EPA, the National Council on Aging, World Wildlife Fund, and National Wildlife Federation, volunteers work to preserve and restore the environment in their own communities. Current projects include pollution control, water source protection, solar energy installations, brown fields, and radon identification. *For information:* EASI, PO Box 250, Catlett, VA 20119; 540-788-3274; www.easi.org.

FOSTER GRANDPARENTS

Foster Grandparents devote their volunteer service to children with special or exceptional needs. They provide emotional support to victims of abuse and neglect, mentor troubled teenagers and young mothers, care for premature infants and children with physical disabilities and severe illnesses, and tutor children who lag behind in reading. Volunteers must be 60 or older, meet certain income-eligibility guidelines, and serve 20 hours a week, usually 4 hours a day Monday through Friday, in facilities in their own neighborhoods.

For this, they receive—in addition to the immense satisfaction—modest tax-free stipends to offset their costs, some meals during service, reimbursement for transportation, an annual physical examination, and accident and liability insurance while on duty.

For information: Contact your local Foster Grandparents program or the Corporation for National Service, 1201 New York Ave. NW, Washington, DC 20525; 800-424-8867; www.cns.gov.

INTERNATIONAL EXECUTIVE SERVICE CORPS

IESC, which is organized and directed by American business executives, is a nonprofit organization that recruits retired, highly skilled executives and technical advisors to assist businesses in the developing nations. It is funded by the U.S. Agency for International Development (AID), overseas clients and foreign governments, and many American corporations.

After being briefed on the country and the client, volunteer executives travel overseas—with their spouses, if they wish—for projects that generally last two to three months. IESC pays for the couple's travel expenses and provides a per diem allowance.

For information: International Executive Service Corps, 333 Ludlow St., Stamford, CT 06902; 800-243-4372 or 203-967-6000; www.iesc.org.

NATIONAL EXECUTIVE SERVICE CORPS

This nonprofit organization performs a unique service. It helps other nonprofit organizations solve their problems by providing retired executives with extensive corporate and professional experience to serve as volunteer consultants. Its services are offered in five basic areas—education, health, the arts, social services, and religion—and the assistance covers everything from organizational structure and financial systems to marketing and funding strategy. Volunteers' expenses are covered.

For information: National Executive Service Corps, 120 Wall St., New York, NY 10005; 212-269-1234; www.help4 nonprofits.org.

NATIONAL PARK SERVICE

If you love the outdoors and have the time, volunteer to work for the National Park Service as a VIP (Volunteers in Parks). VIPs are not limited to over-50s, but a good portion of them are retired people with time, expertise, talent, and interest in forests and wilderness. You may work a few hours a week or a month, seasonally or full-time, and may or may not—depending on the park—wear a uniform or get reimbursed for out-of-pocket expenses. The job possibilities range from working at an information desk to serving as a guide, maintaining trails, driving a shuttle bus, painting fences, designing computer programs, patrolling trails, making wildlife counts, writing visitor brochures, and preparing park events.

For information: Contact the VIP coordinator at the national park where you would like to volunteer and request an application. Or write to Volunteer Coordinator, National Park Service, 18th and C Sts. NW, Ste. 3045, Washington, DC 20240; 202-565-1050; www.nps.gov/volunteer.

NATIONAL TRUST WORKING HOLIDAYS

Britain's National Trust runs hundreds of "working holidays" in England, Wales, and Northern Ireland, inviting volunteers to exchange work for an interesting and low-cost holiday. The Trust, which oversees Britain's historic and environmental treasures, organizes small groups to lend a hand for one-week sessions in such tasks as restoring historic buildings, clearing ponds, or maintaining footpaths. Most programs accept anybody over 18, but several—the Oak Plus Projects—are reserved for enthusiasts between 50 and 70 who are willing to tackle outdoor work.

Lodging is in dormitory-style base camps and the work is paced to allow ample time to relax, take in the local attractions, or go for a stroll.

For information: The National Trust, PO Box 84, Cirencester, Glos, GL7 1ZP, England; workingholidays@smtp.ntrust .org.uk (E-mail); www.nationaltrust.org.uk/volunteers.

PEACE CORPS

It may surprise you to learn that the Peace Corps is a viable choice for idealists of any age. Eighty is the upper age limit for acceptance into the Peace Corps, and since its beginning in 1961, thousands of Senior Volunteers have brought their talents and experience to almost 100 countries all over the world. To become a Senior Volunteer, you must be a U.S. citizen and meet basic legal and medical criteria.

Some assignments require a college or technical-school degree or an experience equivalent. Married couples are eligible and will be assigned together. Service is typically for two years.

What you get in return is the chance to travel, an unforgettable living experience in a foreign land, basic expenses, and housing, plus technical, language, and cultural training. You'll also have a chance to use your expertise constructively in fields such as agriculture, engineering, math/science, home economics, education, skilled trades, forestry and fisheries, and community development.

For information: Peace Corps, 1990 K St. NW, Washington, DC 20526; 800-424-8580; www.peacecorps.gov.

RSVP (RETIRED AND SENIOR VOLUNTEER PROGRAM)

RSVP matches the interests and skills of men and women over the age of 55 with volunteer opportunities in their own communities. Volunteers, who may serve anywhere from a few to over 40 hours a week, may choose to tutor children, help build houses, provide model parenting skills to teen parents, plan community gardens, deliver meals, offer disaster relief to victims of disasters, work in day-care centers, or do whatever their own communities need. They are not paid but they do receive supplemental insurance while on duty, a preservice orientation, and on-the-job training from the agency or organization where they are placed.

For information: Contact your local or regional RSVP office or Corporation for National Service, 1201 New York Ave. NW, Washington, DC 20525; 800-424-8867; www.cns.org.

SENIOR ENVIRONMENTAL EMPLOYMENT PROGRAM (SEE)

The SEE Program, administered by the Environmental Protection Agency (EPA), establishes cooperative agreements with six national organizations to recruit qualified people over the age of 55 to help with environmental problems. The recruits, who work part-time or full-time in EPA offices or in the field, are paid by the hour in jobs ranging from secretarial and clerical work to highly specialized technical and scientific positions. All are designed to assist the agency in protecting and/or cleaning up the environment.

For information: SEE Program, EPA, 401 M St. SW, Washington, DC 20460; 202-260-2574; www.epa.gov/epahrist/see/brochure.

SENIOR COMPANIONS

Senior Companions help frail older adults, adults with disabilities, and adults with serious or terminal illnesses who need extra assistance to live independently in their own homes or communities. They provide companionship and friendship to isolated seniors, assist them with simple chores, and provide needed transportation. Volunteers must be 60 or older, meet certain income eligibility guidelines, and serve 20 hours a week, usually 4 hours a day Monday through Friday. Although they are not paid, they receive a modest tax-free stipend, reimbursement for transportation, some meals during service, on-duty accident and liability insurance, and an annual physical examination.

For information: Corporation for National Service, 1201 New York Ave. NW, Washington, DC 20525; 800-424-8867; www.cns.gov.

SERVICE CORPS OF RETIRED EXECUTIVES (SCORE)

SCORE is a volunteer group of working and retired business leaders who donate their time and talents to counsel owners and would-be owners of small businesses who need expert advice. It offers seminars and workshops plus one-on-one counseling, including counseling via its website. A resource partner of the U.S. Small Business Administration, SCORE has a membership of about 12,000 men and women and 389 chapters around the country.

For information: Contact your local U.S. Small Business Administration office or SCORE, 409 Third St. SW, 6th floor, Washington, DC 20024; 800-634-0245 or 202-205-6762; www.score.org.

SERVICE OPPORTUNITIES FOR OLDER PEOPLE (SOOP)

SOOP, sponsored by the Mennonite Board of Missions and other organizations, provides a way for older people of all persuasions to contribute their experience and skills in a variety of locations throughout the U.S. and Canada. You may sign up for a few weeks or up to six months, living at the site and working to help others in need in whatever way you can, from teaching, building, and child care to home-making, farming, and administering. Once you decide on the kind of work and time commitment you prefer, you make plans with a location coordinator for your assignment and housing. Volunteers usually pay for their own travel, food, and lodging.

For information: Mennonite Board of Missions, PO Box 370, Elkhart, IN 46515; 219-294-7523; www.mbm.org.

FORTY PLUS

Offices in 20 cities throughout the U.S. comprise this non-profit cooperative of unemployed executives, managers, and professionals, men and women, who have earned at least $40,000 a year or are 40 years of age or more. Their objective is to help members conduct effective job searches and find new jobs. There is no paid staff. The members do all the work and help pay expenses by paying $500 upon acceptance and then $100 a month thereafter. They must commit themselves to attend weekly meetings and spend at least two days a week working at the club and assisting others in their search for work.

In return, members are helped to examine their career skills and define their goals, counseled on résumé writing and interview skills, helped to plan marketing strategy, and given job leads. They may also use the premises as a base of operations, with phone answering and mail service, computers, and reference library.

Forty Plus exists at this writing in New York City and Buffalo, New York; Oakland, San Diego, San Jose, and Los Angeles (with a branch in Laguna Hills), California; Fort Collins, Colorado Springs, and Lakewood, Colorado; Columbus, Ohio; Dallas and Houston, Texas; Murray, Ogden, and Provo, Utah; Philadelphia, Pennsylvania; Bellevue, Washington; Washington, D.C.; St. Paul, Minnesota; and Honolulu, Hawaii.

For information: Addresses of locations and descriptive materials are available from Forty Plus of New York, 149 5th Ave., New York, NY 10010; 212-358-7646; www.40plus.org.

SHEPHERD'S CENTERS OF AMERICA (SCA)

An interfaith, nonprofit organization of older adults who volunteer their skills to help seniors in their communities, SCA has about 90 centers in 26 states. Supported by Catholic, Jewish, and Protestant congregations as well as businesses and foundations, the centers operate many programs designed to enable older people to remain in their own homes as active participants in community life. They also encourage intergenerational interaction. Centers offer such in-home services as Telephone Visitors, Family Friends, Meals on Wheels, Handyhands Service, and Respite Care, all provided mostly by volunteers. Programs at the centers include other services, day trips, classes, and courses as well as support groups and referrals. Membership is open to anyone over the age of 55.

For information: Shepherd's Centers of America, 1 W. Armour Blvd., Ste. 201, Kansas City, MO 64111; 800-547-7073; www.shepherdcenters.org.

VOLUNTEER GRANDPARENTS SOCIETY

The objective of this nonprofit organization in Canada is to match volunteer grandparents over the age of 50 with children between the ages of 3 and 12 who have no accessible grandparents. The volunteers, who are not paid and do not commit to a contract or specific hours, establish a relationship of mutual enjoyment, support, and caring and become part of an extended family. They may also spend two to three hours one day a week in elementary school classrooms, to serve as mentors and as a supportive presence for the children. Applicants are interviewed and carefully screened, and matches are based on compatibility as well as on geographic proximity. The organization, which originated in 1973 in Vancouver, has expanded with the development of programs across Canada in addition to several located in British Columbia.

For information: Volunteer Grandparents Society of Canada, 1755 Broadway, Vancouver, BC V6J 4S5; 604-736-8271; www.volunteergrandparents.org.

JOB PROGRAM FOR OLDER WORKERS

Senior Community Service Employment Program (SCSEP), a federally funded program, recruits unemployed low-income men and women over the age of 55, assesses their employment strengths, and hires them for paid jobs in community-service positions. At the same time, the enrollees begin training in new job skills and receive such help as counseling, physical examinations, group meetings, and job fairs while the agency tries to match them with permanent jobs in the private sector. If you qualify and are looking for a paying position, this agency is worth a try.

For information: SCSEP, National Council on the Aging, 409 Third St. SW, Washington, DC 20024; 800-424-9046 or 202-479-1200; www.ncoa.org. Or contact your local, county, or state Office for the Aging.

VOLUNTEERS IN TECHNICAL ASSISTANCE

VITA provides another avenue for helping developing countries. A nonprofit international organization, VITA provides volunteer experts who respond—usually by direct correspondence—to technical inquiries from people in these nations who need assistance in such areas as small-business development, energy applications, agriculture, reforestation, water supply and sanitation, and low-cost housing. Its volunteers also perform other services such as project planning, translations, publications, marketing strategies, evaluations, and technical reports and often become on-site consultants.

There is no minimum age, but you must have enough time to serve. If you become a volunteer, you will not be paid, but you will be reimbursed for your travel and living expenses.

For information: Volunteers in Technical Assistance, 1600 Wilson Blvd., Ste. 710, Arlington, VA 22209; 703-276-1800; www.vita.org.

VOLUNTEER PROGRAMS IN ISRAEL

ACTIVE RETIREES IN ISRAEL (ARI)

Sponsored by B'nai B'rith International, ARI is a volunteer work program for people who are at least 50 and in good health. Volunteers pay for the opportunity to live in the resort city of Netanya and work in the mornings for one or two months in hospitals, forests, kibbutzim, schools, and facilities for the elderly and the handicapped. Afternoons are spent learning Hebrew, while the evenings include concerts, discussion groups, and cultural activities. Guided tours of the country are part of the program. Optional trips to Eilat and Petra in Jordan are available as add-ons to your stay.

For information: ARI, B'nai B'rith Center for Jewish Identity, 1640 Rhode Island Ave. NW, Washington, DC 20036; 800-500-6533 or 202-857-6580; www.bnaibrith.org.

JEWISH NATIONAL FUND

To qualify for the JNF Canadian American Active Retirees in Israel (CA-ARI), a two- to ten-week winter program sponsored by the Jewish National Fund, you must be over 50 and in good physical and mental health. Your time will be spent working five mornings a week, tending the JNF national forests, and, in addition, working at a choice of other jobs. Some volunteers choose to contribute their time in schools, hospitals, homes for the aged, army bases, or universities, while others assist local craftspeople. Afternoons are devoted to planned activities such as sight-seeing trips, cultural and social events, and lectures; and evenings to socializing. Included is a tour of the country and time in Jerusalem.

For information: JNF CA-ARI Program, Missions Dept., 42 E. 69th St., New York, NY 10021; 888-563-0033, ext. 284; www.jnf.org.

VOLUNTEERS FOR ISRAEL

In this volunteer work-and-cultural program for adults 18 and older in Israel, you'll put in eight-hour days for three weeks, working alongside members of the Israel Defense Force. You'll sleep in a segregated dormitory and work in small groups at a reserve or supply military base, doing whatever needs doing most at that moment. You may serve in supply, warehousing, or maintenance of equipment or in social services in hospitals. You'll wear an army uniform with a "Civilian Volunteer" patch. Board, room, and other expenses are free, but you must pay for your own partially subsidized airfare.

For information: Volunteers for Israel, 330 West 42nd St., 16th floor, New York, NY 10036; 212-643-4848; www.vfi-usa.org.

OPERATION ABLE

If you're over 40 and in the market for a job but don't know where to start looking for one, hook up with **Operation ABLE**, a nonprofit organization affiliated with a network of agencies that will help match you with a likely employer. You're in luck if you live in the Chicago area, where there are many regional offices. But there is also a network of independent ABLE-like organizations, modeled after the original, in several other cities, including Boston; Los Angeles; Lincoln, Nebraska; Rockville, Maryland; Southfield, Michigan; and St. Albans, Vermont.

Operation ABLE tries every which way to get you into the working world. It provides job counseling, on-the-job training, group training activities, and individual career assessment and guidance; teaches job-hunting skills; matches older workers with employers; operates a pool of temporaries; and offers many other services.

For information: Operation ABLE, 180 N. Wabash Ave., Chicago, IL 60601; 312-782-3335; www.jobhotline.org.

WINTER, SPRING AND FALL IN NETANYA

Hadassah's Winter in Netanya (WIN), Springtime in Netanya (SPIN), and Fall in Netanya (FIN) programs combine work, vacation, and study in Israel. For one or two months, participants live in a four-star hotel in a Mediterranean resort town 20 miles north of Tel Aviv. They pay for their privileges by donating their mornings to working in hospitals, schools, community centers, and army bases; teaching English to new immigrants; planting gardens; painting murals; and doing carpentry. Afternoons are devoted to optional conversational Hebrew lessons, sight-seeing, and relaxation, while the evenings are reserved for social and cultural events. The participants, many of them retirees, also spend a week in Jerusalem and go on special excursions to such places as Masada and Safed as well as museums, archaeological sites, and a kibbutz.

For information: Hadassah, 50 West 58th St., New York, NY 10019; 212-303-8031 or your local Hadassah chapter; www.hadassah.org.

19

The Over-50 Organizations and What They Can Do for You

When you consider that there are more people in this country over the age of 55 than there are children in elementary and high schools, you can see why we have powerful potential to influence what goes on around here. As the demographic discovery of the times, a group that controls most of the nation's disposable income, we've become a prime marketing target. And, just like any other large group of people, we've got plenty of needs.

A number of organizations in the U.S. and Canada have been formed in recent years to act as advocates for the mature population and to provide us with special programs as well as opportunities to spend our money on their products or services. Here is a brief rundown on them and what they have to offer you. You may want to join more than one of them so you can get the best of each.

AARP

At age 50 you are eligible to join AARP, the extensive non-profit organization that serves as an advocate for the older generation, offers a vast array of services and programs, and sells many kinds of insurance. With more than 32 million members, it is one of the most effective lobbying groups in the country. Its monthly newsletter, *AARP Bulletin*, and bimonthly magazine, *Modern Maturity*, go to more homes than any other publications in the U.S. For a membership fee of $10 for one year or $27 for three years (and that includes a spouse), AARP offers many benefits. Here are some of them:

- Group health insurance, life insurance, auto insurance, homeowner's insurance, mobile-home insurance
- Discounts on airfares, cruises, hotels, motels, auto rentals, and sight-seeing
- A mail-order pharmacy service that delivers prescription and nonprescription drugs
- A motoring plan that includes emergency road and towing services, trip planning, and other benefits
- A national advocacy and lobbying program at all levels of government to develop legislative priorities and represent the interests of older people
- More than 4,000 local chapters with their own activities and volunteer projects
- The Volunteer Center, which matches you with volunteer opportunities in your community
- A series of employment planning workshops called AARP Works for older job hunters

- Special programs in a wide range of areas such as consumer affairs, legal counseling, financial information, housing, health advocacy, voter education, employment planning, independent living, disability initiatives, grandparent information, and public benefits
- Tax-Aide, a program conducted in cooperation with the IRS that helps lower- and moderate-income members with their income tax returns
- 55 ALIVE/Mature Driving, a classroom course developed to refresh your driving skills and, in many states, help you qualify for lower auto insurance rates
- Legal Services Network, which assists members in finding prescreened attorneys to help with legal problems
- Free publications on many subjects relevant to your life

For information: AARP, 601 E St. NW, Washington, DC 20049; 800-424-3410 or 202-434-AARP; www.aarp.org.

CANADIAN SNOWBIRD ASSOCIATION

CSA is an organization formed to represent the interests of Canadian snowbirds, people who flee the winter snow for the sun and palm trees of the U.S. southern states. As their advocate and lobbying group, CSA addresses issues of concern to Canadian seniors such as health care, absentee voting rights, cross-border problems, residency requirements, U.S. tax laws for Canadians wintering abroad, and estate tax rules on Canadian-owned vacation property in the U.S. And it endorses travel insurance as well as out-of-country health insurance.

Membership costs $10 (single) and $15 (couple) per year, and benefits include a magazine, travel offerings, an automobile club, a currency-exchange program, home and automobile insurance, and social gatherings in popular snowbird locations such as Florida, Arizona, Texas, and California.

For information: Canadian Snowbird Association, 180 Lesmill Rd., North York, ON M3B 2T5; 800-265-3200 or 416-391-9000; www.snowbirds.org.

CARP (CANADA'S ASSOCIATION FOR THE FIFTY-PLUS)

Canadians over the age of 50 are invited to join CARP, a national nonprofit association with about 375,000 members, retired and employed. For a membership fee of $15.95 (Canadian) a year for singles or couples, members get many benefits, including discounted rates on out-of-country health insurance, long-term care insurance, extended health and dental plans, and automobile and home insurance. They can also take advantage of an expanded travel program with an auto club and discounts on airfares, travel packages, hotels, and car rentals. Members may also participate in the activities of local chapters in their own communities.

CARP publishes a lively, informative, award-winning magazine called *Fifty-Plus*, with six regular issues per year, plus bonus editions on special subjects such as finances, travel, and retirement. CARP is at the forefront of national and provincial advocacy on issues of great concern to mature Canadians, such as pensions, health care, home care, scams and frauds, and the environment. Free financial seminars are held frequently throughout the country.

For information: CARP, 27 Queen St. East, Ste. 1304, Toronto, ON M5C 2M6; 800-363-9736 (in Canada) or 416-363-8748; www.fifty-plus.net.

CATHOLIC GOLDEN AGE

A Catholic nonprofit organization that is concerned with issues affecting older citizens, such as health care, housing, and Social Security benefits, CGA has well over a million members and more than 200 chapters throughout the country. It offers many good things to its members, who must be over 50. These include spiritual benefits, such as masses and prayers worldwide, and practical benefits, such as discounts on hotels, campgrounds, car rentals, and prescriptions. Other offerings include group insurance plans, pilgrimage and group travel programs, and an automobile club. Membership costs $8 a year or $19 for three years.

For information: Catholic Golden Age, RD2, Box 161, Olyphant, PA 18447; 800-836-5699; www.catholicgolden age.org.

GRAY PANTHERS

A national organization of about 16,000 intergenerational activists, the Gray Panthers work on multiple issues that include peace, jobs for all, antidiscrimination (ageism, sexism, racism), family security, the environment, campaign reform, and the United Nations. They are active in more than 50 local networks across the U.S. in their efforts to promote social justice. For annual membership dues of $20, members receive a bimonthly newsletter, which is also available by subscription

For information: Gray Panthers, 733 15th St. NW, Ste. 437, Washington, DC 20005; 800-280-5362 or 202-737-6637; www.graypanthers.org.

MEMBERS PRIME CLUB

An association for past or present credit-union employees and volunteers who are at least 50 years old and belong to a credit union, MPC (formerly National Association for Retired Credit Union People, or NARCUP) offers a number of benefits to its members. These include an excellent bimonthly magazine called *Prime Times*, a pharmacy discount program, and discounts on hotels, condominiums, airfares, car and RV rentals, cruises, and vacation packages. Annual membership fee is $49.95.

For information: Members Prime Club, NARCUP, PO Box 391, Madison, WI 53701; 888-889-4373 or 608-238-5898; www.cunamutual.com.

NATIONAL ASSOCIATION OF RETIRED FEDERAL EMPLOYEES

As you can probably gather, this is an association of federal retirees and their families. The primary mission of NARFE is to protect the earned benefits of retired federal employees, which it does through its lobbying program in Washington. Members, who pay $20 a year plus local chapter dues, receive a monthly magazine and are entitled to discounts and special services.

For information: NARFE, 606 N. Washington St., Alexandria, VA 22314; 800-627-3394 or 703-838-7760; www .narfe.org.

NATIONAL COUNCIL OF SENIOR CITIZENS

An advocacy organization, NCSC lobbies on the local, state, and national level for legislation benefiting older Americans. With about half a million members, it has carried on many campaigns concerning Medicare, housing, health care, Social Security, and other relevant programs.

Although NCSC's major focus is its legislative program, it also has a local club network, social events, prescription discounts, group rates on supplemental health insurance, automobile insurance, and travel discounts, plus a newspaper that keeps you up to date on all of the above. Membership costs $13 a year or $33 for three years.

For information: National Council of Senior Citizens, 8403 Colesville Rd., Ste. 1200, Silver Springs, MD 20910; 800-333-7212 or 301-578-8800; www.ncscinc.org.

NATIONAL EDUCATION ASSOCIATION–RETIRED

With a membership of more than 163,000 retired education employees from teachers to school bus drivers, NEA–Retired acts as an advocate for their special interests such as pensions and health care and supports public education through legislative lobbying as well as reading programs, mentoring, and intergenerational activities. Among its benefits of membership are life, health, disability, and casualty insurance programs; savings and investment plans; credit and loan programs; and discounts, educational guides, and a bimonthly magazine. Join for $15 a year or $100 for life plus local dues that vary by state.

For information: NEA–Retired, 1201 16th St. NW, Washington, DC 20036; 202-822-7149; www.nea.org/retired.

OLDER WOMEN'S LEAGUE

OWL is a national nonprofit organization with local chapters dedicated to achieving economic, political, and social equality for older women. Anyone, of any age, may join. OWL provides educational materials, training for citizen advocates, and informative publications dealing with the important issues—such as Social Security, health care, retirement benefits, employment discrimination—that face women as they grow older. Annual dues are $25.

For information: Older Women's League, 666 11th St. NW, Washington, DC 20001; 800-825-3695 or 202-783-6686; www.owl-national.org.

THE RETIRED OFFICERS ASSOCIATION

This group is open to anyone who has been a commissioned or warrant officer in the seven U.S. uniformed services. Members receive lobbying representation on Capitol Hill and an excellent magazine that features articles on matters of special interest to them. They may also take advantage of a number of benefits, including discounts on car rentals and motel lodgings, a travel program with "military fares" to many overseas destinations, sports tournaments, a mail-order prescription program, group health and life insurance plans, and a car lease-purchase plan. TROA also has many autonomous local chapters with their own activities and membership fees. Annual dues are $20. Auxiliary members (spouses, widows, or widowers) pay $15 a year.

For information: The Retired Officers Association, 201 N. Washington St., Alexandria, VA 22314; 800-245-8762 or 703-549-2311; www.troa.org.

SEARS MATURE OUTLOOK PLUS

The country's largest retailer, Sears has long sponsored Mature Outlook, a discount club for its customers. Although it is no longer accepting new enrollments, existing members may renew their memberships indefinitely for an annual fee of $19.95.

For new enrollees, it has been replaced by an enhanced version, Mature Outlook Plus, that provides better benefits. They include money coupons to use in Sears stores on both regular and sale items, a free car-buying service, a newsletter, the bimonthly *Mature Outlook Magazine*, and discounts on airfares, cruises, RV rentals, hotels, resorts, restaurants, car rentals, and prescriptions. Annual dues are $39.95 for you, your spouse, and your children.

For information: Mature Outlook Plus, PO Box 9390, Des Moines, IA 50306; 800-688-5665.

Index